## 2000 SUPPLEMI

MW01705925

# FEDERAL COURTS AND THE LAW OF FEDERAL–STATE RELATIONS

FOURTH EDITION

*by*

PETER W. LOW
Vice President and Provost of the University
Hardy Cross Dillard Professor of Law
University of Virginia

JOHN C. JEFFRIES, JR.
Emerson Spies Professor of Law
William L. Matheson & Robert M. Morgenthau Distinguished Professor
University of Virginia

NEW YORK, NEW YORK

**FOUNDATION PRESS**

2000

**ISBN** 1–56662–922–5

*TEXT IS PRINTED ON 10% POST CONSUMER RECYCLED PAPER*

# PREFACE

This Supplement brings **Federal Courts and the Law of Federal-State Relations** (4th ed. 1998) up-to-date through the end of the 1999-2000 Term of the Supreme Court. Recently published scholarship is also referenced.

In compiling this Supplement, we have decided to err on the side of inclusion rather than exclusion. Consequently, the Supplement presents six new main cases from the 1998-99 Term and two from the 1999-2000 Term. It also provides shorter treatment of several others from both Terms. While we do not regard coverage of all these materials as essential, we thought that others would appreciate, as we do, the opportunity to teach recent decisions and thereby to keep abreast of developments in the field.

The new main cases from the 1998-99 Term are:

***Gebser v. Lago Vista Independent School District.*** In *Gebser*, a student brought a title IX damages action against a school district for sexual harassment by a teacher. A closely divided Supreme Court ruled that the district could be held liable only is a supervisor actually knew of the teacher's misconduct or was deliberately indifferent to its existence. The Court reasoned that the fact that the title IX damages action was "judicially implied" rather than legislatively express justified a "measure of latitude" in crafting and limiting the appropriate remedy. The dissenters disagreed, arguing that the limitation of liability was judicial lawmaking. *Gebser* is interesting both in substance and in methodology. Since so much of the debate turns on what inferences, if any, can be drawn from the fact that the private right of action was judicially created, we include it as a new main case in the materials on that subject.

***Federal Election Commission v. Akins.*** *Akins* is the Supreme Court's latest—and very interesting—major pronouncement on standing. A group of voters sued the Federal Election Commission to establish that the American Israel Public Affairs Committee was a "political committee" within the meaning of the Federal Election Campaign Act and was therefore required to make certain disclosures regarding membership, contributions, and expenditures. The Supreme court found that standing under the statute extended to any person "aggrieved" by a Commission decision, including those who were simply opposed to it. Three Justices dissented. Because *Akins* limits—or at least clarifies the limits of—*Lujan v. Defenders* *of Wildlife* (casebook, page 364), we include it as a new main case after *Lujan*.

***Bousley v. United States.*** *Bousley* is a habeas decision allowing a prisoner convicted of "using" a firearm in violation of federal law to raise a later Supreme court decision requiring the government to prove "active employment." *Teague v. Lane* was found inapplicable to cases where the new law was not an innovation of procedure but anew interpretation of the requirements of substantive liability. The Court further ruled that the prisoner's failure to raise this issue at trial (he pled guilty) would be overlooked if he could establish "actual innocence" under the newly announced standard of liability. Justices Scalia and Thomas dissented.

**11th Amendment Decisions.** Additionally, the Court handed down three major 11th amendment decisions during its 1998-99 Term. All answered questions left over after *Seminole Tribe v. Florida*, and all upheld state immunity by a vote of five to four. Although we doubt that students five years from now will be reading all three cases, we have included them in this Supplement to provide a generous opportunity to investigate this area of current controversy and concern.

***Alden v. Maine.*** Probation officers claimed that their employer, the state of Maine, had failed to pay them overtime as required by the Fair Labor Standards Act, which expressly applies to states. They sued first in federal court, but that action was dismissed after *Seminole Tribe* declared that Congress's power to abrogate state immunity did not extend to its powers under article I. The plaintiffs then filed suit in state court, reasoning that the supremacy clause obligated state courts to enforce federal law and that the federal provision giving states immunity from private suit, the 11th amendment, did not apply in state court. The Supreme Court rejected this argument, finding that the 11th amendment evidenced but did not define a preexisting constitutionalization of state sovereign immunity, applicable in both state and federal court.

***College Savings Bank v. Florida Prepaid Postsecondary Education Expense Board.*** College Savings Bank patented and marketed certificates of deposit designed to finance college education. The state of Florida sold a competing product through its agency, the Prepaid Postsecondary Education Expense Board. In this case, College Savings Bank accused the state of Florida of false and misleading advertising in violation of the Lanham Act, which had expressly been made applicable to states by the Trademark Remedy Clarification Act. The chief issue was whether the state's decision to engage in non-core activities subject to federal regulation amounted to consent to be sued or a waiver of sovereign immunity. The Court said no, and expressly overruled whatever was left of *Parden v. Terminal Ry.*

***Florida Postsecondary Education Expense Board v. College Savings Bank.*** In this companion case, announced the same day, College Saving Bank claimed patent infringement. The principal issue in this case was whether the patent laws could be justified under § 5 of the 14th amendment, in which case they could override state sovereign immunity, or whether they necessarily rested on Congress's article I powers, in which case state immunity would prevail. The Court again decided in favor of the state.

Both new main cases from the 1999-2000 Term concern the limitations on habeas corpus enacted by Congress in the Antiterrorism and Effective Death Penalty Act of 1996 (AEDPA). They are the first important interpretations of that statute by the Supreme Court. Both invite consideration of the extent to which the AEDPA has resulted in real change of the rules developed by the Court prior to enactment of the statute:

***Terry Williams v. Taylor.*** *Terry Williams* involved the substantive limitations of the AEDPA on the issues open to litigation in federal habeas review of state criminal convictions. Williams had been convicted of capital murder and sentenced to death. As it reached the Supreme Court, his case turned on whether the judgment of the Virginia Supreme Court refusing to set aside his death sentence was, in the language of the AEDPA, "contrary to, or involved an unreasonable application of, clearly established Federal law, as determined by the Supreme Court of the United States." The Court divided five to four on the meaning of this phrase, with the majority holding that questions of law were to be decided de novo but that applications of correct legal principles could be reversed only if the state court acted unreasonably. The Court then divided six to three on the outcome of the case. Significantly, the majority held that the state Supreme Court had not properly applied the applicable federal law.

***Michael Wayne Williams v. Taylor.*** *Michael Wayne Williams* involved the rules of procedural foreclosure enacted by the AEPDA. The AEDPA provides that if the habeas petitioner has failed "to develop the factual basis of a claim in State court proceedings, the court shall not hold an evidentiary hearing on the claim unless the applicant shows" that several stringent conditions can be met. Williams admitted that he could not meet these conditions, and the state argued that that should be the end of the matter. The Court unanimously disagreed, concluding that he was not required to establish the stringent statutory conditions if he could establish "cause and prejudice" for failing to litigate his claim in the state courts. The Court agreed unanimously, moreover, that he had established "cause" for failing to litigate some of his claims.

## PERMISSION TO DUPLICATE

There are many intersections between **Civil Rights Actions: Enforcing the Constitution** (2000), and **Federal Courts and the Law of Federal-State Relations** (4th ed., 1998). Occasionally, a teacher using one book may wish to use material from the other or its supplement. To facilitate such borrowings, we authorize teachers who have adopted either book to duplicate limited portions of the other or its annual supplement for distribution to their students. We are grateful to Foundation Press for agreeing to make this option available.

PWL
JCJjr

Charlottesville, Virginia
August, 2000

# TABLE OF CONTENTS

## CHAPTER III: CONGRESSIONAL CONTROL OF THE FEDERAL COURTS

### Section 1: The Power to Limit Federal Jurisdiction

### Section 2: Diversity Jurisdiction



### Section 3: The Substance/Procedure Problem



### Section 4: Finality and Appellate Review



## CHAPTER VI: ABSTENTION

### Section 1: General Principles



### Section 3: *Younger* Abstention



### Section 4: Anti-Injunction Act



## PART III: FEDERAL COURT ENFORCEMENT OF FEDERAL RIGHTS

## CHAPTER VII: HABEAS CORPUS

### Section 1: The Scope of Review



### Section 2: Procedural Foreclosure

*

# TABLE OF CASES

Principal cases are in bold type. Non-principal cases are in roman type. References are to Pages.

# TABLE OF SECONDARY AUTHORITIES

Hierarchy, 86 Geo.L.J. 2445 (1998)--pp. 14, 63

Jackson, Principle and Compromise in Constitutional Adjudication: The Eleventh Amendment and State Sovereign Immunity, 75 Notre Dame L. Rev. 953 (2000)--p. 143

Jackson, Seminole Tribe, the Eleventh Amendment, and the Potential Evisceration of Ex Parte Young, 72 N.Y.U.L.Rev. 495 (1997)--p. 145

Jackson, The Infrastructure of Federal Supremacy, 32 Ind.L.Rev. 111 (1998)--p. 2

Jeffries, Disaggregating Constitutional Torts, 110 Yale L.J. ___ (2000)--p. 147

Jeffries, In Praise of the Eleventh Amendment and Section 1983, 84 Va.L.Rev. 49 (1998)--pp. 93, 145

Jeffries, The Right–Remedy Gap in Constitutional Law, 109 Yale L.J. ___ (1999)--p. 148

Karlan, The Irony of Immunity: The Eleventh Amendment, Irreparable Injury, and Section 1983, 53 Stan. L. Rev. ___ (2001)--p. 144

Kelleher, Taking "Substantive Rights" (in the Rules Enabling Act) More Seriously, 74 Notre Dame L.Rev. 47 (1998)--p. 35

Kinports, Implied Waiver After Seminole Tribe, 82 Minn.L.Rev. 793 (1998)--p. 94

Koh, Is International Law Really State Law, 111 Harv.L.Rev. 1824 (1998)--p. 1

Lee, On the Received Wisdom in Federal Courts, 147 U. Pa. L. Rev. 1111 (1999)--p. 15

Lee, Section 2254(d) of the New Habeas Statute: An (Opinionated) User's Manual, 51 Vand.L.Rev. 103 (1998)--p. 62

Lessig, Erie-Effects of Volume 110: An Essay on Context in Interpretive Theory, 110 Harv.L.Rev. 1785 (1997)--p. 1

Liebman and Ryan, "Some Effectual Power": The Quantity and Quality of Decisionmaking Required of Article III Courts, 98 Colum.L.Rev. 696 (1998)--pp. 15, 62

Lilly, Making Sense of Nonsense: Reforming Supplemental Jurisdiction, 74 Ind.L.J. 181 (1998)--p. 34

Lund, The Decline of Federal Common Law, 76 B.U.L. Rev. 895 (1996)--p. 1

Meltzer, Congress, Courts, and Constitutional Remedies, 86 Geo.L.J. 2537 (1998)--pp. 14, 63

Meltzer, State Sovereign Immunity: Five Authors in Search of a Theory, 75 Notre Dame L. Rev. 1011 (2000)--p. 143

Meltzer, The *Seminole* Decision and State Sovereign Immunity, 1996 Sup. Ct. Rev. 1--pp. 94, 144

Monaghan, The Sovereign Immunity "Exception," 110 Harv. L. Rev. 102 (1995)--p. 94

Nahmod, The Restructuring of Narrative and Empathy in Section 1983 Cases, 72 Chi.-Kent L.Rev. 819 (1997)--p. 147

Nelson, Resolving Native American Land Claims and the Eleventh Amendment: Changing the Balance of Power, 39 Villanova L. Rev. 525 (1994)--p. 94

Neuman, Habeas Corpus, Executive Detention, and the Removal of Aliens, 98 Colum.L.Rev. 961 (1998)--p. 38

Note, Rewriting the Great Writ: Standards of Review for Habeas Corpus under the New 28 U.S.C. § 2254, 110 Harv.L.Rev. 1868 (1997)--p. 62

Nowak, The Gang of Five & the Second Coming of an Anti–Reconstruction Supreme Court, 75 Notre Dame L. Rev. 1091 (2000)--p. 143

Oakley, Federal Jurisdiction and the Problem of the Litigative Unit: When Does What "Arise Under" Federal Law, 76 Texas L.Rev. 1829 (1998)--p. 30

Oakley, Integrating Supplemental Jurisdiction and Diversity Jurisdiction: A Progress Report on the Work of the American Law Institute, 74 Ind.L.J. 25 (1998)--p. 34

Orth, History and the Eleventh Amendment, 75 Notre Dame L. Rev. 1147 (2000)--p. 143

Peterson, Controlling the Federal Courts Through the Appropriations Process, [1998] Wisc.L.Rev. 993--p. 14

Pfander, History and State Suability: An "Explanatory" Account of the Eleventh Amendment, 83 Corn.L.Rev. 1269 (1998)--p. 93

Pfander, Once More Unto the Breach: Eleventh Amendment Scholarship and the Court, 75 Notre Dame L. Rev. 817 (2000)--p. 143

Pfander, Supplemental Jurisdiction and Section 1367: The Case for a Sympathetic Textualism, 148 U. Pa. L. Rev. 109 (1999)--p. 34

Pillard, Taking Fiction Seriously: The Strange Results of Public Officials' Individual Liability Under *Bivens*, 88 Geo. L.J. 65 (1999)--p. 147

Pushaw, Congressional Power Over Federal Court Jurisdiction: A Defense of the Neo–Federalist Interpretation of Article III, Brigham Young L.Rev. 847 (1997)--p. 15

2000 SUPPLEMENT

# FEDERAL COURTS AND THE LAW OF FEDERAL–STATE RELATIONS

*

CHAPTER I

# Choice of Law in the Federal System

**Page 12, add at the end of footnote d:**

Compare Jack Goldsmith and Steven.Walt, *Erie* and the Irrelevance of Legal Positivism, 84 Va. L. Rev. 673 (1998), which argues that the historical connection between *Erie* and legal positivism has not been shown and that "*Erie's* commitment to legal positivism is conceptually and normatively independent of its constitutional holding."

**Page 13, Change Footnote 9 to footnote f; add at the end of the footnote:**

For commentary on the implications of *Printz* and an argument in favor of appropriately limited judicial enforcement of federalism limits on Congressional power, see Vicki C. Jackson, Federalism and the Uses and Limits of Law: *Printz* and Principle, 111 Harv. L. Rev. 2181 (1998).

**Page 14, add to the first sentence of footnote g:**

Paul Lund, The Decline of Federal Common Law, 76 B.U. L. Rev. 895 (1996).

**Page 15, add to the second sentence of footnote h:**

; Joel K. Goldstein, Federal Common Law in Admiralty: An Introduction to the Beginning of an Exchange, 43 St. Louis U. L.J. 1337 (1999) (advocating "a fairly robust federal common law-making role for admiralty courts"); Ernest A. Young, The Last Brooding Omnipresence: *Erie Railroad Co. v. Tompkins* and the Unconstitutionality of Preemptive Federal Maritime Law, 43 St. Louis U. L.J. 1349 (1999) (arguing that the "broad role of maritime preemption is unconstitutional"); Robert Force, An Essay on Federal Common Law and Admiralty, 43 St. Louis U. L.J. 1367 (1999) (defending the "constitutional authority [of federal courts] to create substantive rules of maritime law"); Steven F. Friedell, The Diverse Nature of Admiralty Jurisdiction, 43 St. Louis U. L.J. 1389 (1999) (arguing that Congress has confirmed the law-making authority of the federal admiralty courts on numerous occasions).

**Page 15, add at the end of footnote h:**

For reactions, see Harold Hongju Koh, Is International Law Really State Law, 111 Harv. L. Rev. 1824 (1998); Curtis A. Bradley and Jack L. Goldsmith, Federal Courts and the Incorporation of International Law, 111 Harv. L. Rev. 2260 (1998). See also Jack L. Goldsmith, Federal Courts, Foreign Affairs, and Federalism, 83 Va. L. Rev. 1617 (1997); Beth Stephens, The Law of Our Land: Customary International Law as Federal Law After *Erie*, 66 Fordham L. Rev. 393 (1997). For an interesting extrapolation from the Bradley and Goldsmith article cited above, see Lawrence Lessig, *Erie*-Effects of Volume 110: An Essay on Context in Interpretive Theory, 110 Harv. L. Rev. 1785 (1997).

**Page 22, revise the first sentence of Note 5(iii) and substitute a new footnote c:**

Forty-three states, plus the District of Columbia and Puerto Rico, now permit some form of certification of uncertain state law to the highest local court for resolution.[c]

**c.** Bradford R. Clark, Ascertaining the Laws of the Several States: Positivism and Judicial Federalism After *Erie*, 145 U. Pa. L. Rev. 1459, 1548 (1997). Clark examines alternative approaches to uncertain state law and concludes that a presumption in favor of certification is the preferred approach. See also Geri J. Yonover, A Kinder, Gentler *Erie*: Reigning in the Use of Certification, 47 Ark. L. Rev. 305 (1994).

**Page 22, add a footnote after the second sentence in Note 5(iii):**

**d.** For an example of unanimous use of the certification procedure by the Supreme Court seeking the answer to a question of state law that would shape the federal constitutional question presented by a petition for federal habeas corpus, see Fiore v. White, ___ U.S. ___ (1999).

**Page 50, add a new Note:**

**5. The Anti–Commandeering Principle.** In Printz v. United States, 521 U.S. 898 (1997), the Supreme Court ruled that Congress could not constitutionally require local law enforcement to conduct background checks of firearms purchasers, as specified in the Brady Handgun Violence Prevention Act. The Court found the requirement violative of what has been called the anti-commandeering principle, namely, that "[t]he federal government may not compel the states to enact or administer a federal regulatory program." New York v. United States, 505 U.S. 144, 188 (1992).

Although the anti-commandeering principle in terms applies only to executive officers, there is perhaps some tension between that view of state sovereignty as a limit on federal legislative power and the requirement, often associated with *Testa v. Katt*, that state courts hear federal claims. The *Printz* Court distinguished congressional "commandeering" of state judges on the ground that they are bound by the supremacy clause to enforce state law. This reasoning, though not the conclusion to which it leads, is questioned and its implications explored in Martin H. Redish and Steven G. Sklaver, Federal Power to Commandeer State Courts: Implications for the Theory of Judicial Federalism, 32 Ind. L. Rev. 71 (1998), and Vicki C. Jackson, The Infrastructure of Federal Supremacy, 32 Ind. L. Rev. 111 (1998).

The problem became more acute after Alden v. Maine, 527 U.S. 706 (1999) (reprinted, infra, as a main case in this Supplement), where the Supreme Court invoked *Printz* and the anti-commandeering principle in support of its conclusion that Congress lacked power to override state sovereign immunity in state courts. For an anticipatory endorsement of that reasoning and careful examination of its relation to *Testa v. Katt*, see Richard H. Seamon, The Sovereign Immunity of States in Their Own Courts, 37 Brandeis L. Rev. 319 (1998–99).

**Page 92, add at the end of footnote a:**

For an argument that "the Constitution dictates the boundaries" of the adequate and independent state ground doctrine, see Cynthia L. Fountaine, Article III and the Adequate and Independent State Grounds Doctrine, 48 American U. L. Rev. 1053 (1999).

CHAPTER II

# THE POWER OF THE FEDERAL COURTS TO CREATE FEDERAL LAW

**Page 173, add a new main case immediately before Section 3:**

## Gebser v. Lago Vista Independent School District

Supreme Court of the United States, 1998.
524 U.S. 274.

■ JUSTICE O'CONNOR delivered the opinion of the Court.

The question in this case is when a school district may be held liable in damages in an implied right of action under title IX of the Education Amendments of 1972 as amended, 20 U.S.C. § 1681 et seq., for the sexual harassment of a student by one of the district's teachers. We conclude that damages may not be recovered in those circumstances unless an official of the school district who at a minimum has authority to institute corrective measures on the district's behalf has actual notice of, and is deliberately indifferent to, the teacher's misconduct.

I

In the spring of 1991, when petitioner Alida Star Gebser was an eighth-grade student at a middle school in respondent Lago Vista Independent School District (Lago Vista), she joined a high school book discussion group led by Frank Waldrop, a teacher at Lago Vista's high school. Lago Vista received federal funds at all pertinent times. During the book discussion sessions, Waldrop often made sexually suggestive comments to the students. Gebser entered high school in the fall and was assigned to classes taught by Waldrop in both semesters. Waldrop continued to make inappropriate remarks to the students, and he began to direct more of his suggestive comments toward Gebser, including the substantial amount of time that the two were alone in his classroom. He initiated sexual contact with Gebser in the spring, when, while visiting her home ostensibly to give her a book, he kissed and fondled her. The two had sexual intercourse on a number of occasions during the remainder of the school year. . . .

Gebser did not report the relationship to school officials, testifying that while she realized Waldrop's conduct was improper, she was uncertain how to react and she wanted to continue having him as a teacher. In October

1992, the parents of two other students complained to the high school principal about Waldrop's comments in class. The principal arranged a meeting, at which, according to the principal, Waldrop indicated that he did not believe he had made offensive remarks but apologized to the parents and said it would not happen again. The principal also advised Waldrop to be careful about his classroom comments and told the school guidance counselor about the meeting, but he did not report the parents' complaint to Lago Vista's superintendent, who was the district's title IX coordinator. A couple of months later, in January 1993, a police officer discovered Waldrop and Gebser engaging in sexual intercourse and arrested Waldrop. Lago Vista terminated his employment. . . .

Gebser and her mother filed suit against Lago Vista and Waldrop in state court in November 1993, raising claims against the school district under title IX, 42 U.S.C. § 1983, and state negligence law, and claims against Waldrop primarily under state law. . . . After the case was removed, the United States District Court for the Western District of Texas granted summary judgment in favor of Lago Vista on all claims, and remanded the allegations against Waldrop to state court. In rejecting the title IX claim against the school district, the court reasoned that the statute "was enacted to counter *policies* of discrimination . . . in federally funded education programs," and that "[o]nly if school administrators have some type of notice of the gender discrimination and fail to respond in good faith can the discrimination be interpreted as a *policy* of the school district." . . . The Court of Appeals for the Fifth Circuit affirmed . . . and we now affirm.

II

Title IX provides in pertinent part that, "[n]o person . . . shall, on the basis of sex, be excluded from participation in, be denied the benefits of, or be subjected to discrimination under any education program or activity receiving federal financial assistance." 20 U.S.C. § 1681(a). The express statutory means of enforcement is administrative: The statute directs federal agencies who distribute education funding to establish requirements to effectuate the nondiscrimination mandate, and permit the agencies to enforce those requirements through "any means authorized by law," including ultimately the termination of federal funding. § 1682. The Court held in Cannon v. University of Chicago, 441 U.S. 677 (1979), that title IX is also enforceable through an implied private right of action, a conclusion we do not revisit here. We subsequently established in Franklin v. Gwinnett County Public Schools, 503 U.S. 60 (1992), that monetary damages are available in the implied action. . . .

*Franklin* . . . establishes that a school district can be held liable in damages in cases involving a teachers' sexual harassment of a student; the decision, however, does not purport to define the contours of that liability.

We face that issue squarely in this case. Petitioners, joined by the United States as amicus curiae, would invoke standards used by the courts of appeals in title VII cases involving a supervisor's sexual harassment of an employee in the workplace. [One approach, based on common-law agency theory, would impose respondeat superior liability "whenever a teacher's authority over a student facilities the harassment," "irrespective of whether school district officials had any knowledge of the harassment and irrespective of their response upon becoming aware." Alternatively, petitioners argued that liability should be imposed on a theory of constructive notice when the district knew or should have known of the harassment "but failed to uncover and eliminate it."]

In this case ..., petitioners seek not just to establish a title IX violation but to recover *damages* based on theories of respondeat superior and constructive notice. It is that aspect of their action, in our view, which is most critical to resolving the case. Unlike title IX, title VII contains an express cause of action and specifically provides for relief in the form of money damages. Congress ... has directly addressed the subject of damages relief under title VII and has set out the particular situations in which damages are available as well as the maximum amounts recoverable. With respect to title IX, however, the private right of action is judicially implied, and there is thus no legislative expression of the scope of available remedies, including when it is appropriate to award monetary damages. ...

III

Because the private right of action under title IX is judicially implied, we have a measure of latitude to shape a sensible remedial scheme that best comports with the statute. That endeavor inherently entails a degree of speculation, since it addresses an issue on which Congress has not specifically spoken. To guide the analysis, we generally examine the relevant statute to ensure that we do not fashion the parameters of an implied right in an manner at odds with the statutory structure and purpose.

Those considerations, we think, are pertinent not only to the scope of the implied right, but also the scope of the available remedies. ... Applying those principles here, we conclude that it would "frustrate the purposes" of title IX to permit a damages recovery against a school district for a teacher's sexual harassment of a student based on principles of respondeat superior or constructive notice, i.e., without actual notice to a school district official. ...

As a general matter, it does not appear that Congress contemplated unlimited recovery in damages against a funding recipient where the recipient is unaware of discrimination in its programs. When title IX was enacted in 1972, the principal civil rights statutes containing an express right of action did not provide for recovery of monetary damages at all, instead allowing only injunctive and equitable relief. It was not until 1991 that Congress made damages available under title VII, and even then, Congress carefully limited the amount recoverable in any individual case, calibrating the maximum recovery to the size of the employer. Adopting petitioners' position would amount, then, to allowing unlimited recovery of damages under title IX where Congress has not spoken on the subject of either the right or the remedy, and in the face of evidence that when Congress expressly considered both in title VII it restricted the amount of damages available.

Congress enacted title IX in 1972 with two principal objectives in mind: "to avoid the use of federal resources to support discriminatory practices" and "to provide individual citizens effective protection against those practices." *Cannon*, supra, at 704. The statute was modeled after title VI of the Civil Rights Act of 1964, which is parallel to title IX except that it prohibits race discrimination, not sex discrimination, and applies in all programs receiving federal funds, not only in education programs. See 42 U.S.C. § 2000d et seq. The two statutes operate in the same manner, conditioning an offer of federal funding on a promise by the recipient not to discriminate, in what amounts essentially to a contract between the government and the recipient of funds.

That contractual framework distinguishes title IX from title VII, which is framed in terms not of a condition but of an outright prohibition ... [W]hereas title VII aims centrally to compensate victims of discrimination, title IX focuses more on "protecting" individuals from discriminatory practices carried out by recipients of federal funds. That might explain why, when the Court first recognized the implied right under title IX in *Cannon*, the opinion referred to injunctive or equitable relief in a private action, but not to a damages remedy.

Title IX's contractual nature has implications for our construction of the scope of available remedies. When Congress attaches conditions to the award of federal funds under its spending power, ... we examine closely the propriety of private actions holding the recipient liable in monetary damages for noncompliance with the condition. Our central concern ... is with ensuring "that the receiving entity of federal funds [has] notice that it will be liable for a monetary award." *Franklin*, supra, at 74. ... If a school district's liability for a teacher's sexual harassment rests on principles of constructive notice or respondeat superior, it will ... be the case that the recipient of funds was unaware of the discrimination. It is sensible to assume that Congress did not envision a recipient's liability in damages in that situation. See Rosa H. v. San Elizario Independent School Dist., 106 F.3d 648, 654 (5th Cir.1997) ("When the school board accepted federal funds, it agreed not to discriminate on the basis of sex. We think it unlikely that it further agreed to suffer liability whenever its employees discriminate on the basis of sex.").

Most significantly, title IX contains important clues that Congress did not intend to allow recovery in damages where liability rests solely on principles of vicarious liability or constructive notice. Title IX's express means of enforcement—by administrative agencies—operates on an assumption of actual notice to officials of the funding recipient. [A]n agency may not initiate enforcement proceedings until it "has advised the appropriate person or persons of the failure to comply with the requirement and has determined that compliance cannot be secured by voluntary means." 20 U.S.C. § 1682. . . .

Presumably, a central purpose of requiring notice of the violation "to the appropriate person" and an opportunity for voluntary compliance before administrative enforcement proceedings can commence is to avoid diverting education funding from beneficial uses where a recipient was unaware of discrimination in its programs and is willing to institute prompt corrective measures. The scope of private damages relief proposed by petitioners is at odds with that basic objective. . . .

It would be unsound, we think for a statute's *express* system of enforcement to require notice to the recipient and an opportunity to come into voluntary compliance while a judicially *implied* system of enforcement permits substantial liability without regard to the recipient's knowledge or its corrective actions upon receiving notice. Moreover, an award of damages in a particular case might well exceed a recipient's level of federal funding. See Tr. of Oral Arg. 35 (Lago Vista's federal funding for 1992–1993 was roughly $120,000). Where a statute's express enforcement scheme hinges its most severe sanction on notice and unsuccessful efforts to obtain compliance, we cannot attribute to Congress the intention to have implied an enforcement scheme that allows imposition of greater liability without comparable conditions.

IV

Because the express remedial scheme under title IX is predicated upon notice to an "appropriate person" and an opportunity to rectify any violation, we conclude, in the absence of further direction from Congress, that an implied damages remedy should be fashioned along the same lines. An "appropriate person" under § 1682 is, at a minimum, an official of the recipient entity with authority to take corrective action to end the discrimination. Consequently, in cases like this one that do not involve official policy of the recipient entity, we hold that a damages remedy will not lie under title IX unless an official who at a minimum has authority to address the alleged discrimination and to institute correction measures on the recipient's behalf has actual knowledge of discrimination in the recipient's programs and fails adequately to respond.

We think, moreover, that the response must amount to deliberate indifference to discrimination. The administrative enforcement scheme presupposes that an official who is advised of a title IX violation refuses to take action to bring the recipient into compliance. The premise, in other words, is an official decision by the recipient not to remedy the violation. That framework finds rough parallel in the standard of deliberate indifference. . . .

Applying the framework to this case is fairly straightforward, as petitioners do not contend they can prevail under an actual notice standard. ... Petitioners focus primarily on Lago Vista's asserted failure to promulgate and publicize an effective policy and grievance procedure for sexual harassment claims. They point to Department of Education regulations requiring [such procedures]. Lago Vista's alleged failure to comply with the regulations, however, does not establish the requisite actual notice and deliberate indifference. And in any event, the failure to promulgate a grievance procedure does not itself constitute "discrimination" under title IX. ...

V

The number of reported cases involving sexual harassment of students in schools confirms that harassment unfortunately is an all too common aspect of the educational experience. No one questions that a student suffers extraordinary harm when subjected to sexual harassment and abuse by a teacher, and that the teacher's conduct is reprehensible and undermines the basic purposes of the educational system. The issue in this case, however, is whether the independent misconduct of a teacher is attributable to the school district that employs him under a specific federal statute designed primarily to prevent recipients of federal financial assistance from using the funds in a discriminatory manner. Our decision does not affect any right of recovery that an individual may have against a school district as a matter of state law or against the teacher in his individual capacity under state law or under 42 U.S.C. § 1983. Until Congress speaks directly on the subject, however, we will not hold a school district liable in damages under title IX for a teacher's sexual harassment of a student absent actual notice and deliberate indifference. We therefore affirm the judgment of the court of appeals.

■ JUSTICE STEVENS, with whom JUSTICE SOUTER, JUSTICE GINSBURG, and JUSTICE BREYER join, dissenting.

... As a basis for its decision, the majority relies heavily on the notion that because the private cause of action under title IX is "judicially implied," the Court has "a measure of latitude" to use its own judgment in shaping a remedial scheme. This assertion of lawmaking authority is not faithful either to our precedents or to our duty to interpret, rather than to revise, congressional commands. Moreover, the majority's policy judgment about the appropriate remedy in this case thwarts the purposes of title IX.

I

It is important to emphasize that in Cannon v. University of Chicago, 441 U.S. 677 (1979), the court confronted a question of statutory construction. The decision represented our considered judgment about the intent of the Congress that enacted title IX in 1972. After noting that title IX had been patterned after title VI of the Civil Rights Act of 1964, which had been interpreted to include a private right of action, we concluded that Congress intended to authorize the same private enforcement of title IX. As long as the intent of Congress is clear, an implicit command has the same legal force as one that is explicit. . . .

In Franklin v. Gwinnett County Public Schools, 503 U.S. 60 (1992), we unanimously concluded that title IX authorized a high school student who had been sexually harassed by a sports coach/teacher to recover damages from the school district. That conclusion was supported by two considerations. In his opinion for the Court, Justice White first relied on the presumption that Congress intends to authorize "all appropriate remedies" unless it expressly indicates otherwise. He then noted that two amendments to title IX enacted after the decision in *Cannon* had validated *Cannon*'s holding and supported the conclusion that "Congress did not intend to limit the remedies available in a suit brought under title IX." Justice Scalia, concurring in the judgment, agreed that Congress' amendment of title IX to eliminate the states' 11th amendment immunity, see 42 U.S.C. § 2000d–7(a)(1), must be read "not only 'as a validation of *Cannon*'s holding,' but also as an implicit acknowledgment that damages are available."

Because these constructions of the statute have been accepted by Congress and are unchallenged here, they have the same legal effect as if the private cause of action seeking damages had been explicitly, rather than implicitly, authorized by Congress. We should therefore seek guidance from the text of the statute and settled legal principles rather than from our views about sound policy.

II

. . . *Franklin* . . . stands for the proposition that sexual harassment of a student by her teacher violates the duty—assumed by the school district in exchange for federal funds—not to discriminate on the basis of sex, and that a student may recover damages from a school district for such a violation.

Although the opinion the Court announces today is not entirely clear, it does not purport to overrule *Franklin*. Moreover, I do not understand the Court to question the conclusion that an intentional violation of title IX, of the type we recognized in *Franklin*, has been alleged in this case. During her freshman and sophomore years of high school, petitioner Alida Star Gebser was repeatedly subjected to sexual abuse by her teacher, Frank Waldrop, whom she had met in the eighth grade when she joined his high school book discussion group. Waldrop's conduct was surely intentional and it occurred during, and as a part of, a curriculum activity in which he wielded authority over Gebser that had been delegated to him by respondent. . . .

The Court nevertheless holds that the law does not provide a damages remedy for the title IX violation alleged in this case because no official of the school district with "authority to institute corrective measures on the district's behalf" had actual notice of Waldrop's misconduct. That holding is at odds with settled principles of agency law, under which the district is responsible for Waldrop's misconduct because "he was aided in accomplishing the tort by the existence of the agency relation." Restatement (Second) of Agency, § 219(2)(d) (1957). This case presents a paradigmatic example of a tort that was made possible, that was effected, and that was repeated over a prolonged period because of the powerful influence that Waldrop had over Gebser by reason of the authority that his employer, the school district, had delegated to him. As a secondary school teacher, Waldrop exercised even greater authority over his students than employers and supervisors exercise over their employees. His gross misuse of that authority allowed him to abuse this young student's trust.

Reliance on the principle set out in § 219(2)(d) of the Restatement comports with the relevant agency's interpretation of title IX. The United States Department of Education, through its Office for Civil Rights, recently issued a policy "guidance" stating that a school district is liable under title IX if one of its teachers "was aided in carrying out the sexual harassment of students by his or her position of authority with the institution." Dept. of Ed., Office for Civil Rights, Sexual Harassment Guidance: Harassment of Students by School Employees, Other Students, or Third Parties, 62 Fed. Reg. 12034, 12039 (1997). . . .

The reason why the common law imposes liability on the principal in such circumstances is the same as the reason why Congress included the prohibition against discrimination on the basis of sex in title IX: to induce school boards to adopt and enforce practices that will minimize the danger that vulnerable students will be exposed to such odious behavior. The rule that the court has crafted creates the opposite incentive. As long as school boards can insulate themselves from knowledge about this sort of conduct, they can claim immunity from damages liability. . . .

III

The Court advances several reasons why it would "frustrate the purposes" of title IX to allow recovery against a school district that does not have actual notice of a teacher's sexual harassment of a student. As the Court acknowledges, however, the two principal purposes that motivated the enactment of title IX were: (1) " 'to avoid the use of federal resources to support discriminatory practices' "; and (2) " 'to provide individual citizens effective protection against those practices,' " (quoting *Cannon*, supra, at 704). It seems quite obvious that both of these purposes would be served—not frustrated—by providing a damages remedy in a case of this kind. To the extent that the Court's reasons for its policy choice have any merit, they suggest that no damages should ever be awarded in a title IX case—in other words, that our unanimous holding in *Franklin* should be repudiated.

First, the Court observes that at the time title IX was enacted, "the principal civil rights statutes containing an express right of action did not provide for recovery of monetary damages at all." *Franklin*, however, forecloses this reevaluation of legislative intent; in that case, we "evaluate[d] the state of the law when the legislature passed title IX," 503 U.S., at 71, and concluded that "the same contextual approach used to justify an implied right of action more than amply demonstrates the lack of any legislative intent to abandon the traditional presumption in favor of all available remedies," id., at 72. . . .

Second, the Court suggests that the school district did not have fair notice when it accepted federal funding that it might be held liable " 'for a monetary award' " under title IX (quoting *Franklin*, supra, at 74). The Court cannot mean, however, that respondent was not on notice that sexual harassment of a student by a teacher constitutes an "intentional" violation of title IX for which damages are available, because we so held shortly before Waldrop began abusing Gebser. See *Franklin*, supra, at 74–75. . . .

The majority nevertheless takes the position that a school district that accepts federal funds under title IX should not be held liable in damages for an intentional violation of that statute if the district itself "was unaware of the discrimination." The Court reasons that because administrative proceedings to terminate funding cannot be commenced until after the grant recipient has received notice of its noncompliance and the agency determines that voluntary compliance is not possible, there should be no damages liability unless the grant recipient has actual notice of the violation (and thus an opportunity to end the harassment).

The fact that Congress has specified a particular administrative procedure to be followed when a subsidy is to be terminated, however, does not illuminate the question of what the victim of discrimination on the basis of sex must prove in order to recover damages in an implied right of action. Indeed, in *Franklin*, we noted that the Department of Education's Office of Civil Rights had declined to terminate federal funding of the school district at issue—despite its finding that a title IX violation had occurred—because "the district had come into compliance with title IX" after the harassment at issue. That fact did not affect the Court's analysis, much less persuade the Court that a damages remedy was unavailable. Cf. *Cannon*, supra, at 711 ("The fact that other provisions of a complex statutory scheme create express remedies has not been accepted as a sufficient reason for refusing to imply an otherwise appropriate remedy under a separate section"). . . .

## IV

. . . It is possible, of course, that in some cases the recoverable damages, in either a title IX action or a state-law tort action, would exceed the amount of a federal grant. That is surely not relevant to the question whether the school district or the injured student should bear the risk of harm—a risk against which the district, but not the student, can insure. It is not clear to me why the well-settled rules of law that impose responsibility on the principal for the misconduct of its agents should not apply in this case. As a matter of policy, the Court ranks protection of the school district's purse above the protection of immature high school students that those rules would provide. Because those students are members of the class for whose special benefit Congress enacted title IX, that policy choice is not faithful to the intent of the policymaking branch of our government.

I respectfully dissent.

■ JUSTICE GINSBURG, with whom JUSTICE SOUTER and JUSTICE BREYER join, dissenting. . . .

I join [Justice Stevens'] opinion [and add that] I would recognize as an affirmative defense to a title IX charge of sexual harassment, an effective policy for reporting and redressing such misconduct. School districts subject to title IX's governance have been instructed by the Secretary of Education to install procedures for "prompt and equitable resolution" of complaints, 34 CFR § 106.8(b) (1977), and the Department of Education's Office of Civil Rights has detailed elements of an effective grievance process, with specific reference to sexual harassment. 62 Fed. Reg. 12034, 12044–45 (1997).

The burden would be on the school district to show that its internal remedies were adequate publicized and likely would have provided redress without exposing the complainant to undue risk, effort, or expense. Under such a regime, to the extent that a plaintiff unreasonably failed to avail herself of the school district's preventive and remedial measures, and consequently suffered avoidable harm, she would not qualify for title IX relief.

## NOTE ON *GEBSER v. LAGO VISTA*

What question should the Court be asking in this case? Is the issue the standard of liability that the Court thinks most consistent with sound policy (as informed by explicit legislative choices), or is the question one of legislative intent? If the latter, how is that intent to be discerned? Does the (wholly unsurprising) fact that Congress did not impose explicit limits on a liability it did not explicitly create preclude the Court from crafting restrictive standards? Or affirmative defenses? How much of the dispute in this case turns on competing methodologies, and how much springs from differing conceptions of what the law should be?

CHAPTER III

# CONGRESSIONAL CONTROL OF THE FEDERAL COURTS

**Page 215, add a footnote after the words "constitutional rights" in the second sentence of the first full paragraph:**

**e.** Erwin Chemerinsky, A Framework for Analyzing the Constitutionality of Restrictions on Federal Court Jurisdiction in Immigration Cases, 29 U. Memphis L. Rev. 295 (1999), suggests that the Court will need to address this issue because of the exclusions of immigration cases from federal court jurisdiction in the 1996 Antiterrorism and Effective Death Penalty Act, Pub. L. No. 104–132, 110 Stat. 1214 (1996), and the Illegal Immigration Reform and Immigrant Responsibility Act of 1996, Pub. L. No. 104–208, div. C, 110 Stat. 3009 (1996).

**Page 218, add to the second sentence of footnote f:**

Julian Velasco, Congressional Control Over Federal Court Jurisdiction: A Defense of the Traditional View, 46 Catholic U. L. Rev. 671 (1997).

**Page 218, add at the end of footnote f:**

Of course, control over jurisdiction is not the only mechanism through which Congress can influence the actions of the federal courts. See Todd D. Peterson, Controlling the Federal Courts Through the Appropriations Process, [1998] Wisc. L. Rev. 993.

**Page 224, add to the end of footnote c:**

For treatments of *Klein* provoked by 1996 legislation in which Congress restricted federal court authority to impose remedial decrees on state prison systems, to grant writs of habeas corpus, and to review deportation orders, see Lawrence G. Sager, *Klein*'s First Principle: A Proposed Solution, 86 Geo. L.J. 2525 (1998), and the response in Daniel J. Meltzer, Congress, Courts, and Constitutional Remedies, 86 Geo. L.J. 2537 (1998). For additional articles in the same symposium addressing the issues covered in these and the following series of Notes, see Vicki C. Jackson, Introduction: Congressional Control of Jurisdiction and the Future of the Federal Courts—Opposition, Agreement, and Hierarchy, 86 Geo. L.J. 2445 (1998); David Cole, Jurisdiction and Liberty: Habeas Corpus and Due Process as Limits on Congress's Control of Federal Jurisdiction, 86 Geo. L.J. 2481 (1998); John Harrison, Jurisdiction, Congressional Power, and Constitutional Remedies, 86 Geo. L.J. 2513 (1998); Judith Resnick, The Federal Courts and Congress: Additional Sources, Alternative Texts, and Altered Aspirations, 86 Geo. L.J. 2589 (1998).

**Page 232, add to the second sentence of footnote e:**

Julian Velasco, Congressional Control Over Federal Court Jurisdiction: A Defense of the Traditional View, 46 Catholic U. L. Rev. 671 (1997).

**Page 232, add to the end of the first paragraph of footnote e:**

For a friendly elaboration of the Amar position, see Robert J. Pushaw, Jr., Congressional Power Over Federal Court Jurisdiction: A Defense of the Neo–Federalist Interpretation of Article III, [1997] Brigham Young L. Rev. 847.

**Page 232, add to the end of the second paragraph of footnote e:**

See also David E. Engdahl, Intrinsic Limits of Congress' Power Regarding the Judicial Branch, 1999 B.Y.U. L. Rev. 75. Engdahl criticizes Amar's analysis, suggests that one key to the scope of Congressional power over federal court jurisdiction lies in properly understanding the necessary and proper clause, and concludes that "[w]hile Congress may create or abolish inferior tribunals and may shuffle assignments among such federal courts as exist, no category of subject matter jurisdiction, once vested, may be divested from the judiciary as a whole, except by constitutional amendment."

**Page 232, add to the end of the third paragraph of footnote e:**

See also Evan Tsen Lee, On the Received Wisdom in Federal Courts, 147 U. Pa. L. Rev. 1111 (1999), which criticizes the received wisdom that constitutional claims should be channeled to state courts and "attempts to make an affirmative case for the normative attractiveness of a system that generally guarantees federal constitutional claimants at least one full hearing in federal court."

**Page 235, add to footnote o:**

For an interpretation of the Hart dialogue to speak to the essential qualities of art. III adjudication and not the essential quantity of federal court jurisdiction, see James S. Liebman and William F. Ryan, "Some Effectual Power": The Quantity and Quality of Decisionmaking Required of Article III Courts, 98 Colum. L. Rev. 696 (1998).

**Page 238, add at the end of footnote y:**

See also Kevin M. Clermont & Theodore Eisenberg, Do Case Outcomes Really Reveal Anything About the Legal System? Win Rates and Removal Jurisdiction, 83 Cornell L. Rev. 581 (1998), which examines statistics leading them to the conclusions that forum effects outcome and removal takes defendants "to a forum much more favorable."

**Page 298, add at the end of Note 3:**

For analysis of the intersection of non-article III courts and the seventh amendment, see Ellen E. Sward, Legislative Courts, Article III, and the Seventh Amendment, 77 N.C.L. Rev. 1037 (1999). Sward argues that the right to jury trial in civil cases should not necessarily be limited to article III courts but should extend as well to much non-article III adjudication.

**Page 330, at the end of *Plaut*, add a note as follows:**

## NOTE ON *MILLER v. FRENCH*

A variation on the problem in *Plaut* arose in Miller v. French, ___ U.S. ___ (2000), which concerned the "automatic stay" provision of the Prison Litigation Reform Act of 1995. That statute curtails structural reform injunctions against prisons. Basically, § 3626(b) of the statute requires that courts issue or continue such injunctions only if the relief is narrowly drawn and extends no further than is necessary to correct the violation of a federal right. The automatic stay provision, § 3626(e)(2), provides that a motion to terminate prospective relief automatically operates as a stay of that relief after 30 days, or 90 days if extended for "good cause." Under this provision, when a prison subject to a court order regarding conditions of confinement moves to terminate the injunction, the injunction is automatically lifted after a maximum of 90 days, unless the district court denies the motion.

In *Miller*, four inmates challenged this provision as an indirect legislative "suspension" of a final judgment, as condemned in *Plaut*. Speaking for the Court, Justice O'Connor rejected that argument:

> *Plaut* . . . was careful to distinguish the situation before the Court in that case—legislation that attempted to reopen the dismissal of a suit seeking money damages—from legislation that "altered the prospective effect of injunctions entered by Article III courts." . . . Prospective relief under a continuing, executory decree remains subject to alteration due to changes in the underlying law. . . .
>
> By establishing new standards for the enforcement of prospective relief in § 3626(b), Congress has altered the relevant underlying law. The PLRA has restricted courts' authority to issue and enforce prospective relief concerning prison conditions, requiring that such relief be supported by findings and precisely tailored to what is needed to remedy the violation of a federal right. [W]hen Congress changes the law underlying a judgment awarding prospective relief, that relief is no longer enforceable to the extent it is inconsistent with the new law. . . . Although the remedial injunction here is a "final judgment" for purposes of appeal, it is not the "last word of the judicial department." *Plaut*, 514 U.S., at 227. The provision of prospective relief is subject to the continuing supervisory jurisdiction of the court, and therefore may be altered according to subsequent changes in the law.

In reaching this conclusion, the Court relied particularly on Pennsylvania v. Wheeling & Belmont Bridge Co., 59 U.S. (18 How.) 421 (1856) (*Wheeling Bridge II*). In an earlier decision under the same name, the Court had ruled that a bridge across the Ohio River obstructed navigation (because it was too low) and therefore had to be removed. Congress thereafter enacted legislation declaring the bridge a "lawful structure." When the bridge was destroyed in a storm, the state of Pennsylvania sued to enjoin its reconstruction, claiming that the statute was an unconstitutional attempt to annul the Court's judgment requiring removal. In *Wheeling Bridge II*, the Court rejected that contention, saying that the intervening statute had altered the underlying law and rendered the bridge no longer unlawful. The Court noted that an award of damages would have been beyond Congress's power to undo, but concluded that continuing injunction against maintaining the bridge could be rendered invalid by a change in the underlying law. Parallel reasoning suggested that Congress could also change the underlying law governing prison reform injunctions.

Having found no separation-of-powers problem, the Court found that there might be a due process violation if the time limit imposed by the automatic stay provision proved so short that it deprived litigants of a meaningful opportunity to be heard. That issue, not being before the Court, was left to another day.

Justice Breyer, joined by Justice Stevens, dissented. Breyer thought that there was a separation-of-powers problem and that the automatic stay provision could be construed to avoid it by allowing courts to suspend the automatic stay on appropriate facts. Justice Souter, joined by Justice Ginsburg, dissented in part. They agreed with the majority that the statute precluded judicial discretion but believed that there would be a separation-of-powers violation if the time authorized proved insufficient. As there had been no consideration of whether the 90 days allowed by the statute were sufficient in this case, Souter suggested that the case be remanded for consideration of that issue.

CHAPTER IV

# JUSTICIABILITY

**Page 357, add at the end of Note 6:**

In a more recent article, Pushaw argues that "separation of powers in our democracy is frustrated by justiciability doctrines that permit courts to abdicate their role of enforcing federal law." See Robert J. Pushaw, Jr., Justiciability and Separation of Powers: A Neo–Federalist Approach, 81 Corn. L. Rev. 393 (1996). Pushaw includes extensive historical investigation of the origins and development of modern justiciability doctrines.

For another interesting perspective on the constitutional foundation of modern standing law, see Edward A. Hartnett, The Standing of the United States: How Criminal Prosecutions Show That Standing Doctrine Is Looking for Answers in All the Wrong Places, 97 Mich. L. Rev. 2239 (1999). Hartnett suggests that criminal prosecutions demonstrate that "injury in fact," in the sense of "concrete and particularized" harm, need not exist for the United States as plaintiff and consequently that injury is not part of the "irreducible constitutional minimum" of article III.

**Page 382, add a footnote at the end of the first sentence of Note 4:**

**d.** For criticism of a subsequent decision holding that ranchers and other competing users of waters that the U.S. Fish and Wildlife Service had restricted in order to preserve endangered species had standing to challenge such restrictions, see William W. Buzbee, Expanding the Zone, Tilting the Field: Zone of Interests and Article III Standing Analysis After *Bennett v. Spear*, 49 Admin. L. Rev. 763 (1997).

**Page 383, add a new main case before *Raines v. Byrd*:**

## Federal Election Commission v. Akins

Supreme Court of the United States, 1998.
524 U.S. 11.

■ JUSTICE BREYER delivered the opinion of the Court.

The Federal Election Commission (FEC) has determined that the American Israel Public Affairs Committee (AIPAC) is not a "political committee" as defined by the Federal Election Campaign Act of 1971 as amended, 2 U.S.C. § 431(4) (FECA), and, for that reason, the Commission has refused to require AIPAC to make disclosures regarding its membership, contributions, and expenditures that FECA would otherwise require. We hold that respondents, a group of voters, have standing to challenge the

Commission's determination in court, and we remand this case for further proceedings.

I

[T]he act imposes extensive recordkeeping and disclosure requirements upon groups that fall within the act's definition of a "political committee." Those groups must register with the FEC, appoint a treasurer, keep names and addresses of contributors, track and the amount and purpose of disbursements, and file complex FEC reports that include lists of donors giving in excess of $200 per year (often, these donors may be the group's members), contributions, expenditures, and any other disbursements irrespective of their purposes.

The act's use of the word "political committee" calls to mind the term "political action committee" . . ., [but the term] has a much broader scope. The act states that a "political committee" includes "*any* committee, club, association or other group of persons which receives" more than $1,000 in "contributions" or "which makes" more than $1,000 in "expenditures" in any given year. § 431(4)(A) (emphasis added).

This broad definition, however, is less universally encompassing than at first it may seem, for later definitional subsections limit its scope. The act defines the key terms "contribution" and "expenditure" as covering only those contributions and expenditures that are made "for the purpose of influencing any election for Federal office." §§ 431(8)(A)(i), (9)(A)(i). Moreover, the act sets forth detailed categories of disbursements, loans, and assistance-in-kind that do not count as a "contribution" or "expenditure," even when made for election-related purposes. §§ 431(8)(B), (9)(B). In particular, assistance given to help a particular candidate will not count toward the $1,000 "expenditure" ceiling that qualified an organization as a "political committee" if it takes the form of a "communication" by an organization "to its members"—as long as the organization at issue is a "membership organization or corporation" and it is not "organized primarily for the purpose of influencing the nomination . . . or election, of any individual." § 431(9)(B)(iiii).

This case arises out of an effort by respondents, a group of voters with views often opposed to those of AIPAC, to persuade the FEC to treat AIPAC as a "political committee." Respondents filed a complaint with the FEC, stating that AIPAC had made more than $1,000 in qualifying "expenditures" last year, and thereby became a "political committee." . . .

AIPAC asked the FEC to dismiss the complaint. AIPAC described itself as an issue-oriented organization that seeks to maintain friendship and promote goodwill between the United States and Israel. AIPAC conceded that it lobbies elected officials and disseminates information about candidates for public office. But . . . AIPAC denied that it had made the kinds of "expenditures" that matter for FECA purposes. . . .

To put the matter more specifically: AIPAC focused on certain "expenditures" that respondents had claimed were election-related, such as the costs of meetings with candidates, the introduction of AIPAC members to candidates, and the distribution of candidate position papers. AIPAC said that its spending on such activities, even if election-related, fell within a relevant exception. They amounted, said AIPAC, to communications by a membership organization with its members, which the act exempts from its definition of "expenditures." . . .

The FEC's General Counsel concluded that, between 1983 and 1988, AIPAC had indeed funded communications of the sort described. The General Counsel said that those expenditures were campaign related, in that they amounted to advocating the election or defeat of particular candidates. He added that these expenditures were "likely to have crossed the $1,000 threshold." At the same time, the FEC said that, although tit was a "close question," these expenditures were not membership communications, because that exception applies to a membership organization's communications with its members, and most of the persons who belonged to AIPAC did not qualify as "members" for purposes of the act. . . .

The FEC's determination that many of the persons who belonged to AIPAC were not "members" effectively foreclosed any claim that AIPAC's communications did not count as "expenditures" for purposes of determining whether it was a "political committee." . . .

The FEC nonetheless held that AIPAC was not subject to the disclosure requirements, but for a different reason. In the FEC's view, the act's definition of "political committee" includes only those organizations that have as a "major purpose" the nomination or election of candidates. AIPAC, it added, was fundamentally an issue-oriented lobbying organization, not a campaign-related organization, and hence AIPAC fell outside the definition of a "political committee" regardless. The FEC consequently dismissed respondents' complaint.

Respondents filed a petition in federal district court seeking review of the FEC's determination dismissing their complaint. The district court granted summary judgment for the FEC, and a divided panel of the court of appeals affirmed. The en banc court of appeals reversed, however, on the ground that the FEC's "major purpose" test improperly interpreted the act's definition of a "political committee." We granted the government's petition for certiorari. . . .

II

The Solicitor General argues that respondents lack standing to challenge the FEC's decision not to proceed against AIPAC. . . .

We [disagree]. Congress has specifically provided in FECA that "[a]ny person who believes a violation of this act . . . has occurred, may file a complaint with the Commission." § 437g(a)(1). It has added that "[a]ny party aggrieved by an order of the Commission dismissing a complaint filed by such party ... may file a petition" in district court seeking review of that dismissal. § 437g(a)(8)(A). History associates the word "aggrieved" with a congressional intent to cast the standing net broadly—beyond the common-law interests and substantive statutory rights upon which "prudential" standing traditionally rested.

Moreover, prudential standing is satisfied when the injury asserted by a plaintiff " 'arguably [falls] within the zone of interests to be protected to regulated by the statute ... in question.' " National Credit Union Admin. v. First National Bank & Trust Co., 522 U.S. 479, ___ (1998) (quoting Association of Data Processing Service Organizations, Inc. v. Camp, 397 U.S. 150, 153 (1970)). The kind of injury of which respondents complain—their failure to obtain relevant information—is injury of a kind that FECA seeks to address. We have found nothing in the act that suggests Congress intended to exclude voters from the benefits of these provisions, or otherwise to restrict standing, say, to political parties, candidates, or their committees.

Given the language of the statute and the nature of the injury, we conclude that Congress, intending to protect voters such as respondents from suffering the kind of injury here at issue, intended to authorize this kind of suit. Consequently, respondents satisfy "prudential" standing requirements.

Nor do we agree ... that Congress lacks the constitutional power to authorize federal courts to adjudicate this lawsuit. Article III, of course, limits Congress' grant of judicial power to "cases" or "controversies." That limitation means that respondents must show, among other things, an "injury in fact"....

The "injury in fact" that respondents have suffered consists of their inability to obtain information—lists of AIPAC donors (who are, according to AIPAC, its members), and campaign-related contributions and expenditures—that, on respondents' view of the law, the statute requires that AIPAC make public. There is no reason to doubt their claim that the information would help them (and others to whom they would communicate it) to evaluate candidates for public office, especially candidates who received assistance from AIPAC, and to evaluate the role that AIPAC's financial assistance might play in a specific election. Respondents' injury consequently seems concrete and particular. Indeed, this Court has previously held that a plaintiff suffers an "injury in fact" when the plaintiff fails to obtain information which must be publicly disclosed pursuant to a statute. Public Citizen v. Department of Justice, 491 U.S. 440, 449 (1989) (failure to obtain information subject to disclosure under Federal Advisory Committee Act "constitutes a sufficiently distinct injury to provide standing to sue").

The dissent refers to United States v. Richardson, 418 U.S. 166 (1974), a case in which a plaintiff sought information (details of Central Intelligence Agency expenditures) to which, he said, the Constitution's accounts clause, art. I, § 9, cl. 7, entitled him. The Court held that the plaintiff there lacked article III standing. The dissent says that *Richardson* and this case are "indistinguishable." But as the parties' briefs suggest—for they do not mention *Richardson*—that case does not control the outcome here.

*Richardson*'s plaintiff claimed that a statute permitting the CIA to keep its expenditures nonpublic violated the accounts clause, which requires that "a regular Statement and Account of the Receipts and Expenditures of all public Money shall be published from time to time." The Court held that the plaintiff lacked standing because there was "no 'logical nexus' between the [plaintiff's] asserted status of taxpayer and the claimed failure of the Congress to require the Executive to supply a more detailed report of the [CIA's] expenditures." 418 U.S., at 175 (quoting Flast v. Cohen, 392 U.S. 83, 102 (1968), for the proposition that in "taxpayer standing" cases, there must be "a logical nexus between the status asserted and the claim sought to be adjudicated").

In this case, however, the "logical nexus" inquiry is not relevant. Here, there is no constitutional provision requiring the demonstration of the "nexus" the Court believed must be shown in *Richardson* and *Flast*. Rather, there is a statute which, as we previously pointed out, does seek to protect individuals such as respondents from the kind of harm they say they have suffered, i.e., failing to receive particular information about campaign-related activities. . . .

The fact that the Court in *Richardson* focused upon taxpayer standing, not voter standing, places that case at still a greater distance from the case before us. . . .

The FEC's strongest argument is its contention that this lawsuit involves only a "generalized grievance." The Solicitor General points out that respondents' asserted harm (their failure to obtain information) is one which is " 'shared in substantially equal measure by all or a large class of citizens,' " quoting Warth v. Seldin, 422 U.S. 490, 499 (1975). This Court, he adds, has often said that "generalized grievance[s]" are not the kinds of harms that confer standing. See also Lujan v. Defenders of Wildlife, 504 U.S. 555, 573–74 (1992); Allen v. Wright, 468 U.S. 737, 755–56 (1984); [and others]. . . .

The kind of judicial language to which the FEC points, however, invariably appears in cases where the harm at issue is not only widely shared, but is also of an abstract and indefinite nature—for example, harm to the "common concern for obedience to law." L. Singer & Sons v. Union Pacific R. Co., 311 U.S. 295, 303 (1940); see also *Allen*, supra, 468 U.S., at 754. Cf. *Lujan*, supra, 504 U.S., at 572–78 (injury to interest in seeing that certain procedures are followed not normally sufficient by itself to confer standing). The abstract nature of the harm—for example, injury to the interest in seeing that the law is obeyed—deprives the case of the concrete specificity that characterized those controversies which were "the traditional concern of the courts at Westminster,'' and which today prevents a plaintiff from obtaining what would, in effect, amount to an advisory opinion.

Often the fact that an interest is abstract and the fact that it is widely shared go hand in hand. But their association is not invariable, and where a harm is concrete, though widely shared, the Court has found ''injury in fact.'' See *Public Citizen*, supra, 491 U.S. at 449–50. Thus the fact that a political forum may be more readily available where an injury is widely shared (while counseling against, say, interpreting a statute as conferring standing) does not, by itself, automatically disqualify an interest for article III purposes. Such an interest, where sufficiently concrete, may count as an ''injury in fact.'' This conclusion seems particularly obvious where (to use a hypothetical example) large numbers of individuals suffer the same common-law injury (say, a widespread mass tort), or where large numbers of voters suffer interference with voting rights conferred by law. We conclude that similarly, the informational injury at issue here, directly related to voting, the most basic of political rights, is sufficiently concrete and specific such that the fact that it is widely shared does not deprive Congress of constitutional power to authorize its vindication in the federal courts.

Respondents have also satisfied the remaining two constitutional standing requirements. The harm asserted is ''fairly traceable'' to the FEC's decision about which respondents complain. Of course, . . . it is possible that even had the FEC agreed with respondents' view of the law, it would still have decided in the exercise of its discretion not to require the AIPAC to produce the information. Yet that fact does not destroy article III ''causation,'' for we cannot know that the FEC would have exercised its prosecutorial discretion in this way. Agencies often have discretion about whether or not to take a particular action. Yet those adversely affected by a discretionary agency decision generally have standing to complain that the agency based its decision upon an improper legal ground. If a reviewing court agrees that the agency misinterpreted the law, it will set aside the agency's action and remand the case—even though the agency (like a new jury after a mistrial) might later, in the exercise of its lawful discretion, reach the same result for a different reason. Thus respondents' ''injury in fact'' is ''fairly traceable'' to the FEC's decision not to issue its complaint, even though the FEC might reach the same result exercising its discretionary powers lawfully. For similar reasons, the courts in this case can ''redress'' respondents' ''injury in fact.''

Finally, the FEC argues that we should deny respondents standing because this case involves an agency's decision not to undertake an enforcement action—an area generally not subject to judicial review. In Heckler v. Chaney, 470 U.S. 821, 832 (1985), this Court noted that agency enforcement decisions ''ha[ve] traditionally been 'committed to agency discretion,' '' and concluded that Congress did not intend to alter that tradition in enacting the APA. We deal here with a statute that explicitly indicates to the contrary.

In sum, respondents, as voters, have satisfied both prudential and constitutional standing requirements. They may bring this petition for a declaration that the FEC's dismissal of their complaint was unlawful. . . .

■ JUSTICE SCALIA, with whom JUSTICE O'CONNOR and JUSTICE THOMAS join, dissenting.

The provision of law at issue in this case is an extraordinary one, conferring upon a private person the ability to bring an executive agency into court to compel its enforcement of the law against a third party. . . . If provisions such as the present one were commonplace, the role of the executive branch in our system of separated and equilibrated powers would be greatly reduced, and that of the judiciary greatly expanded.

Because this provision is so extraordinary, we should be particularly careful not to expand it beyond its fair meaning. In my view, the Court's opinion does that. Indeed, it expands the meaning beyond what the Constitution permits.

I

It is clear that the Federal Election Campaign Act does not intend that *all* persons filing complaints with the Commission have the right to seek judicial review of the rejection of their complaints. This is evident from the fact that the act permits a complaint to be filed by "[a]ny *person* who believes a violation of this act . . . has occurred," 2 U.S.C. § 437g(a)(1) (emphasis added), but accords a right to judicial relief only to "[a]ny *party aggrieved* by an order of the Commission dismissing a complaint filed by such party," 2 U.S.C. § 437g(a)(8)(A) (emphasis added). The interpretation that the Court gives the latter provision deprives it of almost all its limiting force. *Any voter* can sue to compel the agency to require registration of an entity as a political committee, even though the "aggrievement" consists of nothing more than the deprivation of access to information whose public availability would have been one of the consequences of registration.

This seems to me too much of a stretch. It should be borne in mind that the agency action complained of here is not the refusal to make available information in its possession that the act requires to be disclosed. A person demanding provision of information that the law requires the agency to furnish . . . can reasonably be described as being "aggrieved" by the agency's refusal to provide it. What the respondents complain of in this suit, however, is not the refusal to provide information, but the refusal (for an allegedly improper reason) to commence an agency enforcement action against a third person. That refusal *itself* plainly does not render respondents "aggrieved" within the meaning of the act, for in that case there would have been no reason for the act to differentiate between "person" in subsection (a)(1) and "party aggrieved" in subsection (a)(8). . . .

And finally, a narrower reading of "party aggrieved" is supported by the doctrine of constitutional doubt, which counsels us to interpret statutes, if possible, in such fashion as to avoid grave constitutional questions. . . .

II

In United States v. Richardson, 418 U.S. 166 (1974), we dismissed for lack of standing a suit whose "aggrievement" was precisely the "aggrievement" respondents assert here: the government's unlawful refusal to place information within the public domain. The only difference, in fact, is that the aggrievement there was more direct, since the government already had the information within its possession, whereas here the respondents seek enforcement action that will bring information within the government's possession and *then* require the information to be made public. The plaintiff in *Richardson* challenged the government's failure to disclose the expenditures of the Central Intelligence Agency (CIA), in alleged violation of the constitutional requirement, art. I, § 9, cl. 7, that "a regular Statement and Account of the Receipts and Expenditures of all public Money shall be published from time to time." We held that such a claim was a nonjusticiable "generalized grievance" because "the impact on [plaintiff] is plainly undifferentiated and common to all members of the public."

It was alleged in *Richardson* that the government had denied a right conferred by the Constitution, whereas respondents here assert a right conferred by statute—but of course "there is absolutely no basis for making the article III inquiry turn on the source of the asserted right." Lujan v. Defenders of Wildlife, 504 U.S. 555, 576 (1992). The Court today distinguishes *Richardson* on a different basis—a basis that reduces it from a landmark constitutional holding to a curio. According to the Court, "*Richardson* focused upon taxpayer standing, . . . not voter standing." In addition to being a silly distinction, . . . this is also a distinction that the Court in *Richardson* went out of its way explicitly to eliminate. It is true enough that the narrow question presented in *Richardson* was " '[w]hether a federal taxpayer has standing.' " 418 U.S., at 167. But the *Richardson* Court did not hold only, as the Court today suggests, that the plaintiff failed to qualify for the exception to the rule of no taxpayer standing established by the "logical nexus" test of Flast v. Cohen, 392 U.S. 83 (1968). The plaintiff's complaint in *Richardson* had also alleged that he was " 'a member of the electorate,' " 418 U.S., at 167 n.1, and he asserted injury in that capacity as well. The *Richardson* opinion treated that as fairly included within the taxpayer-standing question, or at least as plainly distinguishable from it. . . .Fairly read, and applying a fair understanding of its important purposes, *Richardson* is indistinguishable from the present case.

The Court's opinion asserts that our language disapproving generalized grievances "invariably appears in cases where the harm at issue is not only widely shared, but is also of an abstract and indefinite nature." . . . But . . . the Court is wrong to think that generalized grievances have only concerned us when they are abstract. One need go no further than *Richardson* to prove that—unless the Court believes that deprivation of information is an abstract injury, in which event this case could be disposed of on that much broader ground.

What is noticeably lacking in the Court's discussion of our generalized-grievance jurisprudence is all reference to two words that have figured in it prominently: "particularized" and "undifferentiated." "Particularized" means that "the injury must affect the plaintiff in a personal and individual way." *Lujan*, supra, 504 U.S., at 560 n.1. If the effect is "undifferentiated and common to all members of the public," *Richardson*, supra, 418 U.S., at 177, the plaintiff has a "generalized grievance" that must be pursued by political rather than judicial means. These terms explain why it is a gross oversimplification to reduce the concept of a generalized grievance to nothing more than "the fact that [the grievance] is widely shared, thereby enable the concept to be dismissed as a standing principle by such examples as 'large numbers of individuals suffer[ing] the same common-law injury (say, a widespread mass tort), or . . . large numbers of voters suffer[ing] interference with voting rights conferred by law.' " The exemplified injuries are widely shared, to be sure, but each individual suffers a particularized and differentiated harm. One tort victim suffers a burnt leg, another a burnt arm—or even if both suffer burnt arms they are *different* arms. One voter suffers the deprivation of *his* franchise, another the deprivation of *hers*. With the generalized grievance, on the other hand, the injury or deprivation is not only widely shared but is *undifferentiated*. The harm caused to Mr. Richardson by the alleged disregard of the statement-of-accounts clause was precisely the same as the harm caused to everyone else: unavailability of a description of CIA expenditures. Just as the (more indirect) harm caused to Mr. Akins by the allegedly unlawful failure to enforce FECA is precisely the same as the harm caused to everyone else: unavailability of a description of AIPAC's activities.

The Constitution's line of demarcation between the executive power and the judicial power presupposes a common understanding of the type of interest needed to sustain a "case or controversy" against the executive in the courts. A system in which the citizenry at large could sue to compel executive compliance with the law would be a system in which the courts, rather than the president, are given the primary responsibility to "take Care that the Laws be faithfully executed," art. II, § 3. We do not have such a system because the common understanding of the interest necessary so sustain suit has included the requirement, affirmed in *Richardson*, that the complained-of injury be particularized and differentiated, rather than common to all the electorate. When the executive can be directed by the courts, at the instance of any voter, to remedy a deprivation which affects the entire electorate in precisely the same way—and particularly when that deprivation (here, the unavailability of information) is one inseverable part of a larger enforcement scheme—there has occurred a shift of political responsibility to a branch designed not to protect the public at large but to protect individual rights. "To permit Congress to convert the undifferentiated public interest in executive officers' compliance with the law into an 'individual right' vindicable in the courts is to permit Congress to transfer from the president to the courts the chief executive's most important constitutional duty...." *Lujan*, supra, 504 U.S. at 577. If today's decision is correct, it is within the power of Congress to authorize any interested person to manage (through the courts) the executive's enforcement of any law that includes a requirement for the filing and public availability of a piece of paper. This is not the system we have had, and is not the system we should desire.

**Page 388, add a footnote at the end of *Raines v. Byrd*:**

**a.** For commentary on *Raines*, see Neal Devins and Michael A. Fitts, The Triumph of Timing: *Raines v. Byrd* and the Modern Supreme Court's Attempt to Control Constitutional Confrontations, 86 Geo. L. J. 351 (1997). [Footnote by eds.]

**Page 414, add at end of Note 9 prior to Subsection C:**

See also John F. Duffy, Administrative Common Law in Judicial Review, 77 Texas L. Rev. 113 (1998).

**Page 418, add a new Note, as follows:**

**4A. *City of Erie v. Pap's "Kandyland."*** The Supreme Court appeared to follow, but not acknowledge, Chief Justice Rehnquist's approach in City of Erie v. Pap's A.M., tdba "Kandyland," ___ U.S. ___ (2000). When the City of Erie passed an ordinance aimed at nude dancing, Pap's, operator of an establishment known as "Kandyland," raised a first amendment challenge. Eventually, the Pennsylvania Supreme Court ruled in the plaintiff's favor and enjoined enforcement of the ordinance. Thereafter, Pap's closed Kandyland and sold the building to a developer. Pap's sole shareholder, who was of an age to retire, submitted an affidavit recounting those facts and confirming that neither he nor the corporation had any current interest in nude dancing nor any intention to own or operate such an establishment in the future. Based on these facts, the case looked moot. The problem, however, was that if mootness deprived the Court of jurisdiction to reach the merits, it also lacked jurisdiction to direct a vacatur by the state court. See ASARCO, Inc. v. Kadish, 490 U.S. 605, 621 n.1 (1989). That would mean that the judgment against Erie would remain in effect. Additionally, the Justices were irritated that the facts suggesting mootness had not been mentioned in Pap's response to the city's petition for certiorari but had first been raised in a motion to dismiss filed after certiorari was granted.

Speaking for the Court, Justice O'Connor found that the case was not moot. The Court refused to credit the owner's affidavit, noting that "Pap's is still incorporated under Pennsylvania law, and it could again decide to operate a nude dancing establishment in Erie." O'Connor noted that the city had an "ongoing injury because it is barred from enforcing the public nudity provisions of its ordinance," and concluded, somewhat obliquely, that "to the extent Pap's has an interest in resuming operations, it has an interest in preserving the judgment of the Pennsylvania Supreme Court." On the merits, the Court concluded that the ordinance was not unconstitutional.

Justice Scalia, joined by Justice Thomas, dissented on the mootness issue, arguing that the unfortunate situation of leaving in place an erroneous decision of the Pennsylvania Supreme Court did not justify "entertain[ing] a suit that the Constitution places beyond our power."

CHAPTER V

# SUBJECT MATTER JURISDICTION

**Page 459, add a new Note:**

**7a. *City of Chicago v. International College of Surgeons.*** The interrelationship between federal question jurisdiction, removal, review of state administrative action, and supplemental jurisdiction was elaborated by a divided Court in City of Chicago v. International College of Surgeons, 522 U.S. 156 (1997). The College of Surgeons (ICS) owned two properties on North Lake Shore Drive in Chicago. The Chicago Landmarks Commission had determined that two mansions on ICS property were historical landmarks, but ICS wished to sell the property to a developer for construction of a high-rise condominium. ICS's application for permission to demolish the mansions was denied by the Landmarks Commission. ICS then sought administrative review of the Commission's decision in the Circuit Court of Cook County pursuant to the Illinois Administrative Review Law. It also challenged the decision on a number of federal and state constitutional grounds.

The City removed the case to federal court. The District Court exercised jurisdiction over both the federal and state claims, ultimately ruling for the City on all counts. The Court of Appeals reversed, holding that the case had been improperly removed. The Supreme Court disagreed. It held the case properly removable, and upheld the District Court's jurisdiction over both federal and state claims.

For the Court, Justice O'Connor began by observing that it "is true ... that the federal constitutional claims were raised by way of a cause of action created by state law, namely, the Illinois Administrative Review Law." But, quoting Franchise Tax Board of California v. Construction Laborers Vacation Trust for Southern California, 463 U.S. 1 (1983), " '[even though state law creates [a party's] cause of action, its case might 'arise under' the laws of the United States if a well-pleaded complaint established that its right to relief under state law requires resolution of a substantial question of federal law.]' " Given this, and given that the state claims for relief derived "from a common nucleus of operative fact" (quoting *United Mine Workers v. Gibbs*), the supplemental jurisdiction statute authorized the district court to hear all of the claims.

Joined by Justice Stevens, Justice Ginsburg had a different take. She saw the case as "a watershed decision" because it authorized, in her view, a "cross system appeal":

> "This now-federal case originated as an appeal in state court from a municipal agency's denials of demolition permits. The review that state law provides is classically appellate in character—on the agency's record, not de novo. Nevertheless, the court decides today that this standard brand of appellate review can be shifted from the appropriate state tribunal to a federal court of first instance at the option of either party—plaintiff originally or defendant by removal. ... After today, litigants asserting federal-question ... jurisdiction may routinely lodge in federal courts direct appeals from the actions of all manner of local (county and municipal) agencies, boards, and commissions. Exercising this cross-system appellate authority, federal courts may now directly superintend local agencies by affirming, reversing, or modifying their administrative rulings."

The Court's response was that "[o]f course, to say that the terms of § 1367(a) authorize the district courts to exercise supplemental jurisdiction over state law claims for on-the-record review of administrative decisions does not mean that the jurisdiction *must* be exercised in all cases." Accordingly, it remanded for consideration whether the district court should have refused to hear the state claims based on abstention principles or the discretion to deny supplemental jurisdiction contained in *Gibbs* and 28 U.S.C. § 1367(c).

For a general discussion of how to determine the existence of federal question jurisdiction using as the point of departure *City of Chicago*, *Merrill Dow*, *Franchise Tax Board* (the next main case), and the less well known case of Christianson v. Colt Industries Operating Corp., 486 U.S. 800 (1988), see John B. Oakley, Federal Jurisdiction and the Problem of the Litigative Unit: When Does What "Arise Under" Federal Law, 76 Texas L. Rev. 1829 (1998).

**7b. The Primacy of Subject Matter Jurisdiction.** Rule 12(h)(3) of the Federal Rules of Civil Procedure provides that "[w]henever it appears by suggestion of the parties or otherwise that the court lacks jurisdiction of the subject matter, the court shall dismiss the action." It is standard lore that this requirement operates at all levels of adjudication. If an appellate court notices at any stage of the proceedings that the district court lacked subject matter jurisdiction, it is obliged to order dismissal of the case for lack of jurisdiction and is foreclosed from reaching the merits of the case.[j]

**(i) Hypothetical Jurisdiction: *Steel Co. v. Citizens for a Better Environment*.** In Steel Co. v. Citizens for a Better Environment, 523 U.S. 83 (1998), six Justices concluded that the plaintiff lacked article

**j.** "[I]f the record discloses that the lower court was without jurisdiction this Court will notice the defect, although the parties make no contention concerning it. [This Court will then have] jurisdiction on appeal, not of the merits but merely for the purpose of correcting the error of the lower court in entertaining the suit." United States v. Corrick, 298 U.S. 435, 440 (1936).

III standing to bring suit under a federal statute. The other three thought that the federal statute should not be interpreted to authorize the suit. In the course of his opinion for the Court on the standing question, Justice Scalia described a jurisdictional practice that had grown up in the Courts of Appeals:

> "[S]everal Courts of Appeals ... find it proper to proceed immediately to the merits ... despite jurisdictional objections, at least where (1) the merits question is more readily resolved, and (2) the prevailing party on the merits would be the same as the prevailing party were jurisdiction denied. The Ninth Circuit has denominated this practice—which it characterizes as 'assuming' jurisdiction for the purpose of deciding the merits—the 'doctrine of hypothetical jurisdiction.' "

Justice Scalia made it clear that such a doctrine was unacceptable:

> "We decline to endorse such an approach because it carries the courts beyond the bounds of authorized judicial action and thus offends fundamental principles of separation of powers. This conclusion should come as no surprise, since it is reflected in a long and venerable line of our cases. [Citations omitted.] This Court's insistence that proper jurisdiction appear begins at least as early as 1804, when we set aside a judgment for the defendant at the instance of the losing plaintiff *who had himself* failed to allege the basis for federal jurisdiction. Capron v. Van Noorden, 6 U.S. (2 Cranch) 126 (1804)."

Justice Scalia examined a line of Supreme Court cases that had been cited by the Courts of Appeals in support of its asserted authority. He distinguished them all and continued:

> "While some of the above cases must be acknowledged to have diluted the absolute purity of the rule that article III jurisdiction is always an antecedent question, none of them even approaches approval of a doctrine of 'hypothetical jurisdiction' that enables a court to resolve contested questions of law when its jurisdiction is in doubt. Hypothetical jurisdiction produces nothing more than a hypothetical judgment—which comes to the same thing as an advisory opinion, disapproved by this Court from the beginning. Much more than legal niceties are at stake here. The statutory and (especially) constitutional elements of jurisdiction are an essential ingredient of separation and equilibration of powers, restraining the courts from acting at certain times, and even restraining them from acting permanently regarding certain subjects. For a court to pronounce upon the meaning or the constitutionality of a state or federal law when it has no jurisdiction to do so is, by very definition, for a court to act ultra vires."

Two Justices in the majority reserved judgment about whether the opinion should be read as an absolute prohibition. Joined by Justice Kennedy, Justice O'Connor wrote separately to say that, while she agreed "that federal courts should be certain of their jurisdiction before reaching the merits of a case," she nonetheless thought that "the Court's opinion should not be read as cataloguing an exhaustive list of circumstances under which federal courts may exercise judgment in 'reserv[ing] difficult questions of . . . jurisdiction when the case alternatively could be resolved on the merits in favor of the same party.' Norton v. Mathews, 427 U.S. 524, 532 (1976)."

Justice Breyer went further. He said:

> "I agree with the Court that the respondent in this case lacks article III standing. I further agree that federal courts often and typically should decide standing questions at the outset of a case. That order of decision (first jurisdiction then the merits) helps better to restrict the use of the federal courts to those adversarial disputes that article III defines as the federal judiciary's business. But my qualifying words 'often' and 'typically' are important. The Constitution, in my view, does not require us to replace those words with the word 'always.' The Constitution does not impose a rigid judicial 'order of operations,' when doing so would cause serious practical problems.
>
> "This Court has previously made clear that courts may 'reserve [ ] difficult questions of . . . jurisdiction when the case alternatively could be resolved on the merits in favor of the same party.' Norton v. Mathews, 427 U.S. 524, 532 (1976). That rule makes theoretical sense, for the difficulty of the jurisdictional question makes reasonable the court's jurisdictional assumption. And that rule makes enormous practical sense. Whom does it help to have appellate judges spend their time and energy puzzling over the correct answer to an intractable jurisdictional matter, when (assuming an easy answer on the substantive merits) the same party would win or lose regardless? More importantly, to insist upon a rigid 'order of operations' in today's world of federal court caseloads that have grown enormously over a generation means unnecessary delay and consequent added cost. It means a more cumbersome system. It thereby increases, to at least a small degree, the risk of the 'justice delayed' that means 'justice denied.' "
>
> "For this reason, I would not make the ordinary sequence an absolute requirement. Nor, even though the case before us is ordinary, not exceptional, would I simply reserve judgment about the matter."[k]

**k.** For an extensive consideration of *Steel*, its Court of Appeals antecedents, and its likely effect on future decisions in the Courts of Appeals, see Scott C. Idelman, The

**(ii) In Personam v. Subject Matter Jurisdiction: *Ruhrgas AG v. Marathon Oil Co.*** Ruhrgas AG v. Marathon Oil Co., 526 U.S. 574 (1999), involved an easy question of in personam jurisdiction and a hard question of subject matter jurisdiction (in this case, whether diversity or federal question jurisdiction could be established). Writing for a unanimous Court, Justice Ginsburg adhered to *Steel*, but held it appropriate to address the issue of in personam jurisdiction without resolving the question of subject matter jurisdiction:

> "This case concerns the authority of the federal courts to adjudicate controversies. Jurisdiction to resolve cases on the merits requires both authority over the category of claim in suit (subject-matter jurisdiction) and authority over the parties (personal jurisdiction), so that the court's decision will bind them. In Steel Co. v. Citizens for Better Environment, 523 U.S. 83 (1998), this Court adhered to the rule that a federal court may not hypothesize subject-matter jurisdiction for the purpose of deciding the merits. *Steel Co.* is the backdrop for the issue now before us: If, as *Steel Co.* held, jurisdiction generally must precede merits in dispositional order, must subject-matter jurisdiction precede personal jurisdiction on the decisional line? Or, do federal district courts have discretion to avoid a difficult question of subject-matter jurisdiction when the absence of personal jurisdiction is the surer ground? . . .
>
> "We hold that in cases removed from state court to federal court, as in cases originating in federal court, there is no unyielding jurisdictional hierarchy. Customarily, a federal court first resolves doubts about its jurisdiction over the subject matter, but there are circumstances in which a district court appropriately accords priority to a personal jurisdiction inquiry. The proceeding before us is such a case. . . .
>
> "The Court of Appeals accorded priority to the requirement of subject-matter jurisdiction because it is nonwaivable and delimits federal-court power, while restrictions on a court's jurisdiction over the person are waivable and protect individual rights. The character of the two jurisdictional bedrocks unquestionably differs. Subject-matter limitations on federal jurisdiction serve institutional interests. They keep the federal courts within the bounds the Constitution and Congress have prescribed. Accordingly, subject-

Demise of Hypothetical Jurisdiction in the Federal Courts, 52 Vand. L. Rev. 235 (1999). Idelman concludes that "[w]hile the outward form and even the doctrinal core of hypothetical jurisdiction may have been eliminated by the Court's formalist decree, its value and thus its essence will long persist in the deliberations, and quite possibly the decisions, of the lower federal bench."

matter delineations must be policed by the courts on their own initiative even at the highest level. . . .

"These distinctions do not mean that subject-matter jurisdiction is ever and always the more 'fundamental.' . . . While *Steel Co.* reasoned that subject-matter jurisdiction necessarily precedes a ruling on the merits, the same principle does not dictate a sequencing of jurisdictional issues. . . . It is hardly novel for a federal court to choose among threshold grounds for denying audience to a case on the merits. Thus, as the Court observed in *Steel Co.*, district courts do not overstep article III limits when they decline jurisdiction of state-law claims on discretionary grounds without determining whether those claims fall within their pendent jurisdiction, see Moor v. County of Alameda, 411 U.S. 693, 715–16 (1973), or abstain under Younger v. Harris, 401 U.S. 37 (1971), without deciding whether the parties present a case or controversy, see Ellis v. Dyson, 421 U.S. 426, 433–34 (1975). . . .

"Where, as here, . . . a district court has before it a straightforward personal jurisdiction issue presenting no complex question of state law, and the alleged defect in subject-matter jurisdiction raises a difficult and novel question, the court does not abuse its discretion by turning directly to personal jurisdiction."

**Page 500, add to the last paragraph of Note 2:**

Robert G. Bone, Revisiting the Policy Case for Supplement Jurisdiction, 74 Ind. L.J. 139 (1998); Edward H. Cooper, An Alternative and Discretionary § 1367, 74 Ind. L.J. 153 (1998); Howard P. Fink, Supplemental Jurisdiction—Take it to the Limit!, 74 Ind. L.J. 161 (1998); William A. Fletcher, "Common Nucleus of Operative Fact" and Defensive Set–Off: Beyond the *Gibbs* Test, 74 Ind. L.J. 171 (1998); Richard D. Freer, Toward a Principled Statutory Approach to Supplemental Jurisdiction in Diversity of Citizenship Cases, 74 Ind. L.J. 5 (1998); Graham C. Lilly, Making Sense of Nonsense: Reforming Supplemental Jurisdiction, 74 Ind. L.J. 181 (1998); John B. Oakley, Intergrating Supplemental Jurisdiction and Diversity Jurisdiction: A Progress Report on the Work of the American Law Institute, 74 Ind. L.J. 25 (1998); James E. Pfander, Supplemental Jurisdiction and Section 1367: The Case for a Sympathetic Textualism, 148 U. Pa. L. Rev. 109 (1999); Peter Raven–Hansen, The Forgotten Proviso of § 1376(b) (And Why We Forgot), 74 Ind. L.J. 197 (1998); Thomas D. Rowe, Jr., 1367 and All That: Recodifying Supplemental Jurisdiction, 74 Ind. L.J. 53 (1998); David L. Shapiro, Supplemental Jurisdiction: A Confession, An Avoidance, and a Proposal, 74 Ind. L.J. 211 (1998); Joan Steinman, Crosscurrents: Supplemental Jurisdiction, Removal, and the ALI Revision Project, 74 Ind. L.J. 75 (1998); Arthur D. Wolf, Comment on the Supplemental–Jurisdiction Statute: 28 U.S.C. § 1367, 74 Ind. L.J. 223 (1998); Stephen C. Yeazell, Teaching Supplemental Jurisdiction, 74 Ind. L.J. 241 (1998).

**Page 518, add at the end of footnote c:**

*Gasperini* has engendered a new round of debate in the *Erie* literature. See, e.g., C. Douglas Floyd, *Erie* Awry: A Comment on *Gasperini v. Center for Humanities, Inc.*, [1997] Brigham Young L. Rev. 267; Richard D. Freer, Some Thoughts on the State of *Erie* After *Gasperini*, 76 Texas L. Rev. 1637 (1998); Thomas D. Rowe, Jr., Not Bad for Government Work: Does Anyone Else Think the Supreme Court is Doing a Halfway Decent Job in its *Erie-Hanna* Jurisprudence?, 73 Notre Dame L. Rev. 963 (1998).

**Page 529, add to footnote a:**

For a more general discussion of how the Supreme Court should interpret the limitations of the Rules Enabling Act, see Leslie M. Kelleher, Taking "Substantive Rights" (in the Rules Enabling Act) More Seriously, 74 Notre Dame L. Rev. 47 (1998).

**Page 538, add to last paragraph of Note 6:**

Joseph P. Bauer, The *Erie* Doctrine Revisited: How a Conflicts Perspective Can Aid the Analysis, 74 Notre Dame L. Rev. 1235 (1999); John T. Cross, The *Erie* Doctrine in Equity, 60 La. L. Rev. 173 (1999);

**Page 552, add to footnote f:**

For an elaborate criticism of *Swint* and an argument in favor of a properly circumscribed doctrine of pendent appellate jurisdiction applicable to all categories of interlocutory review, see Joan Steinman, The Scope of Appellate Jurisdiction: Pendent Appellate Jurisdiction Before and After *Swint*, 49 Hastings L.J. 1337 (1998).

**Page 568, add at the end of footnote d:**

Jefferson v. City of Tarrant, 522 U.S. 75 (1997) (confining *Ritchie* to its precise circumstances).

# CHAPTER VI

# ABSTENTION

**Page 590, add a footnote at the end of Note 1:**

**a.** Yet another abstention rationale is known as the "*Rooker-Feldman* doctrine," under which lower federal courts are said to have no jurisdiction to hear functional appeals from state court decisions or to decide questions that are "inextricably intertwined" with prior state court judgments. The doctrine derives from Rooker v. Fidelity Trust Co., 263 U.S. 413 (1923), and District of Columbia Court of Appeals v. Feldman, 460 U.S. 462 (1983).

There are no recent Supreme Court explications of the doctrine, but as applied by the lower federal courts it appears to have broader preclusive effect than the normal application of res judicata principles. For a defense of the doctrine and an exploration of situations where it can legitimately be applied, see Suzanna Sherry, Judicial Federalism in the Trenches: The *Rooker–Feldman* Doctrine in Action, 74 Notre Dame L. Rev. 1085 (1999). The doctrine is also the subject of a Symposium in the Notre Dame Law Review. See Thomas D. Rowe, Jr., *Rooker–Feldman*: Worth Only the Powder to Blow It Up?, 74 Notre Dame L. Rev. 1081 (1999); Suzanna Sherry, Judicial Federalism in the Trenches: The *Rooker–Feldman* Doctrine in Action, 74 Notre Dame L. Rev. 1085 (1999); Barry Friedman & James E. Gaylord, *Rooker–Feldman*, from the Ground Up, 74 Notre Dame L. Rev. 1129 (1999); Susan Bandes, The *Rooker–Feldman* Doctrine: Evaluating Its Jurisdictional Status, 74 Notre Dame L. Rev. 1175 (1999); Jack M. Beermann, Comments on *Rooker–Feldman* or Let State Law Be Our Guide, 74 Notre Dame L. Rev. 1209 (1999).

**Page 596, add at the end of paragraph of Note 6:**

For an argument endorsing, on both historical and contemporary grounds, greater federal judicial review of state agency, see Ann Woolhandler and Michael G. Collins, Judicial Federalism and the Administrative States, 87 Cal. L. Rev. 613 (1999).

**Page 629, add at the end of footnote k:**

Brian Stagner, Avoiding Abstention: The *Younger* Exceptions, 29 Texas Tech L. Rev. 137 (1998). Based on cases litigated in the lower courts, Stagner adds two other exceptions to the *Younger* list: a colorable claim of double jeopardy; and waiver by the state of a *Younger* argument.

**Page 680, add at the end of footnote f:**

See also Lonny Sheinkopf Hoffman, Removal Jurisdiction and the All Writs Act, 148 U. Pa. L. Rev. 401 (1999), and Joan Steinman, The Newest Frontier of Judicial Activism: Removal Under the All Writs Act, 80 Boston U. L. Rev. 773 (2000), which consider federal court use of the All Writs Act (28 U.S.C. § 1651(a)) as the basis for removal of state claims that threaten a prior federal court order.

**Page 683, add a footnote at the end of Note 4:**

**h.** Can a defendant in state court remove to federal court on the ground that the plaintiff's claim is precluded by a prior federal court judgment? The Court said "no" in Rivet v. Regions Bank of Louisiana, 522 U.S. 470 (1998): "Under the well-pleaded complaint rule, [claim] preclusion [is] a defensive plea involving no recasting of the plaintiff's complaint, and is therefore not a proper basis for removal."

# CHAPTER VII

# HABEAS CORPUS

**Page 686, add after the Duker citation in footnote a:**

For debate about application of the suspension clause in the context of executive detention, see Gerald L. Neuman, Habeas Corpus, Executive Detention, and the Removal of Aliens, 98 Colum. L. Rev. 961 (1998), and the response in Richard H. Fallon, Jr., Applying the Suspension Clause to Immigration Cases, 98 Colum. L. Rev. 1068 (1998).

**Page 709, add to footnote b:**

Alan Clarke, Habeas Corpus: The Historical Debate, 13 N.Y. Law School J. Human Rights 375 (1998).

**Page 718, add to footnote c:**

For comparison of the Court's criminal cases dealing with the retroactivity of constitutional decisions to their civil counterparts, see Pamela J. Stephens, The New Retroactivity Doctrine: Equality, Reliance and Stare Decisis, 48 Syracuse L. Rev. 1515 (1998).

**Page 722, add a footnote after the citation in Note 6:**

**f.** For a panel discussion criticizing the statute before it was enacted convened by the ABA Section of Individual Rights and Responsibilities, see Capital Punishment: Is There Any Habeas Left in This Corpus?, 27 Loyola U. Chi. L.J. 523 (1996). See also Stephen B. Bright, Is Fairness Irrelevant?: The Evisceration of Federal Habeas Corpus Review and Limits on the Ability of State Courts to Protect Fundamental Rights, 54 Wash. & Lee L. Rev. 1 (1997).

**Page 722, omit *Lindh v. Murphy* and the Notes on the 1966 Legislation, pages 722–743, and substitute the following:**

## Terry Williams v. Taylor

Supreme Court of the United States, 2000.
___ U.S. ___.

■ JUSTICE STEVENS announced the judgment of the Court and delivered the opinion of the Court with respect to Parts, I, III, and IV, and an opinion with respect to Parts II and V.*

The questions presented are whether Terry Williams' constitutional right to the effective assistance of counsel as defined in Strickland v.

* Justice Souter, Justice Ginsburg, and Justice Breyer join this opinion in its entirety. Justice O'Connor and Justice Kennedy join Parts I, III, and IV of this opinion.

Washington, 466 U.S. 668 (1984), was violated, and whether the judgment of the Virginia Supreme Court refusing to set aside his death sentence "was contrary to, or involved an unreasonable application of, clearly established Federal law, as determined by the Supreme Court of the United States," within the meaning of 28 U.S.C. § 2254(d)(1) (1994 ed., Supp. III). We answer both questions affirmatively.

## I

On November 3, 1985, Harris Stone was found dead in his residence on Henry Street in Danville, Virginia. Finding no indication of a struggle, local officials determined that the cause of death was blood alcohol poisoning, and the case was considered closed. Six months after Stone's death, Terry Williams, who was then incarcerated in the "I" unit of the city jail for an unrelated offense, wrote a letter to the police stating that he had killed " 'that man down on Henry Street' " and also stating that he " 'did it' " to that " 'lady down on West Green Street' " and was " 'very sorry.' " The letter was unsigned, but it closed with a reference to "I cell." The police readily identified Williams as its author, and, on April 25, 1986, they obtained several statements from him. In one Williams admitted that, after Stone refused to lend him " 'a couple of dollars,' " he had killed Stone with a mattock and took the money from his wallet. In September 1986, Williams was convicted of robbery and capital murder.

At Williams' sentencing hearing, the prosecution proved that Williams had been convicted of armed robbery in 1976 and burglary and grand larceny in 1982. The prosecution also introduced the written confessions that Williams had made in April. The prosecution described two auto thefts and two separate violent assaults on elderly victims perpetrated after the Stone murder. On December 4, 1985, Williams had started a fire outside one victim's residence before attacking and robbing him. On March 5, 1986, Williams had brutally assaulted an elderly woman on West Green Street—an incident he had mentioned in his letter to the police. That confession was particularly damaging because other evidence established that the woman was in a "vegetative state" and not expected to recover. Williams had also been convicted of arson for setting a fire in the jail while awaiting trial in this case. Two expert witnesses employed by the State testified that there was a "high probability" that Williams would pose a serious continuing threat to society.

The evidence offered by Williams' trial counsel at the sentencing hearing consisted of the testimony of Williams' mother, two neighbors, and a taped excerpt from a statement by a psychiatrist. One of the neighbors had not been previously interviewed by defense counsel, but was noticed by counsel in the audience during the proceedings and asked to testify on the spot. The three witnesses briefly described Williams as a "nice boy" and not a violent person. The recorded psychiatrist's testimony did little more than relate Williams' statement during an examination that in the course of one of his earlier robberies, he had removed the bullets from a gun so as not to injure anyone.

In his cross-examination of the prosecution witnesses, Williams' counsel repeatedly emphasized the fact that Williams had initiated the contact with the police that enabled them to solve the murder and to identify him as the perpetrator of the recent assaults, as well as the car thefts. In closing argument, Williams' counsel characterized Williams' confessional statements as "dumb," but asked the jury to give weight to the fact that he had "turned himself in, not on one crime but on four ... that the [police otherwise] would not have solved." The weight of defense counsel's closing, however, was devoted to explaining that it was difficult to find a reason why the jury should spare Williams' life.[2]

The jury found a probability of future dangerousness and unanimously fixed Williams' punishment at death. The trial judge concluded that such punishment was "proper" and "just" and imposed the death sentence. The Virginia Supreme Court affirmed the conviction and sentence. It rejected Williams' argument that when the trial judge imposed sentence, he failed to give mitigating weight to the fact that Williams had turned himself in.

*State Habeas Corpus Proceedings*

In 1988 Williams filed for state collateral relief in the Danville Circuit Court. The petition was subsequently amended, and the Circuit Court (the same judge who had presided over Williams' trial and sentencing) held an evidentiary hearing on Williams' claim that trial counsel had been ineffective. Based on the evidence adduced after two days of hearings, Judge Ingram found that Williams' conviction was valid, but that his trial attorneys had been ineffective during sentencing. Among the evidence reviewed that had not been presented at trial were documents prepared in connection with Williams' commitment when he was 11 years old that dramatically described mistreatment, abuse, and neglect during his early childhood, as well as testimony that he was "borderline mentally retarded," had suffered repeated head injuries, and might have mental impairments organic in origin. The habeas hearing also revealed that the same experts who had testified on the State's behalf at trial believed that Williams, if kept in a "structured environment," would not pose a future danger to society.

**2.** In defense counsel's words: "I will admit too that it is very difficult to ask you to show mercy to a man who maybe has not shown much mercy himself. I doubt very seriously that he thought much about mercy when he was in Mr. Stone's bedroom that night with him. I doubt very seriously that he had mercy very highly on his mind when he was walking along West Green and the incident with Alberta Stroud. I doubt very seriously that he had mercy on his mind when he took two cars that didn't belong to him. Admittedly it is very difficult to get us and ask that you give this man mercy when he has shown so little of it himself. But I would ask that you would."

Counsel's failure to discover and present this and other significant mitigating evidence was "below the range expected of reasonable, professional competent assistance of counsel." Counsel's performance thus "did not measure up to the standard required under the holding of Strickland v. Washington, 466 U.S. 668 (1984), and [if it had,] there is a reasonable probability that the result of the sentencing phase would have been different." [Acting under the applicable state procedures,] Judge Ingram therefore recommended [to the Virginia Supreme Court] that Williams be granted a rehearing on the sentencing phase of his trial.

The Virginia Supreme Court did not accept that recommendation. Although it assumed, without deciding, that trial counsel had been ineffective, it disagreed with the trial judge's conclusion that Williams had suffered sufficient prejudice to warrant relief. [T]he court concluded that there was no reasonable possibility that the omitted evidence would have affected the jury's sentencing recommendation, and that Williams had failed to demonstrate that his sentencing proceeding was fundamentally unfair.

*Federal Habeas Corpus Proceedings*

Having exhausted his state remedies, Williams sought a federal writ of habeas corpus pursuant to 28 U.S.C. § 2254. After reviewing the state habeas hearing transcript and the state courts' findings of fact and conclusions of law, the federal trial judge agreed with the Virginia trial judge: The death sentence was constitutionally infirm.

[T]he judge ... identified five categories of mitigating evidence that counsel had failed to introduce,[4] and he rejected the argument that counsel's failure to conduct an adequate investigation had been a strategic decision to rely almost entirely on the fact that Williams had voluntarily confessed.

According to Williams' trial counsel's testimony before the state habeas court, counsel did not fail to seek Williams' juvenile and social services records because he thought they would be counterproductive, but because counsel erroneously believed that " 'state law didn't permit it.' " Counsel also acknowledged in the course of the hearings that information about Williams' childhood would have been important in mitigation. And counsel's failure to contact a potentially persuasive character witness was likewise not a conscious strategic choice, but simply a failure to return that

**4.** "(i) Counsel did not introduce evidence of the Petitioner's background.... (ii) Counsel did not introduce evidence that Petitioner was abused by his father. (iii) Counsel did not introduce testimony from correctional officers who were willing to testify that defendant would not pose a danger while incarcerated. Nor did counsel offer prison commendations awarded to Williams for his help in breaking up a prison drug ring and for returning a guard's wallet. (iv) Several character witnesses were not called to testify.... [T]he testimony of Elliott, a respected CPA in the community, could have been quite important to the jury.... (v) Finally, counsel did not introduce evidence that Petitioner was borderline mentally retarded, though he was found competent to stand trial."

witness' phone call offering his service. Finally, even if counsel neglected to conduct such an investigation at the time as part of a tactical decision, the District Judge found, tactics as a matter of reasonable performance could not justify the omissions.

Turning to the prejudice issue, the judge determined that there was " 'a reasonable probability that, but for counsel's unprofessional errors, the result of the proceeding would have been different.' *Strickland*, 466 U.S. at 694." He found that the Virginia Supreme Court had erroneously assumed that Lockhart v. Fretwell, 506 U.S. 364 (1993), had modified the *Strickland* standard for determining prejudice, and that it had made an important error of fact in discussing its finding of no prejudice.[5]...

The Federal Court of Appeals reversed. ...[6] We granted certiorari, and now reverse.

II

... The warden here contends that federal habeas corpus relief is prohibited by the amendment to 28 U.S.C. § 2254, enacted as a part of the Antiterrorism and Effective Death Penalty Act of 1996 (AEDPA). The relevant portion of that amendment provides:

> (d) An application for a writ of habeas corpus on behalf of a person in custody pursuant to the judgment of a State court shall not be granted with respect to any claim that was adjudicated on the merits in State court proceedings unless the adjudication of the claim—
>
> > (1) resulted in a decision that was contrary to, or involved an unreasonable application of, clearly established Federal law, as determined by the Supreme Court of the United States....

... The inquiry mandated by the amendment relates to the way in which a federal habeas court exercises its duty to decide constitutional questions; the amendment does not alter the underlying grant of jurisdiction in § 2254(a). When federal judges exercise their federal-question jurisdiction under the "judicial Power" of Article III of the Constitution, it

5. "Specifically, the Virginia Supreme Court found no prejudice, reasoning: 'The mitigation evidence that the prisoner says, in retrospect, his trial counsel should have discovered and offered barely would have altered the profile of this defendant that was presented to the jury. At most, this evidence would have shown that numerous people, mostly relatives, thought that defendant was nonviolent and could cope very well in a structured environment.' The Virginia Supreme Court ignored or overlooked the evidence of Williams' difficult childhood and abuse and his limited mental capacity. It is also unreasonable to characterize the additional evidence as coming from 'mostly relatives.' ... Bruce Elliott, a respected professional in the community, and several correctional officers offered to testify on Williams behalf."

6. Like the Virginia Supreme Court, the Court of Appeals assumed, without deciding, that the performance of trial counsel fell below an objective standard of reasonableness.

is "emphatically the province and duty" of those judges to "say what the law is." Marbury v. Madison, 5 U.S. (1 Cranch) 137 (1803). At the core of this power is the federal courts' independent responsibility—independent from its coequal branches in the Federal Government, and independent from the separate authority of the several States—to interpret federal law. A construction of AEDPA that would require the federal courts to cede this authority to the courts of the States would be inconsistent with the practice that federal judges have traditionally followed in discharging their duties under Article III of the Constitution. If Congress had intended to require such an important change in the exercise of our jurisdiction, we believe it would have spoken with much greater clarity than is found in the text of AEDPA.

This basic premise informs our interpretation of both parts of § 2254(d)(1): first, the requirement that the determinations of state courts be tested only against "clearly established Federal law, as determined by the Supreme Court of the United States," and second, the prohibition on the issuance of the writ unless the state court's decision is "contrary to, or involved an unreasonable application of," that clearly established law. We address each part in turn.

*The "clearly established law" requirement*

In Teague v. Lane, 489 U.S. 288 (1989), we held that the petitioner was not entitled to federal habeas relief because he was relying on a rule of federal law that had not been announced until after his state conviction became final. The antiretroactivity rule recognized in *Teague*, which prohibits reliance on "new rules," is the functional equivalent of a statutory provision commanding exclusive reliance on "clearly established law." Because there is no reason to believe that Congress intended to require federal courts to ask both whether a rule sought on habeas is "new" under *Teague*—which remains the law—and also whether it is "clearly established" under AEDPA, it seems safe to assume that Congress had congruent concepts in mind. It is perfectly clear that AEDPA codifies *Teague* to the extent that *Teague* requires federal habeas courts to deny relief that is contingent upon a rule of law not clearly established at the time the state conviction became final.

*Teague*'s core principles are therefore relevant to our construction of this requirement. Justice Harlan recognized the "inevitable difficulties" that come with "attempting 'to determine whether a particular decision has really announced a 'new' rule at all or whether it has simply applied a well-established constitutional principle to govern a case which is closely analogous to those which have been previously considered in the prior case law.' " Mackey v. United States, 401 U.S. 667, 695 (quoting Desist v.

United States, 394 U.S. 244, 263 (1969)). But *Teague* established some guidance for making this determination, explaining that a federal habeas court operates within the bounds of comity and finality if it applies a rule "dictated by precedent existing at the time the defendant's conviction became final." *Teague*, 489 U.S., at 301 (emphasis deleted). A rule that "breaks new ground or imposes a new obligation on the States or the Federal Government," ibid., falls outside this universe of federal law.

To this, AEDPA has added, immediately following the "clearly established law" requirement, a clause limiting the area of relevant law to that "determined by the Supreme Court of the United States." 28 U.S.C. § 2254(d)(1). If this Court has not broken sufficient legal ground to establish an asked-for constitutional principle, the lower federal courts cannot themselves establish such a principle with clarity sufficient to satisfy the AEDPA bar. In this respect, we agree with the Seventh Circuit that this clause "extends the principle of *Teague* by limiting the source of doctrine on which a federal court may rely in addressing the application for a writ." Lindh v. Murphy, 96 F.3d 856, 869 (7th Cir. 1996). As that court explained:

> This is a retrenchment from former practice, which allowed the United States courts of appeals to rely on their own jurisprudence in addition to that of the Supreme Court. The novelty in this portion § 2254(d)(1) is not the "contrary to" part but the reference to "Federal law, *as determined by the Supreme Court of the United States*" (emphasis added). This extends the principle of *Teague* by limiting the source of doctrine on which a federal court may rely in addressing the application for a writ. It does not, however, purport to limit the federal courts' independent interpretive authority with respect to federal questions.

A rule that fails to satisfy the foregoing criteria is barred by *Teague* from application on collateral review, and, similarly, is not available as a basis for relief in a habeas case to which AEDPA applies.

In the context of this case, we also note that, as our precedent interpreting *Teague* has demonstrated, rules of law may be sufficiently clear for habeas purposes even when they are expressed in terms of a generalized standard rather than as a bright-line rule. As Justice Kennedy has explained:

> If the rule in question is one which of necessity requires a case-by-case examination of the evidence, then we can tolerate a number of specific applications without saying that those applications themselves create a new rule.... Where the beginning point is a rule of this general application, a rule designed for the specific purpose of evaluating a myriad of factual contexts, it will be the infrequent case that yields a result so novel that it forges a new rule, one not dictated by precedent.

Wright v. West, 505 U.S. 277, 308–09 (1992) (opinion concurring in judgment). Moreover, the determination whether or not a rule is clearly established at the time a state court renders its final judgment of conviction is a question as to which the "federal courts must make an independent evaluation." Id., at 305 (O'Connor, J., concurring in judgment); accord id., at 307 (Kennedy, J., concurring).

It has been urged, in contrast, that we should read *Teague* and its progeny to encompass a broader principle of deference requiring federal courts to "validat[e] 'reasonable, good-faith interpretations' of the law" by state courts. The position has been bolstered with references to our statements elucidating the "new rule" inquiry as one turning on whether "reasonable jurists" would agree the rule was not clearly established. This presumption of deference was in essence the position taken by three Members of this Court in *Wright*, 505 U.S., at 290–91 (opinion of Thomas, J.) ("[A] federal habeas court 'must defer to the state court's decision rejecting the claim unless that decision is patently unreasonable' ").

*Teague*, however, does not extend this far. The often repeated language that *Teague* endorses "reasonable, good-faith interpretations" by state courts is an explanation of policy, not a statement of law. The *Teague* cases reflect this Court's view that habeas corpus is not to be used as a second criminal trial, and federal courts are not to run roughshod over the considered findings and judgments of the state courts that conducted the original trial and heard the initial appeals. On the contrary, we have long insisted that federal habeas courts attend closely to those considered decisions, and give them full effect when their findings and judgments are consistent with federal law. But as Justice O'Connor explained in *Wright*, 505 U.S., at 305:

> [T]he duty of the federal court in evaluating whether a rule is "new" is not the same as deference; ... *Teague* does not direct federal courts to spend less time or effort scrutinizing the existing federal law, on the ground that they can assume the state courts interpreted it properly.
>
> [T]he maxim that federal courts should "give great weight to the considered conclusions of a coequal state judiciary" ... does not mean that we have held in the past that federal courts must presume the correctness of a state court's legal conclusions on habeas, or that a state court's incorrect legal determination has ever been allowed to stand because it was reasonable. We have always held that federal courts, even on habeas, have an independent obligation to say what the law is.

We are convinced that in the phrase, "clearly established law," Congress did not intend to modify that independent obligation.

*The "contrary to, or an unreasonable application of," requirement*

The message that Congress intended to convey by using the phrases, "contrary to" and "unreasonable application of" is not entirely clear. The prevailing view in the Circuits is that the former phrase requires de novo review of "pure" questions of law and the latter requires some sort of "reasonability" review of so-called mixed questions of law and fact.

We are not persuaded that the phrases define two mutually exclusive categories of questions. Most constitutional questions that arise in habeas corpus proceedings—and therefore most "decisions" to be made—require the federal judge to apply a rule of law to a set of facts, some of which may be disputed and some undisputed. For example, an erroneous conclusion that particular circumstances established the voluntariness of a confession, or that there exists a conflict of interest when one attorney represents multiple defendants, may well be described either as "contrary to" or as an "unreasonable application of" the governing rule of law. In constitutional adjudication, as in the common law, rules of law often develop incrementally as earlier decisions are applied to new factual situations. But rules that depend upon such elaboration are hardly less lawlike than those that establish a bright-line test.

Indeed, our pre-AEDPA efforts to distinguish questions of fact, questions of law, and "mixed questions," and to create an appropriate standard of habeas review for each, generated some not insubstantial differences of opinion as to which issues of law fell into which category of question, and as to which standard of review applied to each. We thus think the Fourth Circuit was correct when it attributed the lack of clarity in the statute, in part, to the overlapping meanings of the phrases "contrary to" and "unreasonable application of."

The statutory text likewise does not obviously prescribe a specific, recognizable standard of review for dealing with either phrase. Significantly, it does not use any term, such as "de novo" or "plain error," that would easily identify a familiar standard of review. Rather, the text is fairly read simply as a command that a federal court not issue the habeas writ unless the state court was wrong as a matter of law or unreasonable in its application of law in a given case. The suggestion that a wrong state-court "decision"—a legal judgment rendered "after consideration of *facts, and . . . law*," Black's Law Dictionary 407 (6th ed. 1990) (emphasis added)—may no longer be redressed through habeas (because it is unreachable under the "unreasonable application" phrase) is based on a mistaken insistence that the § 2254(d)(1) phrases have not only independent, but mutually exclusive, meanings. Whether or not a federal court can issue the writ "under [the] 'unreasonable application' clause," the statute is clear that habeas may issue under § 2254(d)(1) if a state court "decision" is "contrary to . . . clearly established Federal law." We thus anticipate that there will be a variety of cases, like this one, in which both phrases may be implicated.

Even though we cannot conclude that the phrases establish "a body of rigid rules," they do express a "mood" that the federal judiciary must respect. In this respect, it seems clear that Congress intended federal judges to attend with the utmost care to state-court decisions, including all of the reasons supporting their decisions, before concluding that those proceedings were infected by constitutional error sufficiently serious to warrant the issuance of the writ. Likewise, the statute in a separate provision provides for the habeas remedy when a state-court decision "was based on an unreasonable determination of the facts *in light of the evidence presented in the State court proceeding*." 28 U.S.C. § 2254(d)(2) (1994 ed., Supp. III) (emphasis added). While this provision is not before us in this case, it provides relevant context for our interpretation of § 2254(d)(1); in this respect, it bolsters our conviction that federal habeas courts must make as the starting point of their analysis the state courts' determinations of fact, including that aspect of a "mixed question" that rests on a finding of fact. AEDPA plainly sought to ensure a level of "deference to the determinations of state courts," provided those determinations did not conflict with federal law or apply federal law in an unreasonable way. Congress wished to curb delays, to prevent "retrials" on federal habeas, and to give effect to state convictions to the extent possible under law. When federal courts are able to fulfill these goals within the bounds of the law, AEDPA instructs them to do so.

On the other hand, it is significant that the word "deference" does not appear in the text of the statute itself. Neither the legislative history, nor the statutory text, suggests any difference in the so-called "deference" depending on which of the two phrases is implicated.[13] Whatever "deference" Congress had in mind with respect to both phrases, it surely is not a requirement that federal courts actually defer to a state-court application of the federal law that is, in the independent judgment of the federal court, in error. As Judge Easterbrook noted with respect to the phrase "contrary to":

> Section 2254(d) requires us to give state courts' opinions a respectful reading, and to listen carefully to their conclusions, but when the state court addresses a legal question, it is the law "as determined by the Supreme Court of the United States" that prevails.

*Lindh*, 96 F.3d, at 869.

Our disagreement with Justice O'Connor about the precise meaning of the phrase "contrary to," and the word "unreasonable," is, of course,

**13.** As Judge Easterbrook has noted, the statute surely does not require the kind of "deference" appropriate in other contexts: "It does not tell us to 'defer' to state decisions, as if the Constitution means one thing in Wisconsin and another in Indiana. Nor does it tell us to treat state courts the way we treat federal administrative agencies. Deference after the fashion of Chevron U.S.A. Inc. v. Natural Resources Defense Council, Inc., 467 U.S. 837 (1984), depends on delegation. Congress did not delegate interpretive or executive power to the state courts. They exercise powers under their domestic law, constrained by the Constitution of the United States. 'Deference' to the jurisdictions bound by those constraints is not sensible." Lindh v. Murphy, 96 F.3d 856, 868 (7th Cir. 1996) (en banc).

important, but should affect only a narrow category of cases. The simplest and first definition of "contrary to" as a phrase is "in conflict with." Webster's Ninth New Collegiate Dictionary 285 (1983). In this sense, we think the phrase surely capacious enough to include a finding that the state-court "decision" is simply "erroneous" or wrong. (We hasten to add that even "diametrically different" from, or "opposite" to, an established federal law would seem to include "decisions" that are wrong in light of that law.) And there is nothing in the phrase "contrary to"—as Justice O'Connor appears to agree—that implies anything less than independent review by the federal courts. Moreover, state-court decisions that do not "conflict" with federal law will rarely be "unreasonable" under either her reading of the statute or ours. We all agree that state-court judgments must be upheld unless, after the closest examination of the state-court judgment, a federal court is firmly convinced that a federal constitutional right has been violated. Our difference is as to the cases in which, at first-blush, a state-court judgment seems entirely reasonable, but thorough analysis by a federal court produces a firm conviction that that judgment is infected by constitutional error. In our view, such an erroneous judgment is "unreasonable" within the meaning of the act even though that conclusion was not immediately apparent.

In sum, the statute directs federal courts to attend to every state-court judgment with utmost care, but it does not require them to defer to the opinion of every reasonable state-court judge on the content of federal law. If, after carefully weighing all the reasons for accepting a state court's judgment, a federal court is convinced that a prisoner's custody—or, as in this case, his sentence of death—violates the Constitution, that independent judgment should prevail. Otherwise the federal "law as determined by the Supreme Court of the United States" might be applied by the federal courts one way in Virginia and another way in California. In light of the well-recognized interest in ensuring that federal courts interpret federal law in a uniform way, we are convinced that Congress did not intend the statute to produce such a result.

III

In this case, Williams contends that he was denied his constitutionally guaranteed right to the effective assistance of counsel when his trial lawyers failed to investigate and to present substantial mitigating evidence to the sentencing jury. The threshold question under AEDPA is whether Williams seeks to apply a rule of law that was clearly established at the time his state-court conviction became final. That question is easily answered because the merits of his claim are squarely governed by our holding in Strickland v. Washington, 466 U.S. 668 (1984).

We explained in *Strickland* that a violation of the right on which Williams relies has two components:

> First, the defendant must show that counsel's performance was deficient. This requires showing that counsel made errors so serious that counsel was not functioning as the "counsel" guaranteed the defendant by the Sixth Amendment. Second, the defendant must show that the deficient performance prejudiced the defense. This requires showing that counsel's errors were so serious as to deprive the defendant of a fair trial, a trial whose result is reliable.

To establish ineffectiveness, a "defendant must show that counsel's representation fell below an objective standard of reasonableness." To establish prejudice he "must show that there is a reasonable probability that, but for counsel's unprofessional errors, the result of the proceeding would have been different. A reasonable probability is a probability sufficient to undermine confidence in the outcome."

It is past question that the rule set forth in *Strickland* qualifies as "clearly established Federal law, as determined by the Supreme Court of the United States." ... Williams is therefore entitled to relief if the Virginia Supreme Court's decision rejecting his ineffective-assistance claim was either "contrary to, or involved an unreasonable application of," that established law. It was both.

IV

The Virginia Supreme Court erred in holding that our decision in Lockhart v. Fretwell, 506 U.S. 364 (1993), modified or in some way supplanted the rule set down in *Strickland*. It is true that while the *Strickland* test provides sufficient guidance for resolving virtually all ineffective-assistance-of-counsel claims, there are situations in which the overriding focus on fundamental fairness may affect the analysis. Thus, on the one hand, as *Strickland* itself explained, there are a few situations in which prejudice may be presumed. And, on the other hand, there are also situations in which it would be unjust to characterize the likelihood of a different outcome as legitimate "prejudice." Even if a defendant's false testimony might have persuaded the jury to acquit him, it is not fundamentally unfair to conclude that he was not prejudiced by counsel's interference with his intended perjury. Nix v. Whiteside, 475 U.S. 157, 175–76 (1986).

Similarly, in *Lockhart*, we concluded that, given the overriding interest in fundamental fairness, the likelihood of a different outcome attributable to an incorrect interpretation of the law should be regarded as a potential "windfall" to the defendant rather than the legitimate "prejudice" contemplated by our opinion in *Strickland*. The death sentence that Arkansas had imposed on Bobby Ray Fretwell was based on an aggravating circumstance (murder committed for pecuniary gain) that duplicated an element of the underlying felony (murder in the course of a robbery). Shortly before the trial, the United States Court of Appeals for the Eighth Circuit had held that such "double counting" was impermissible, but Fretwell's lawyer (presumably because he was unaware of the [relevant] decision) failed to object to the use of the pecuniary gain aggravator. Before Fretwell's claim for federal habeas corpus relief reached this Court, the [Eighth Circuit] case was overruled. Accordingly, even though the Arkansas trial judge probably would have sustained a timely objection to the double counting, it had become clear that the State had a right to rely on the disputed aggravating circumstance. Because the ineffectiveness of Fretwell's counsel had not deprived him of any substantive or procedural right to which the law entitled him, we held that his claim did not satisfy the "prejudice" component of the *Strickland* test.

Cases such as *Nix* and *Lockhart* do not justify a departure from a straightforward application of *Strickland* when the ineffectiveness of counsel does deprive the defendant of a substantive or procedural right to which the law entitles him. In the instant case, it is undisputed that Williams had a right—indeed, a constitutionally protected right—to provide the jury with the mitigating evidence that his trial counsel either failed to discover or failed to offer.

Nevertheless, the Virginia Supreme Court read our decision in *Lockhart* to require a separate inquiry into fundamental fairness even when Williams is able to show that his lawyer was ineffective and that his ineffectiveness probably affected the outcome of the proceeding. ... Unlike the Virginia Supreme Court, the state trial judge omitted any reference to *Lockhart* and simply relied on our opinion in *Strickland* as stating the correct standard for judging ineffective-assistance claims. ... The trial judge analyzed the ineffective-assistance claim under the correct standard; the Virginia Supreme Court did not.

We are likewise persuaded that the Virginia trial judge correctly applied both components of that standard to Williams' ineffectiveness claim. Although he concluded that counsel competently handled the guilt phase of the trial, he found that their representation during the sentencing phase fell short of professional standards—a judgment barely disputed by the State in its brief to this Court. The record establishes that counsel did not begin to prepare for that phase of the proceeding until a week before the trial. They failed to conduct an investigation that would have uncovered extensive records graphically describing Williams' nightmarish childhood, not because of any strategic calculation but because they incorrectly thought that state law barred access to such records. Had they done so, the jury would have learned that Williams' parents had been imprisoned for the criminal neglect of Williams and his siblings,[19] that Williams had been

**19.** Juvenile records contained the following description of his home: "The home was a complete wreck.... There were several places on the floor where someone had had a bowel movement. Urine was standing in several places in the bedrooms. There were dirty dishes scattered over the kitchen, and it was impossible to step any place on the kitchen floor where there was no trash.... The children were all dirty and none of them had on under-pants. Noah and Lula were so intoxicated, they could not find any clothes for the severely and repeatedly beaten by his father, that he had been committed to the custody of the social services bureau for two years during his parents' incarceration (including one stint in an abusive foster home), and then, after his parents were released from prison, had been returned to his parents' custody.

Counsel failed to introduce available evidence that Williams was "borderline mentally retarded" and did not advance beyond sixth grade in school. They failed to seek prison records recording Williams' commendations for helping to crack a prison drug ring and for returning a guard's missing wallet, or the testimony of prison officials who described Williams as among the inmates "least likely to act in a violent, dangerous or provocative way." Counsel failed even to return the phone call of a certified public accountant who had offered to testify that he had visited Williams frequently when Williams was incarcerated as part of a prison ministry program, that Williams "seemed to thrive in a more regimented and structured environment," and that Williams was proud of the carpentry degree he earned while in prison.

Of course, not all of the additional evidence was favorable to Williams. The juvenile records revealed that he had been thrice committed to the juvenile system—for aiding and abetting larceny when he was 11 years old, for pulling a false fire alarm when he was 12, and for breaking and entering when he was 15. But as the Federal District Court correctly observed, the failure to introduce the comparatively voluminous amount of evidence that did speak in Williams' favor was not justified by a tactical decision to focus on Williams' voluntary confession. Whether or not those omissions were sufficiently prejudicial to have affected the outcome of sentencing, they clearly demonstrate that trial counsel did not fulfill their obligation to conduct a thorough investigation of the defendant's background.

We are also persuaded, unlike the Virginia Supreme Court, that counsel's unprofessional service prejudiced Williams within the meaning of *Strickland*. After hearing the additional evidence developed in the postconviction proceedings, the very judge who presided at Williams' trial and who once determined that the death penalty was "just" and "appropriate," concluded that there existed "a reasonable probability that the result of the sentencing phase would have been different" if the jury had heard that evidence. . . .

The Virginia Supreme Court's own analysis of prejudice reaching the contrary conclusion was . . . unreasonable in at least two respects. First, as we have already explained, the State Supreme Court mischaracterized at best the appropriate rule, made clear by this Court in *Strickland*, for determining whether counsel's assistance was effective within the meaning

children, nor were they able to put the clothes on them. . . . The children had to be put in Winslow Hospital, as four of them, by that time, were definitely under the influence of whiskey."

of the Constitution. While it may also have conducted an "outcome determinative" analysis of its own, it is evident to us that the court's decision turned on its erroneous view that a "mere" difference in outcome is not sufficient to establish constitutionally ineffective assistance of counsel. Its analysis in this respect was thus not only "contrary to," but also, inasmuch as the Virginia Supreme Court relied on the inapplicable exception recognized in *Lockhart*, an "unreasonable application of" the clear law as established by this Court.

Second, the State Supreme Court's prejudice determination was unreasonable insofar as it failed to evaluate the totality of the available mitigation evidence—both that adduced at trial, and the evidence adduced in the habeas proceeding—in reweighing it against the evidence in aggravation. [T]he state court failed even to mention the sole argument in mitigation that trial counsel did advance—Williams turned himself in, alerting police to a crime they otherwise would never have discovered, expressing remorse for his actions, and cooperating with the police after that. While this, coupled with the prison records and guard testimony, may not have overcome a finding of future dangerousness, the graphic description of Williams' childhood, filled with abuse and privation, or the reality that he was "borderline mentally retarded," might well have influenced the jury's appraisal of his moral culpability. The circumstances recited in his several confessions are consistent with the view that in each case his violent behavior was a compulsive reaction rather than the product of cold-blooded premeditation. Mitigating evidence unrelated to dangerousness may alter the jury's selection of penalty, even if it does not undermine or rebut the prosecution's death-eligibility case. The Virginia Supreme Court did not entertain that possibility. It thus failed to accord appropriate weight to the body of mitigation evidence available to trial counsel.

V

In our judgment, the state trial judge was correct both in his recognition of the established legal standard for determining counsel's effectiveness, and in his conclusion that the entire postconviction record, viewed as a whole and cumulative of mitigation evidence presented originally, raised "a reasonable probability that the result of the sentencing proceeding would have been different" if competent counsel had presented and explained the significance of all the available evidence. It follows that the Virginia Supreme Court rendered a "decision that was contrary to, or involved an unreasonable application of, clearly established Federal law." Williams' constitutional right to the effective assistance of counsel as defined in Strickland v. Washington, 466 U.S. 668 (1984), was violated.

Accordingly, the judgment of the Court of Appeals is reversed, and the case is remanded for further proceedings consistent with this opinion.

It is so ordered.

■ JUSTICE O'CONNOR delivered the opinion of the Court with respect to Part II (except as to the footnote), concurred in part, and concurred in the judgment.*

. . . I agree . . . that the Virginia Supreme Court's adjudication of Terry Williams' application for state habeas corpus relief . . . "resulted in a decision that was contrary to, or involved an unreasonable application of, clearly established Federal law, as determined by the Supreme Court of the United States." . . . I . . . join Parts I, III, and IV of the Court's opinion. Because I disagree, however, with the interpretation of § 2254(d)(1) set forth in Part II of Justice Stevens' opinion, I write separately to explain my views.

I

Before 1996, this Court held that a federal court entertaining a state prisoner's application for habeas relief must exercise its independent judgment when deciding both questions of constitutional law and mixed constitutional questions (i.e., application of constitutional law to fact). In other words, a federal habeas court owed no deference to a state court's resolution of such questions of law or mixed questions. [O]ur precedents dictated that a federal court should grant a state prisoner's petition for habeas relief if that court were to conclude in its independent judgment that the relevant state court had erred on a question of constitutional law or on a mixed constitutional question.

If today's case were governed by the federal habeas statute prior to Congress' enactment of AEDPA in 1996, I would agree with Justice Stevens that Williams' petition for habeas relief must be granted if we, in our independent judgment, were to conclude that his Sixth Amendment right to effective assistance of counsel was violated.

II

A

Williams' case is not governed by the pre–1996 version of the habeas statute. Because he filed his petition in December 1997, Williams' case is governed by the statute as amended by AEDPA. . . . Accordingly, for Williams to obtain federal habeas relief, he must first demonstrate that his case satisfies the condition set by § 2254(d)(1). That provision modifies the role of federal habeas courts in reviewing petitions filed by state prisoners.

Justice Stevens' opinion in Part II essentially contends that § 2254(d)(1) does not alter the previously settled rule of independent review. Indeed, the opinion concludes its statutory inquiry with the somewhat empty finding that § 2254(d)(1) does no more than express a " 'mood'

* Justice Kennedy joins this opinion in its entirety. The Chief Justice and Justice Thomas join this opinion with respect to Part II. Justice Scalia joins this opinion with respect to Part II, except as to the footnote.

that the federal judiciary must respect." For Justice Stevens, the congressionally enacted "mood" has two important qualities. First, "federal courts [must] attend to every state-court judgment with utmost care" by "carefully weighing all the reasons for accepting a state court's judgment." Second, if a federal court undertakes that careful review and yet remains convinced that a prisoner's custody violates the Constitution, "that independent judgment should prevail." ...

Justice Stevens arrives at his erroneous interpretation by means of one critical misstep. He fails to give independent meaning to both the "contrary to" and "unreasonable application" clauses of the statute. ... By reading § 2254(d)(1) as one general restriction on the power of the federal habeas court, Justice Stevens manages to avoid confronting the specific meaning of the statute's "unreasonable application" clause and its ramifications for the independent-review rule. ... Section 2254(d)(1) defines two categories of cases in which a state prisoner may obtain federal habeas relief with respect to a claim adjudicated on the merits in state court. Under the statute, a federal court may grant a writ of habeas corpus if the relevant state-court decision was either (1) "*contrary to* ... clearly established Federal law, as determined by the Supreme Court of the United States," or (2) "*involved an unreasonable application of* ... clearly established Federal law, as determined by the Supreme Court of the United States." (Emphases added.)

The Court of Appeals for the Fourth Circuit properly accorded both the "contrary to" and "unreasonable application" clauses independent meaning. The Fourth Circuit's interpretation of § 2254(d)(1) in Williams' case relied, in turn, on that court's previous decision in Green v. French, 143 F.3d 865 (4th Cir. 1998). ... With respect to the first of the two statutory clauses, the Fourth Circuit held in *Green* that a state-court decision can be "contrary to" this Court's clearly established precedent in two ways. First, a state-court decision is contrary to this Court's precedent if the state court arrives at a conclusion opposite to that reached by this Court on a question of law. Second, a state-court decision is also contrary to this Court's precedent if the state court confronts facts that are materially indistinguishable from a relevant Supreme Court precedent and arrives at a result opposite to ours.

The word "contrary" is commonly understood to mean "diametrically different," "opposite in character or nature," or "mutually opposed." Webster's Third New International Dictionary 495 (1976). The text of § 2254(d)(1) therefore suggests that the state court's decision must be substantially different from the relevant precedent of this Court. The Fourth Circuit's interpretation of the "contrary to" clause accurately reflects this textual meaning. A state-court decision will certainly be contrary to our clearly established precedent if the state court applies a rule that contradicts the governing law set forth in our cases. Take, for example, our decision in Strickland v. Washington, 466 U.S. 668 (1984). If a state court were to reject a prisoner's claim of ineffective assistance of counsel on the grounds that the prisoner had not established by a preponderance of the evidence that the result of his criminal proceeding would have been different, that decision would be "diametrically different," "opposite in character or nature," and "mutually opposed" to our clearly established precedent because we held in *Strickland* that the prisoner need only demonstrate a "reasonable probability that ... the result of the proceeding would have been different." A state-court decision will also be contrary to this Court's clearly established precedent if the state court confronts a set of facts that are materially indistinguishable from a decision of this Court and nevertheless arrives at a result different from our precedent. Accordingly, in either of these two scenarios, a federal court will be unconstrained by § 2254(d)(1) because the state-court decision falls within that provision's "contrary to" clause.

On the other hand, a run-of-the-mill state-court decision applying the correct legal rule from our cases to the facts of a prisoner's case would not fit comfortably within § 2254(d)(1)'s "contrary to" clause. Assume, for example, that a state-court decision on a prisoner's ineffective-assistance claim correctly identifies *Strickland* as the controlling legal authority and, applying that framework, rejects the prisoner's claim. Quite clearly, the state-court decision would be in accord with our decision in *Strickland* as to the legal prerequisites for establishing an ineffective-assistance claim, even assuming the federal court considering the prisoner's habeas application might reach a different result applying the *Strickland* framework itself. It is difficult, however, to describe such a run-of-the-mill state-court decision as "diametrically different" from, "opposite in character or nature" from, or "mutually opposed" to *Strickland*, our clearly established precedent. Although the state-court decision may be contrary to the federal court's conception of how *Strickland* ought to be applied in that particular case, the decision is not "mutually opposed" to *Strickland* itself.

Justice Stevens would instead construe § 2254(d)(1)'s "contrary to" clause to encompass such a routine state-court decision. That construction, however, saps the "unreasonable application" clause of any meaning. If a federal habeas court can, under the "contrary to" clause, issue the writ whenever it concludes that the state court's application of clearly established federal law was incorrect, the "unreasonable application" clause becomes a nullity. We must, however, if possible, give meaning to every clause of the statute. Justice Stevens not only makes no attempt to do so, but also construes the "contrary to" clause in a manner that ensures that the "unreasonable application" clause will have no independent meaning. We reject that expansive interpretation of the statute. Reading § 2254(d)(1)'s "contrary to" clause to permit a federal court to grant relief in cases where a state court's error is limited to the manner in which it applies Supreme Court precedent is suspect given the logical and natural fit of the neighboring "unreasonable application" clause to such cases.

The Fourth Circuit's interpretation of the "unreasonable application" clause of § 2254(d)(1) is generally correct. That court held in *Green* that a state-court decision can involve an "unreasonable application" of this Court's clearly established precedent in two ways. First, a state-court decision involves an unreasonable application of this Court's precedent if the state court identifies the correct governing legal rule from this Court's cases but unreasonably applies it to the facts of the particular state prisoner's case. Second, a state-court decision also involves an unreasonable application of this Court's precedent if the state court either unreasonably extends a legal principle from our precedent to a new context where it should not apply or unreasonably refuses to extend that principle to a new context where it should apply.

A state-court decision that correctly identifies the governing legal rule but applies it unreasonably to the facts of a particular prisoner's case certainly would qualify as a decision "involv[ing] an unreasonable application of . . . clearly established Federal law." . . .*

The Fourth Circuit also held in *Green* that state-court decisions that unreasonably extend a legal principle from our precedent to a new context where it should not apply (or unreasonably refuse to extend a legal principle to a new context where it should apply) should be analyzed under § 2254(d)(1)'s "unreasonable application" clause. Although that holding may perhaps be correct, the classification does have some problems of precision. Just as it is sometimes difficult to distinguish a mixed question of law and fact from a question of fact, it will often be difficult to identify separately those state-court decisions that involve an unreasonable application of a legal principle (or an unreasonable failure to apply a legal principle) to a new context. Indeed, on the one hand, in some cases it will be hard to distinguish a decision involving an unreasonable extension of a legal principle from a decision involving an unreasonable application of law to facts. On the other hand, in many of the same cases it will also be difficult to distinguish a decision involving an unreasonable extension of a legal principle from a decision that "arrives at a conclusion opposite to that reached by this Court on a question of law." Today's case does not require us to decide how such "extension of legal principle" cases should be treated under § 2254(d)(1). For now it is sufficient to hold that when a state-court decision unreasonably applies the law of this Court to the facts of a prisoner's case, a federal court applying § 2254(d)(1) may conclude that the state-court decision falls within that provision's "unreasonable application" clause.

* The legislative history of § 2254(d)(1) also supports this interpretation. See, e.g., 142 Cong. Rec. 7799 (1996) (remarks of Sen. Specter) ("[U]nder the bill deference will be owed to state courts' decisions on the application of federal law to the facts. Unless it is unreasonable, a state court's decision applying the law to the facts will be upheld"); 141 Cong. Rec. 14666 (1995) (remarks of Sen. Hatch) ("[W]e allow a federal court to overturn a state court decision only if it is contrary to clearly established federal law or if it involves an 'unreasonable application' of clearly established federal law to the facts").

B

There remains the task of defining what exactly qualifies as an "unreasonable application" of law under § 2254(d)(1). The Fourth Circuit held in *Green* that a state-court decision involves an "unreasonable application of ... clearly established Federal law" only if the state court has applied federal law "in a manner that reasonable jurists would all agree is unreasonable." The placement of this additional overlay on the "unreasonable application" clause was erroneous. It is difficult to fault the Fourth Circuit for using this language given the fact that we have employed nearly identical terminology to describe the related inquiry undertaken by federal courts in applying the nonretroactivity rule of *Teague*. For example, in Lambrix v. Singletary, 520 U.S. 518 (1997), we stated that a new rule is not dictated by precedent unless it would be "apparent to *all reasonable jurists*." (Emphasis added). In Graham v. Collins, 506 U.S. 461 (1993), another nonretroactivity case, we employed similar language, stating that we could not say "that *all reasonable jurists* would have deemed themselves compelled to accept Graham's claim in 1984." (Emphasis added.)

Defining an "unreasonable application" by reference to a "reasonable jurist," however, is of little assistance to the courts that must apply § 2254(d)(1) and, in fact, may be misleading. Stated simply, a federal habeas court making the "unreasonable application" inquiry should ask whether the state court's application of clearly established federal law was objectively unreasonable. The federal habeas court should not transform the inquiry into a subjective one by resting its determination instead on the simple fact that at least one of the Nation's jurists has applied the relevant federal law in the same manner the state court did in the habeas petitioner's case. The "all reasonable jurists" standard would tend to mislead federal habeas courts by focusing their attention on a subjective inquiry rather than on an objective one. ...

The term "unreasonable" is no doubt difficult to define. That said, it is a common term in the legal world and, accordingly, federal judges are familiar with its meaning. For purposes of today's opinion, the most important point is that an unreasonable application of federal law is different from an incorrect application of federal law. ... Congress specifically used the word "unreasonable," and not a term like "erroneous" or "incorrect." Under § 2254(d)(1)'s "unreasonable application" clause, then, a federal habeas court may not issue the writ simply because that court concludes in its independent judgment that the relevant state-court decision applied clearly established federal law erroneously or incorrectly. Rather, that application must also be unreasonable. ...

Throughout this discussion the meaning of the phrase "clearly established Federal law, as determined by the Supreme Court of the United States" has been put to the side. That statutory phrase refers to the holdings, as opposed to the dicta, of this Court's decisions as of the time of the relevant state-court decision. In this respect, the "clearly established

Federal law'' phrase bears only a slight connection to our *Teague* jurisprudence. With one caveat, whatever would qualify as an old rule under our *Teague* jurisprudence will constitute ''clearly established Federal law, as determined by the Supreme Court of the United States'' under § 2254(d)(1). The one caveat, as the statutory language makes clear, is that § 2254(d)(1) restricts the source of clearly established law to this Court's jurisprudence.

In sum, § 2254(d)(1) places a new constraint on the power of a federal habeas court to grant a state prisoner's application for a writ of habeas corpus with respect to claims adjudicated on the merits in state court. Under § 2254(d)(1), the writ may issue only if one of the following two conditions is satisfied—the state-court adjudication resulted in a decision that (1) ''was contrary to . . . clearly established Federal law, as determined by the Supreme Court of the United States,'' or (2) ''involved an unreasonable application of . . . clearly established Federal law, as determined by the Supreme Court of the United States.'' Under the ''contrary to'' clause, a federal habeas court may grant the writ if the state court arrives at a conclusion opposite to that reached by this Court on a question of law or if the state court decides a case differently than this Court has on a set of materially indistinguishable facts. Under the ''unreasonable application'' clause, a federal habeas court may grant the writ if the state court identifies the correct governing legal principle from this Court's decisions but unreasonably applies that principle to the facts of the prisoner's case.

III

Although I disagree with Justice Stevens concerning the standard we must apply under § 2254(d)(1) in evaluating Terry Williams' claims on habeas, I agree with the Court that the Virginia Supreme Court's adjudication of Williams' claim of ineffective assistance of counsel resulted in a decision that was both contrary to and involved an unreasonable application of this Court's clearly established precedent. Specifically, I believe that the Court's discussion in Parts III and IV is correct and that it demonstrates the reasons that the Virginia Supreme Court's decision in Williams' case, even under the interpretation of § 2254(d)(1) I have set forth above, was both contrary to and involved an unreasonable application of our precedent.

First, I agree with the Court that our decision in *Strickland* undoubtedly qualifies as ''clearly established Federal law, as determined by the Supreme Court of the United States,'' within the meaning of § 2254(d)(1). Second, I agree that the Virginia Supreme Court's decision was contrary to that clearly established federal law to the extent it held that our decision in Lockhart v. Fretwell, 506 U.S. 364 (1993), somehow modified or supplanted the rule set forth in *Strickland*. . . .

Third, I also agree with the Court that, to the extent the Virginia Supreme Court did apply *Strickland*, its application was unreasonable. As the Court correctly recounts, Williams' trial counsel failed to conduct investigation that would have uncovered substantial amounts of mitigation evidence. ... The consequence of counsel's failure to conduct the requisite, diligent investigation into his client's troubling background and unique personal circumstances manifested itself during his generic, unapologetic closing argument, which provided the jury with no reasons to spare petitioner's life. ... Based on its consideration of all of this evidence, the same trial judge that originally found Williams' death sentence "justified and warranted," concluded that trial counsel's deficient performance prejudiced Williams, and accordingly recommended that Williams be granted a new sentencing hearing. The Virginia Supreme Court's decision reveals an obvious failure to consider the totality of the omitted mitigation evidence. For that reason, and the remaining factors discussed in the Court's opinion, I believe that the Virginia Supreme Court's decision "involved an unreasonable application of ... clearly established Federal law, as determined by the Supreme Court of the United States."

Accordingly, although I disagree with the interpretation of § 2254(d)(1) set forth in Part II of Justice Stevens' opinion, I join Parts I, III, and IV of the Court's opinion and concur in the judgment of reversal.

■ CHIEF JUSTICE REHNQUIST, with whom JUSTICE SCALIA and JUSTICE THOMAS join, concurring in part and dissenting in part.

I agree with the Court's interpretation of 28 U.S.C. § 2254(d)(1), see ante (opinion of O'Connor, J.), but disagree with its decision to grant habeas relief in this case.

There is "clearly established Federal law, as determined by [this Court]" that governs petitioner's claim of ineffective assistance of counsel: Strickland v. Washington, 466 U.S. 668 (1984). Thus, we must determine whether the Virginia Supreme Court's adjudication was "contrary to" or an "unreasonable application of" *Strickland*.

Generally, in an ineffective-assistance-of-counsel case where the state court applies *Strickland*, federal habeas courts can proceed directly to "unreasonable application" review. But, according to the substance of petitioner's argument, this could be one of the rare cases where a state court applied the wrong Supreme Court precedent, and, consequently, reached an incorrect result. Petitioner argues, and the Court agrees, that the Virginia Supreme Court improperly held that Lockhart v. Fretwell, 506 U.S. 364 (1993), "modified or in some way supplanted" the rule set down in *Strickland*. I agree that such a holding would be improper. But the Virginia Supreme Court did not so hold as it did not rely on *Lockhart* to reach its decision.

Before delving into the evidence presented at the sentencing proceeding, the Virginia Supreme Court stated:

> We shall demonstrate that the criminal proceeding sentencing defendant to death was not fundamentally unfair or unreliable,

> and that the prisoner's assertions about the potential effects of the omitted proof do not establish a "reasonable probability" that the result of the proceeding would have been different, nor any probability sufficient to undermine confidence in the outcome. Therefore, any ineffective assistance of counsel did not result in actual prejudice to the accused.

Williams v. Warden, 254 Va. 16, 25, 487 S.E.2d 194, 199 (1997).

While the first part of this statement refers to *Lockhart*, the rest of the statement is straight out of *Strickland*. Indeed, after the initial allusion to *Lockhart*, the Virginia Supreme Court's analysis explicitly proceeds under *Strickland* alone. Because the Virginia Supreme Court did not rely on *Lockhart* to make its decision, and, instead, appropriately relied on *Strickland*, that court's adjudication was not "contrary to" this Court's clearly established precedent

The question then becomes whether the Virginia Supreme Court's adjudication resulted from an "unreasonable application of" *Strickland*. In my view, it did not.

I, like the Virginia Supreme Court and the Federal Court of Appeals below, will assume without deciding that counsel's performance fell below an objective standard of reasonableness. As to the prejudice inquiry, I agree with the Court of Appeals that evidence showing that petitioner presented a future danger to society was overwhelming. As that court stated:

> The murder of Mr. Stone was just one act in a crime spree that lasted most of Williams's life. Indeed, the jury heard evidence that, in the months following the murder of Mr. Stone, Williams savagely beat an elderly woman, stole two cars, set fire to a home, stabbed a man during a robbery, set fire to the city jail, and confessed to having strong urges to choke other inmates and to break a fellow prisoner's jaw.

In *Strickland*, we said that both the performance and prejudice components of the ineffectiveness inquiry are mixed questions of law and fact. It is with this kind of a question that the "unreasonable application of" clause takes on meaning. While the determination of "prejudice" in the legal sense may be a question of law, the subsidiary inquiries are heavily factbound.

Here, there was strong evidence that petitioner would continue to be a danger to society, both in and out of prison. It was not, therefore, unreasonable for the Virginia Supreme Court to decide that a jury would not have been swayed by evidence demonstrating that petitioner had a terrible childhood and a low IQ. The potential mitigating evidence that may have countered the finding that petitioner was a future danger was testimony that petitioner was not dangerous while in detention. But, again, it is not unreasonable to assume that the jury would have viewed this mitigation as unconvincing upon hearing that petitioner set fire to his cell while awaiting trial for the murder at hand and has repeated visions of harming other inmates.

Accordingly, I would hold that habeas relief is barred by 28 U.S.C. § 2254(d).

NOTES ON THE 1996 LEGISLATION

**1. Questions and Comments on *Terry Williams v. Taylor*.** In her opinion stating the Court's interpretation of § 2254(d), Justice O'Connor describes two distinct types of cases. In the first, to be decided under the "contrary to" clause, "a federal habeas court may grant the writ if the state court arrives at a conclusion opposite to that reached by this Court on a question of law or if the state court decides a case differently than this Court has on a set of materially indistinguishable facts." In the second, to be decided under the "unreasonable application" clause, "a federal habeas court may grant the writ if the state court identifies the correct governing legal principle from this Court's decisions but unreasonably applies that principle to the facts of the prisoner's case."

Speaking for four Justices on this point, Justice Stevens saw but a single category:

> We are not persuaded that the phrases define two mutually exclusive categories of questions. Most constitutional questions that arise in habeas corpus proceedings—and therefore most "decisions" to be made—require the federal judge to apply a rule of law to a set of facts, some of which may be disputed and some undisputed. For example, an erroneous conclusion that particular circumstances established the voluntariness of a confession, or that there exists a conflict of interest when one attorney represents multiple defendants, may well be described either as "contrary to" or as an "unreasonable application of "the governing rule of law.

Justice Stevens adds that the difference between his view and that of the Court "is, of course, important, but should affect only a narrow category of cases." What, exactly, are the "important" differences between the two opinions? Will they "affect only a narrow category of cases"? Quite apart from subtle (or "important") differences in how the interpretation of § 2254(d) is stated, at the end of the day how did the law change in 1996? Will the 1996 revision of § 2254(d) have a significant impact on federal habeas litigation?

Consider, in this respect, the division of the Court on the ultimate outcome in *Terry Williams*. Recall that three Justices (Thomas, joined by Rehnquist and Scalia) concluded in Wright v. West, 505 U.S. 277 (1992), that federal habeas courts " 'must defer to the state court's decision rejecting the claim unless that decision is patently unreasonable.' " The remainder of the Court adhered to the pre–1966 doctrine that questions of law and mixed questions of law and fact were to be decided de novo by federal habeas courts. After *Terry Williams*, can it be said that § 2254(d) codified the Thomas position in *Wright v. West*? Or does *Terry Williams* reflect, essentially, the same split among the Justices seen in *Wright v. West*?

Finally, what are the incentives for state-court decisionmaking established by § 2254(d)? Should a state supreme court ignore Court of Appeals decisions and focus only on "clearly established Federal law, as determined by the Supreme Court of the United States"? Should it refuse to recognize the implications of a line of Supreme Court decisions and focus only on what has been "clearly established" to date?

**2. Additional Ambiguities.** [Here read Note 3, page 742. Add two new paragraphs at the end of the Note:]

> Notice that Justice O'Connor states in *Terry Williams* that the statutory phrase "clearly established Federal law, as determined by the Supreme Court of the United States" in § 2254(d) "refers to the holdings, as opposed to the dicta, of this Court's decisions *as of the time of the relevant state-court decision*." [Emphasis added.] Does this mean, contrary to *Teague*, that there are no occasions when "new" Supreme Court decisions will be applied on federal habeas corpus?
>
> Consider the following hypothetical. Assume the state courts, following established Supreme Court precedent, uphold a criminal conviction because they conclude that the underlying conduct on which the conviction was based was not protected speech under the First Amendment. Assume also (a) that the relevant Supreme Court precedents are later overruled, meaning that the underlying conduct is now protected speech; and (b) that collateral attack is no longer available in the state courts. If the convicted defendant then seeks federal habeas, what result?

**Page 741, add new footnote after second paragraph of Note 1:**

**a.** For an extensive elaboration of this position and criticism of the result in *Lindh*, see James S. Liebman and William F. Ryan, "Some Effectual Power": The Quantity and Quality of Decisionmaking Required of Article III Courts, 98 Colum. L. Rev. 696 (1998). For a response to Liebman and Ryan, see Kent S. Scheidegger, Habeas Corpus, Relitigation, and the Legislative Power, 98 Colum. L. Rev. 888 (1998).

**Page 742, add a footnote after the first question at the top of the page:**

**a.** The early case law in the circuit courts is examined and an analysis of the appropriate standards of review is presented in Evan Tsen Lee, Section 2254(d) of the New Habeas Statute: An (Opinionated) User's Manual, 51 Vand. L. Rev. 103 (1998). See also Note, Rewriting the Great Writ: Standards of Review for Habeas Corpus under the New 28 U.S.C. § 2254, 110 Harv. L. Rev. 1868 (1997). Both authors disagree with Yackle's interpretation. Yackle has argued elsewhere that the new habeas provisions "are unlikely to have large-scale, systematic effects on the outcomes in habeas corpus ... cases." Mark Tushnet & Larry Yackle, Symbolic Statutes and Real Laws: The Pathologies of the Antiterrorism and Effective Death Penalty Act and the Prison Litigation Reform Act, 47 Duke L.J. 1 (1997).

**Page 743, add a new Note:**

4. **Bibliography.** A symposium in the Georgetown Law Journal entitled Congress and the Courts: Jurisdiction and Remedies contains six articles provoked in part by the 1996 habeas legislation: Vicki C. Jackson, Introduction: Congressional Control of Jurisdiction and the Future of the Federal Courts—Opposition, Agreement, and Hierarchy, 86 Geo. L.J. 2445 (1998); David Cole, Jurisdiction and Liberty: Habeas Corpus and Due Process as Limits on Congress's Control of Federal Jurisdiction, 86 Geo. L.J. 2481 (1998); John Harrison, Jurisdiction, Congressional Power, and Constitutional Remedies, 86 Geo. L.J. 2513 (1998); Lawrence G. Sager, *Klein*'s First Principle: A Proposed Solution, 86 Geo. L.J. 2525 (1998); Daniel J. Meltzer, Congress, Courts, and Constitutional Remedies, 86 Geo. L.J. 2537 (1998); Judith Resnick, The Federal Courts and Congress: Additional Sources, Alternative Texts, and Altered Aspirations, 86 Geo. L.J. 2589 (1998).

**Page 754, add a footnote after the second sentence of the first full paragraph:**

**f.** Suppose the ineffective assistance claim could have been presented to the state courts but was not. Does the failure properly to exhaust that claim mean that it cannot be asserted as cause for the procedural default of another claim? The Court answered "yes" in Edwards v. Carpenter, ___ U.S. ___ (2000). The habeas petitioner is required to establish "cause and prejudice" to excuse failure to raise the ineffective assistance claim in order for it to suffice as "cause" for the failure to raise the other claim. Joined by Justice Stevens, Justice Breyer dissented from this holding, concluding that it "unnecessarily adds to [the] complexity [of the Court's habeas jurisprudence]."—[Footnote by eds.]

**Page 756, add a footnote after the first of the three questions at the end of Note 6:**

**h.** In Edwards v. Carpenter, ___ U.S. ___ (2000), the state courts had declined to hear an ineffective assistance of counsel claim because a state procedural rule had not been followed. The District Court concluded that the claim could nonetheless be heard on federal habeas because inconsistent application of the state's procedural rule rendered it "inadequate" to bar federal habeas review. The Court of Appeals decided the case on another ground and the Supreme Court reversed. In its list of options open on remand, the Supreme Court said that the Court of Appeals "may conclude, as did the District Court, that the [state procedural rule] does not constitute an adequate procedural ground to bar federal habeas review of the ineffective-assistance claim. We express no view as to [this issue]." In its earlier description of the District Court holding, the Supreme Court cited Ford v. Georgia, 498 U.S. 411, 423–24 (1991), for the proposition that a "state procedural default is not an 'independent and adequate state ground' barring subsequent federal review unless the state rule was 'firmly established and regularly followed' at the time it was applied."

**Page 756, add a footnote at the end of Note 6:**

**i.** The Court held in Trest v. Cain, 522 U.S. 87 (1997), that circuit courts are not *required* to raise a procedural default sua sponte that the parties did not raise or argue. Rather, procedural default is normally a defense that the state is obligated to raise and preserve. The Court declined to decide, however, whether circuit courts are *permitted* to rely on a procedural default that the state has waived or failed to raise.

**Page 757, add at end of first paragraph of Note 8:**

; Larry W. Yackle, The American Bar Association and Federal Habeas Corpus, 61 Law & Contemp Probs. 171 (1998).

**Page 763, omit the Notes on Procedural Foreclosure under the 1996 Legislation and substitute the following:**

## Michael Wayne Williams v. Taylor

Supreme Court of the United States, 2000.
___ U.S. ___.

■ JUSTICE KENNEDY delivered the opinion of the Court.

Petitioner Michael Wayne Williams received a capital sentence for the murders of Morris Keller, Jr., and Keller's wife, Mary Elizabeth. Petitioner later sought a writ of habeas corpus in federal court. Accompanying his petition was a request for an evidentiary hearing on constitutional claims which, he alleged, he had been unable to develop in state-court proceedings. The question in this case is whether 28 U.S.C. § 2254(e)(2) (1994 ed., Supp. III), as amended by the Antiterrorism and Effective Death Penalty Act of 1996 (AEDPA), 110 Stat. 1214, bars the evidentiary hearing petitioner seeks. If petitioner "has failed to develop the factual basis of [his] claim[s] in State court proceedings," his case is subject to § 2254(e)(2), and he may not receive a hearing because he concedes his inability to satisfy the statute's further stringent conditions for excusing the deficiency.

I

On the evening of February 27, 1993, Verena Lozano James dropped off petitioner and his friend Jeffrey Alan Cruse near a local store in a rural area of Cumberland County, Virginia. The pair planned to rob the store's employees and customers using a .357 revolver petitioner had stolen in the course of a quadruple murder and robbery he had committed two months earlier. Finding the store closed, petitioner and Cruse walked to the Kellers' home. Petitioner was familiar with the couple, having grown up down the road from where they lived. He told Cruse they would have "a couple thousand dollars." Cruse, who had been holding the .357, handed the gun to petitioner and knocked on the door. When Mr. Keller opened the door, petitioner pointed the gun at him as the two intruders forced their way inside. Petitioner and Cruse forced Mr. Keller to the kitchen, where they discovered Mrs. Keller. Petitioner ordered the captives to remove their clothing. While petitioner kept guard on the Kellers, Cruse searched the house for money and other valuables. He found a .38–caliber handgun and bullets. Upon Cruse's return to the kitchen, petitioner had Cruse tie their captives with telephone cords. The Kellers were confined to separate closets while the intruders continued ransacking the house.

When they gathered all they wanted, petitioner and Cruse decided to rape Mrs. Keller. With Mrs. Keller pleading with them not to hurt her or her husband, petitioner raped her. Cruse did the same. Petitioner then ordered the Kellers to shower and dress and "take a walk" with him and Cruse. As they were leaving, petitioner told Mrs. Keller he and Cruse were going to burn down the house. Mrs. Keller begged to be allowed to retrieve her marriage license, which she did, guarded by petitioner.

As the prosecution later presented the case, details of the murders were as follows. Petitioner, now carrying the .38, and Cruse, carrying the .357, took the Kellers to a thicket down a dirt road from the house. With petitioner standing behind Mr. Keller and Cruse behind Mrs. Keller, petitioner told Cruse, "We'll shoot at the count of three." At the third count, petitioner shot Mr. Keller in the head, and Mr. Keller collapsed to the ground. Cruse did not shoot Mrs. Keller at the same moment. Saying "he didn't want to leave no witnesses," petitioner urged Cruse to shoot Mrs. Keller. Cruse fired one shot into her head. Despite his wound, Mr. Keller stood up, but petitioner shot him a second time. To ensure the Kellers were dead, petitioner shot each of them two or three more times.

After returning to the house and loading the stolen property into the Kellers' jeep, petitioner and Cruse set fire to the house and drove the jeep to Fredericksburg, Virginia, where they sold some of the property. They threw the remaining property and the .357 revolver into the Rappahannock River and set fire to the jeep.

Pursuing a lead from Verena James, the police interviewed Cruse about the fire at the Kellers' home. Petitioner had fled to Florida. Cruse provided no useful information until the police discovered the bodies of the victims, at which point Cruse consulted counsel. In a plea bargain Cruse agreed to disclose the details of the crimes in exchange for the Commonwealth's promise not to seek the death penalty against him. Cruse described the murders but made no mention of his own act of rape. When the Commonwealth discovered the omission, it revoked the plea agreement and charged Cruse with capital murder.

Petitioner was arrested and charged with robbery, abduction, rape, and the capital murders of the Kellers. At trial in January 1994, Cruse was the Commonwealth's main witness. He recounted the murders as we have just described. Cruse testified petitioner raped Mrs. Keller, shot Mr. Keller at least twice, and shot Mrs. Keller several times after she had been felled by Cruse's bullet. He also described petitioner as the mastermind of the murders. The circumstances of the first plea agreement between the Commonwealth and Cruse and its revocation were disclosed to the jury.

Testifying on his own behalf, petitioner admitted he was the first to shoot Mr. Keller and it was his idea to rob the store and set fire to the house. He denied, however, raping or shooting Mrs. Keller, and claimed to have shot Mr. Keller only once. Petitioner blamed Cruse for the remaining shots and disputed some other parts of Cruse's testimony.

The jury convicted petitioner on all counts. After considering the aggravating and mitigating evidence presented during the sentencing phase, the jury found the aggravating circumstances of future dangerousness and vileness of the crimes and recommended a death sentence. The trial court imposed the recommended sentence. The Supreme Court of Virginia affirmed petitioner's convictions and sentence and we denied certiorari. In a separate proceeding, Cruse pleaded guilty to the capital murder of Mrs. Keller and the first-degree murder of Mr. Keller. After the prosecution asked the sentencing court to spare his life because of his testimony against petitioner, Cruse was sentenced to life imprisonment.

Petitioner filed a habeas petition in state court alleging, in relevant part, that the Commonwealth failed to disclose a second agreement it had reached with Cruse after the first one was revoked. The new agreement, petitioner alleged, was an informal undertaking by the prosecution to recommend a life sentence in exchange for Cruse's testimony. Finding no merit to petitioner's claims, the Virginia Supreme Court dismissed the habeas petition, and we again denied certiorari.

Petitioner filed a habeas petition in the United States District Court for the Eastern District of Virginia on November 20, 1996. In addition to his claim regarding the alleged undisclosed agreement between the Commonwealth and Cruse, the petition raised three claims relevant to questions now before us. First, petitioner claimed the prosecution had violated Brady v. Maryland, 373 U.S. 83 (1963), in failing to disclose a report of a confidential pre-trial psychiatric examination of Cruse. Second, petitioner alleged his trial was rendered unfair by the seating of a juror who at voir dire had not revealed possible sources of bias. Finally, petitioner alleged one of the prosecutors committed misconduct in failing to reveal his knowledge of the juror's possible bias.

The District Court ... dismissed the petition, having determined petitioner could not satisfy § 2254(e)(2)'s requirements.

The Court of Appeals affirmed. [W]e stayed petitioner's execution and granted certiorari to decide whether § 2254(e)(2) precludes him from receiving an evidentiary hearing on his claims. We now affirm in part and reverse in part.

II

A

Petitioner filed his federal habeas petition after AEDPA's effective date, so the statute applies to his case. See Lindh v. Murphy, 521 U.S. 320,

326–27 (1997). The Commonwealth argues AEDPA bars petitioner from receiving an evidentiary hearing on any claim whose factual basis was not developed in state court, absent narrow circumstances not applicable here. Petitioner did not develop, or raise, his claims of juror bias, prosecutorial misconduct, or the prosecution's alleged *Brady* violation regarding Cruse's psychiatric report until he filed his federal habeas petition. Petitioner explains he could not have developed the claims earlier because he was unaware, through no fault of his own, of the underlying facts. As a consequence, petitioner contends, AEDPA erects no barrier to an evidentiary hearing in federal court.

Section 2254(e)(2), the provision which controls whether petitioner may receive an evidentiary hearing in federal district court on the claims that were not developed in the Virginia courts, becomes the central point of our analysis. It provides as follows:

> If the applicant has failed to develop the factual basis of a claim in State court proceedings, the court shall not hold an evidentiary hearing on the claim unless the applicant shows that—
>
> (A) the claim relies on—
>
> (i) a new rule of constitutional law, made retroactive to cases on collateral review by the Supreme Court, that was previously unavailable; or
>
> (ii) a factual predicate that could not have been previously discovered through the exercise of due diligence; and
>
> (B) the facts underlying the claim would be sufficient to establish by clear and convincing evidence that but for constitutional error, no reasonable factfinder would have found the applicant guilty of the underlying offense.

By the terms of its opening clause the statute applies only to prisoners who have "failed to develop the factual basis of a claim in State court proceedings." If the prisoner has failed to develop the facts, an evidentiary hearing cannot be granted unless the prisoner's case meets the other conditions of § 2254(e)(2). Here, petitioner concedes his case does not comply with § 2254(e)(2)(B), so he may receive an evidentiary hearing only if his claims fall outside the opening clause.

There was no hearing in state court on any of the claims for which petitioner now seeks an evidentiary hearing. That, says the Commonwealth, is the end of the matter. In its view petitioner, whether or not through his own fault or neglect, still "failed to develop the factual basis of a claim in State court proceedings." Petitioner, on the other hand, says the phrase "failed to develop" means lack of diligence in developing the claims, a defalcation he contends did not occur since he made adequate efforts during state-court proceedings to discover and present the underlying facts. The Court of Appeals agreed with petitioner's interpretation of

§ 2254(e)(2) but believed petitioner had not exercised enough diligence to avoid the statutory bar. We agree with petitioner and the Court of Appeals that "failed to develop" implies some lack of diligence; but, unlike the Court of Appeals, we find no lack of diligence on petitioner's part with regard to two of his three claims.

B

We start, as always, with the language of the statute. Section 2254(e)(2) begins with a conditional clause, "[i]f the applicant has failed to develop the factual basis of a claim in State court proceedings," which directs attention to the prisoner's efforts in state court. We ask first whether the factual basis was indeed developed in state court, a question susceptible, in the normal course, of a simple yes or no answer. Here the answer is no.

The Commonwealth would have the analysis begin and end there. Under its no-fault reading of the statute, if there is no factual development in the state court, the federal habeas court may not inquire into the reasons for the default when determining whether the opening clause of § 2254(e)(2) applies. We do not agree with the Commonwealth's interpretation of the word "failed."

We do not deny "fail" is sometimes used in a neutral way, not importing fault or want of diligence. So the phrase "We fail to understand his argument" can mean simply "We cannot understand his argument." This is not the sense in which the word "failed" is used here, however.

We give the words of a statute their " 'ordinary, contemporary, common meaning,' " absent an indication Congress intended them to bear some different import. [Citations omitted.] In its customary and preferred sense, "fail" connotes some omission, fault, or negligence on the part of the person who has failed to do something. See, e.g., Webster's New International Dictionary 910 (2d ed.1939) (defining "fail" as "to be wanting; to fall short; to be or become deficient in any measure or degree," and "failure" as "a falling short," "a deficiency or lack," and an "[o]mission to perform"); Webster's New International Dictionary 814 (3d ed.1993) ("to leave some possible or expected action unperformed or some condition unachieved"). See also Black's Law Dictionary 594 (6th ed.1990) (defining "fail" as "[f]ault, negligence, or refusal"). To say a person has failed in a duty implies he did not take the necessary steps to fulfill it. He is, as a consequence, at fault and bears responsibility for the failure. In this sense, a person is not at fault when his diligent efforts to perform an act are thwarted, for example, by the conduct of another or by happenstance. Fault lies, in those circumstances, either with the person who interfered with the accomplishment of the act or with no one at all. We conclude Congress used the word "failed" in the sense just described. Had Congress intended a no-fault standard, it would have had no difficulty in making its intent plain. It would have had to do no more than use, in lieu of the phrase "has failed to," the phrase "did not."

Under the opening clause of § 2254(e)(2), a failure to develop the factual basis of a claim is not established unless there is lack of diligence, or some greater fault, attributable to the prisoner or the prisoner's counsel. In this we agree with the Court of Appeals and with all other courts of appeals which have addressed the issue.

Our interpretation of § 2254(e)(2)'s opening clause has support in Keeney v. Tamayo–Reyes, 504 U.S. 1 (1992), a case decided four years before AEDPA's enactment. In *Keeney*, a prisoner with little knowledge of English sought an evidentiary hearing in federal court, alleging his nolo contendere plea to a manslaughter charge was not knowing and voluntary because of inaccuracies in the translation of the plea proceedings. The prisoner had not developed the facts of his claim in state collateral proceedings, an omission caused by the negligence of his state postconviction counsel. The Court characterized this as the "prisoner's failure to develop material facts in state court." We required the prisoner to demonstrate cause and prejudice excusing the default before he could receive a hearing on his claim, unless the prisoner could "show that a fundamental miscarriage of justice would result from failure to hold a federal evidentiary hearing."

Section 2254(e)(2)'s initial inquiry into whether "the applicant has failed to develop the factual basis of a claim in State court proceedings" echoes *Keeney*'s language regarding "the state prisoner's failure to develop material facts in state court." In *Keeney*, the Court borrowed the cause and prejudice standard applied to procedurally defaulted claims, see Wainwright v. Sykes, 433 U.S. 72, 87–88 (1977), deciding there was no reason "to distinguish between failing to properly assert a federal claim in state court and failing in state court to properly develop such a claim." As is evident from the similarity between the Court's phrasing in *Keeney* and the opening clause of § 2254(e)(2), Congress intended to preserve at least one aspect of *Keeney*'s holding: prisoners who are at fault for the deficiency in the state-court record must satisfy a heightened standard to obtain an evidentiary hearing. To be sure, in requiring that prisoners who have not been diligent satisfy § 2254(e)(2)'s provisions rather than show cause and prejudice, and in eliminating a freestanding "miscarriage of justice" exception, Congress raised the bar *Keeney* imposed on prisoners who were not diligent in state-court proceedings. Contrary to the Commonwealth's position, however, there is no basis in the text of § 2254(e)(2) to believe Congress used "fail" in a different sense than the Court did in *Keeney* or otherwise intended the statute's further, more stringent requirements to control the availability of an evidentiary hearing in a broader class of cases than were covered by *Keeney*'s cause and prejudice standard.

In sum, the opening clause of § 2254(e)(2) codifies *Keeney*'s threshold standard of diligence, so that prisoners who would have had to satisfy

*Keeney*'s test for excusing the deficiency in the state-court record prior to AEDPA are now controlled by § 2254(e)(2). When the words of the Court are used in a later statute governing the same subject matter, it is respectful of Congress and of the Court's own processes to give the words the same meaning in the absence of specific direction to the contrary. See Lorillard v. Pons, 434 U.S. 575, 581 (1978) ("[W]here ... Congress adopts a new law incorporating sections of a prior law, Congress normally can be presumed to have had knowledge of the interpretation given to the incorporated law, at least insofar as it affects the new statute").

Interpreting § 2254(e)(2) so that "failed" requires lack of diligence or some other fault avoids putting it in needless tension with § 2254(d). A prisoner who developed his claim in state court and can prove the state court's decision was "contrary to, or an unreasonable application of, clearly established federal law, as determined by the Supreme Court of the United States," is not barred from obtaining relief by § 2254(d)(1). See Terry Williams v. Taylor, ___ U.S. ___ (2000) (opinion of O'Connor, J.). If the opening clause of § 2254(e)(2) covers a request for an evidentiary hearing on a claim which was pursued with diligence but remained undeveloped in state court because, for instance, the prosecution concealed the facts, a prisoner lacking clear and convincing evidence of innocence could be barred from a hearing on the claim even if he could satisfy § 2254(d). See 28 U.S.C. § 2254(e)(2)(B). The "failed to develop" clause does not bear this harsh reading, which would attribute to Congress a purpose or design to bar evidentiary hearings for diligent prisoners with meritorious claims just because the prosecution's conduct went undetected in state court. We see no indication that Congress by this language intended to remove the distinction between a prisoner who is at fault and one who is not.

The Commonwealth argues a reading of "failed to develop" premised on fault empties § 2254(e)(2)(A)(ii) of its meaning. To treat the prisoner's lack of diligence in state court as a prerequisite for application of § 2254(e)(2), the Commonwealth contends, renders a nullity of the statute's own diligence provision requiring the prisoner to show "a factual predicate [of his claim] could not have been previously discovered through the exercise of due diligence." § 2254(e)(2)(A)(ii). We disagree.

The Commonwealth misconceives the inquiry mandated by the opening clause of § 2254(e)(2). The question is not whether the facts could have been discovered but instead whether the prisoner was diligent in his efforts. The purpose of the fault component of "failed" is to ensure the prisoner undertakes his own diligent search for evidence. Diligence for purposes of the opening clause depends upon whether the prisoner made a reasonable attempt, in light of the information available at the time, to investigate and pursue claims in state court; it does not depend, as the Commonwealth would have it, upon whether those efforts could have been successful. Though lack of diligence will not bar an evidentiary hearing if efforts to discover the facts would have been in vain, see § 2254(e)(2)(A)(ii), and there is a convincing claim of innocence, see § 2254(e)(2)(B), only a prisoner who has neglected his rights in state court need satisfy these conditions. The statute's later reference to diligence pertains to cases in which the facts could not have been discovered, whether there was diligence or not. In this important respect § 2254(e)(2)(A)(ii) bears a close resemblance to (e)(2)(A)(i), which applies to a new rule that was not available at the time of the earlier proceedings. Cf. Gutierrez v. Ada, 528 U.S. ___, ___ (2000) ("[W]ords and people are known by their companions"). In these two parallel provisions Congress has given prisoners who fall within § 2254(e)(2)'s opening clause an opportunity to obtain an evidentiary hearing where the legal or factual basis of the claims did not exist at the time of state-court proceedings.

We are not persuaded by the Commonwealth's further argument that anything less than a no-fault understanding of the opening clause is contrary to AEDPA's purpose to further the principles of comity, finality, and federalism. There is no doubt Congress intended AEDPA to advance these doctrines. Federal habeas corpus principles must inform and shape the historic and still vital relation of mutual respect and common purpose existing between the States and the federal courts. In keeping this delicate balance we have been careful to limit the scope of federal intrusion into state criminal adjudications and to safeguard the States' interest in the integrity of their criminal and collateral proceedings. . . .

It is consistent with these principles to give effect to Congress' intent to avoid unneeded evidentiary hearings in federal habeas corpus, while recognizing the statute does not equate prisoners who exercise diligence in pursuing their claims with those who do not. Principles of exhaustion are premised upon recognition by Congress and the Court that state judiciaries have the duty and competence to vindicate rights secured by the Constitution in state criminal proceedings. Diligence will require in the usual case that the prisoner, at a minimum, seek an evidentiary hearing in state court in the manner prescribed by state law. "Comity . . . dictates that when a prisoner alleges that his continued confinement for a state court conviction violates federal law, the state courts should have the first opportunity to review this claim and provide any necessary relief." O'Sullivan v. Boerckel, 526 U.S. 838, 844 (1999). For state courts to have their rightful opportunity to adjudicate federal rights, the prisoner must be diligent in developing the record and presenting, if possible, all claims of constitutional error. If the prisoner fails to do so, himself or herself contributing to the absence of a full and fair adjudication in state court, § 2254(e)(2) prohibits an evidentiary hearing to develop the relevant claims in federal court, unless the statute's other stringent requirements are met. Federal courts sitting in habeas are not an alternative forum for trying facts and issues which a prisoner made insufficient effort to pursue in state proceedings. Yet comity is not served by saying a prisoner "has failed to develop the factual basis of a claim" where he was unable to develop his claim in state court despite diligent effort. In that circumstance, an evidentiary hearing is not barred by § 2254(e)(2).

III

Now we apply the statutory test. If there has been no lack of diligence at the relevant stages in the state proceedings, the prisoner has not "failed to develop" the facts under § 2254(e)(2)'s opening clause, and he will be excused from showing compliance with the balance of the subsection's requirements. We find lack of diligence as to one of the three claims but not as to the other two.

A

Petitioner did not exercise the diligence required to preserve the claim that nondisclosure of Cruse's psychiatric report was in contravention of Brady v. Maryland, 373 U.S. 83 (1963). The report concluded Cruse "ha[d] little recollection of the [murders of the Kellers], other than vague memories, as he was intoxicated with alcohol and marijuana at the time." The report had been prepared in September 1993, before petitioner was tried; yet it was not mentioned by petitioner until he filed his federal habeas petition and attached a copy of the report. Petitioner explained that an investigator for his federal habeas counsel discovered the report in Cruse's court file but state habeas counsel had not seen it when he had reviewed the same file. State habeas counsel averred as follows:

> Prior to filing [petitioner's] habeas corpus petition with the Virginia Supreme Court, I reviewed the Cumberland County court files of [petitioner] and of his co-defendant, Jeffrey Cruse. . . . I have reviewed the attached psychiatric evaluation of Jeffrey Cruse. . . . I have no recollection of seeing this report in Mr. Cruse's court file when I examined the file. Given the contents of the report, I am confident that I would remember it.

The trial court was not satisfied with this explanation for the late discovery. Nor are we.

There are repeated references to a "psychiatric" or "mental health" report in a transcript of Cruse's sentencing proceeding, a copy of which petitioner's own state habeas counsel attached to the state habeas petition he filed with the Virginia Supreme Court. The transcript reveals that Cruse's attorney described the report with details that should have alerted counsel to a possible *Brady* claim. As Cruse's attorney said:

> The psychiatric report . . . point[s] out that [Cruse] is significantly depressed. He suffered from post traumatic stress. His symptoms include nightmares, sleeplessness, sobbing, reddening of the face, severe depression, flash backs. . . . [T]he psychological report states he is overwhelmed by feelings of guilt and shame in his actions. He is numb. He is trying to suppress his feelings, but when he has feelings, there is only pain and sadness.

The description accords with the contents of the psychiatric report, which diagnosed Cruse as suffering from post-traumatic stress disorder:

> [Cruse] has recurrent nightmares and visualizes the face of the woman that he killed. When attempting to describe this nightmare, he breaks openly into tears and his face reddens. ... He continues to feel worthless as a person.... He has no hope for his future and has been thinking of suicide constantly. ... He does describe inability to sleep, often tossing and turning, waking up, and feeling fatigued during the day. ... He described neurovegetative symptoms of major depression and post-traumatic nightmares, recurrent in nature, of the [murders].

The transcript put petitioner's state habeas counsel on notice of the report's existence and possible materiality. The sole indication that counsel made some effort to investigate the report is an October 30, 1995, letter to the prosecutor in which counsel requested "[a]ll reports of physical and mental examinations, scientific tests, or experiments conducted in connection with the investigation of the offense, including but not limited to: [a]ll psychological test or polygraph examinations performed upon any prosecution witness and all documents referring or relating to such tests...." After the prosecution declined the requests absent a court order, it appears counsel made no further efforts to find the specific report mentioned by Cruse's attorney. Given knowledge of the report's existence and potential importance, a diligent attorney would have done more. Counsel's failure to investigate these references in anything but a cursory manner triggers the opening clause of § 2254(e)(2).

As we hold there was a failure to develop the factual basis of this *Brady* claim in state court, we must determine if the requirements in the balance of § 2254(e)(2) are satisfied so that petitioner's failure is excused. Subparagraph (B) of § 2254(e)(2) conditions a hearing upon a showing, by clear and convincing evidence, that no reasonable factfinder would have found petitioner guilty of capital murder but for the alleged constitutional error. Petitioner concedes he cannot make this showing, and the case has been presented to us on that premise. For these reasons, we affirm the Court of Appeals' judgment barring an evidentiary hearing on this claim.

B

We conclude petitioner has met the burden of showing he was diligent in efforts to develop the facts supporting his juror bias and prosecutorial misconduct claims in collateral proceedings before the Virginia Supreme Court.

Petitioner's claims are based on two of the questions posed to the jurors by the trial judge at voir dire. First, the judge asked prospective jurors, "Are any of you related to the following people who may be called as witnesses?" Then he read the jurors a list of names, one of which was "Deputy Sheriff Claude Meinhard." Bonnie Stinnett, who would later become the jury foreperson, had divorced Meinhard in 1979, after a 17–year marriage with four children. Stinnett remained silent, indicating the answer was "no." Meinhard, as the officer who investigated the crime scene and interrogated Cruse, would later become the prosecution's lead-off witness at trial.

After reading the names of the attorneys involved in the case, including one of the prosecutors, Robert Woodson, Jr., the judge asked, "Have you or any member of your immediate family ever been represented by any of the aforementioned attorneys?" Stinnett again said nothing, despite the fact Woodson had represented her during her divorce from Meinhard.

In an affidavit she provided in the federal habeas proceedings, Stinnett claimed "[she] did not respond to the judge's [first] question because [she] did not consider [herself] 'related' to Claude Meinhard in 1994 [at voir dire ]. . . . Once our marriage ended in 1979, I was no longer related to him." As for Woodson's earlier representation of her, Stinnett explained as follows:

> When Claude and I divorced in 1979, the divorce was uncontested and Mr. Woodson drew up the papers so that the divorce could be completed. Since neither Claude nor I was contesting anything, I didn't think Mr. Woodson "represented" either one of us.

Woodson provided an affidavit in which he admitted "[he] was aware that Juror Bonnie Stinnett was the ex-wife of then Deputy Sheriff Claude Meinhard and [he] was aware that they had been divorced for some time." Woodson stated, however, "[t]o [his] mind, people who are related only by marriage are no longer 'related' once the marriage ends in divorce." Woodson also "had no recollection of having been involved as a private attorney in the divorce proceedings between Claude Meinhard and Bonnie Stinnett." He explained that "[w]hatever [his] involvement was in the 1979 divorce, by the time of trial in 1994 [he] had completely forgotten about it."

Even if Stinnett had been correct in her technical or literal interpretation of the question relating to Meinhard, her silence after the first question was asked could suggest to the finder of fact an unwillingness to be forthcoming; this in turn could bear on the veracity of her explanation for not disclosing that Woodson had been her attorney. Stinnett's failure to divulge material information in response to the second question was misleading as a matter of fact because, under any interpretation, Woodson had acted as counsel to her and Meinhard in their divorce. Coupled with Woodson's own reticence, these omissions as a whole disclose the need for an evidentiary hearing. It may be that petitioner could establish that Stinnett was not impartial, see Smith v. Phillips, 455 U.S. 209, 217, 219–21 (1982), or that Woodson's silence so infected the trial as to deny due process, see Donnelly v. DeChristoforo, 416 U.S. 637, 647–48 (1974).

. . . The trial record contains no evidence which would have put a reasonable attorney on notice that Stinnett's non-response was a deliberate omission of material information. State habeas counsel did attempt to investigate petitioner's jury, though prompted by concerns about a different juror. Counsel filed a motion for expert services with the Virginia Supreme Court, alleging "irregularities, improprieties and omissions exist[ed] with respect to the empaneling [sic] of the jury." Based on these suspicions, counsel requested funding for an investigator "to examine all circumstances relating to the empanelment of the jury and the jury's consideration of the case." The Commonwealth opposed the motion, and the Virginia Supreme Court denied it and dismissed the habeas petition, depriving petitioner of a further opportunity to investigate. The Virginia Supreme Court's denial of the motion is understandable in light of petitioner's vague allegations, but the vagueness was not the fault of petitioner. Counsel had no reason to believe Stinnett had been married to Meinhard or been represented by Woodson. The underdevelopment of these matters was attributable to Stinnett and Woodson, if anyone. We do not suggest the State has an obligation to pay for investigation of as yet undeveloped claims; but if the prisoner has made a reasonable effort to discover the claims to commence or continue state proceedings, § 2254(e)(2) will not bar him from developing them in federal court.

The Court of Appeals held state habeas counsel was not diligent because petitioner's investigator on federal habeas discovered the relationships upon interviewing two jurors who referred in passing to Stinnett as "Bonnie Meinhard." The investigator later confirmed Stinnett's prior marriage to Meinhard by checking Cumberland County's public records. [The Court of Appeals noted: "The documents supporting [petitioner's] Sixth Amendment claims have been a matter of public record since Stinnett's divorce became final in 1979. Indeed, because [petitioner's] federal habeas counsel located those documents, there is little reason to think that his state habeas counsel could not have done so as well."] We should be surprised, to say the least, if a district court familiar with the standards of trial practice were to hold that in all cases diligent counsel must check public records containing personal information pertaining to each and every juror. Because of Stinnett and Woodson's silence, there was no basis for an investigation into Stinnett's marriage history. Section 2254(e)(2) does not apply to petitioner's related claims of juror bias and prosecutorial misconduct.

We further note the Commonwealth has not argued that petitioner could have sought relief in state court once he discovered the factual bases of these claims some time between appointment of federal habeas counsel on July 2, 1996, and the filing of his federal habeas petition on November 20, 1996. As an indigent, petitioner had 120 days following appointment of state habeas counsel to file a petition with the Virginia Supreme Court. Va.Code Ann. § 8.01–654.1 (1999). State habeas counsel was appointed on August 10, 1995, about a year before petitioner's investigator on federal habeas uncovered the information regarding Stinnett and Woodson. As state postconviction relief was no longer available at the time the facts came to light, it would have been futile for petitioner to return to the Virginia courts. In these circumstances, though the state courts did not have an opportunity to consider the new claims, petitioner cannot be said to have failed to develop them in state court by reason of having neglected to pursue remedies available under Virginia law.

Our analysis should suffice to establish cause for any procedural default petitioner may have committed in not presenting these claims to the Virginia courts in the first instance. Questions regarding the standard for determining the prejudice that petitioner must establish to obtain relief on these claims can be addressed by the Court of Appeals or the District Court in the course of further proceedings. These courts, in light of cases such as *Smith*, supra, at 215 ("[T]he remedy for allegations of juror partiality is a hearing in which the defendant has the opportunity to prove actual bias"), will take due account of the District Court's earlier decision to grant an evidentiary hearing based in part on its belief that "Juror Stinnett deliberately failed to tell the truth on voir dire."

IV

Petitioner alleges the Commonwealth failed to disclose an informal plea agreement with Cruse. The Court of Appeals rejected this claim on the merits under § 2254(d)(1), so it is unnecessary to reach the question whether § 2254(e)(2) would permit a hearing on the claim.

The decision of the Court of Appeals is affirmed in part and reversed in part. The case is remanded for further proceedings consistent with this opinion.

It is so ordered.

## NOTES ON PROCEDURAL FORECLOSURE UNDER THE 1996 LEGISLATION

**1. Effect of Prior Litigation of the Facts in State Court.** Section 2254(e)(1) provides that:

> In a proceeding instituted by an application for a writ of habeas corpus by a person in custody pursuant to the judgment of a State court, a determination of a factual issue made by a State court shall be presumed to be correct. The applicant shall have the burden of rebutting the presumption of correctness by clear and convincing evidence.

This provision repudiates the *Townsend v. Sain* approach to relitigation of facts that have previously been litigated in state court.[a] Gone is the discretion of the federal habeas court to hold a hearing in any case "where the material facts are in dispute." Gone also is the requirement that a

**a.** Larry W. Yackle disagrees. See Federal Evidentiary Hearings Under the New Habeas Corpus Statute, 6 B.U. Pub. Interest L.J. 135 (1996).

hearing be held in any case where the standard of a "full and fair hearing" in the state court has not been met. Instead, the findings of the state court "shall be presumed to be correct" and the federal habeas applicant has the burden of rebutting the presumption by the heightened standard of "clear and convincing evidence."

**2. Questions and Comments on *Michael Wayne Williams v. Taylor*.** As the Court unanimously holds in *Michael Wayne Williams*, the *Sykes* "cause and prejudice" standard, as applied in *Keeney v. Tamayo-Reyes*, survives the enactment of § 2254(e)(2). If the federal habeas applicant can show "cause and prejudice" to excuse the procedural default of failing to raise a claim in state court, the restrictive provisions of § 2254(e)(2)(A) and (B) do not apply and a hearing can be held by the federal habeas court.

Consider the impact of this interpretation of § 2254(e)(2). If "cause and prejudice" cannot be established to excuse a procedural default in state court, then the restrictions of § 2254(e)(2)(A) and (B) will come into play. Are there likely to be many situations when "cause and prejudice" cannot be established but the standards of § 2254(e)(2)(A) and (B) could be? Suppose a federal habeas court believes that cause and prejudice cannot be shown, but that "a fundamental miscarriage of justice would result from failure to hold a federal evidentiary hearing." What is it to do then? Will all such cases fit into § 2254(e)(2)(A) and (B)?

If "cause and prejudice" can be established, on the other hand, the applicant is entitled to a hearing. What happens then? Does the federal habeas court consider the constitutional claim de novo and grant the relief the state court should have granted if the claim had been properly raised? What else could it do? Can it consider Court of Appeals decisions, or is it limited by analogy to § 2254(d) to "clearly established Federal law, as determined by the Supreme Court of the United States"? Can it extend the federal law even slightly beyond what has been "clearly established"?

On another point, is it surprising that the Court was unanimous in its application of the "cause" standard to Williams' claims relating to juror bias and prosecutorial misconduct? What of the Court of Appeals' point that "because [petitioner's] federal habeas counsel located [the relevant] documents, there is little reason to think that his state habeas counsel could not have done so as well"?

Finally, the Supreme Court held in *Michael Wayne Williams* that the petitioner had established "cause" for two of his claims. How is he to show "prejudice" on remand? Is he to be afforded a hearing at which he "has the opportunity to show actual bias" by the juror? Or must he first establish "prejudice" in order to get such a hearing? If the former, does this mean that only "cause" need be shown in order to get a hearing? If the latter, how could the defendant show what it would take a hearing to demonstrate?

**3. The New Legislation in Capital Cases.** [Here read Note 3 on pages 764–65.]

**Page 780, replace footnote b:**

**b.** This includes discretionary review in the highest court of the state. But there is ambiguity about whether such review must be sought if the highest state court has made it clear that routine presentation of all possible claims is unwelcome because its function is to hear only questions of statewide importance. See O'Sullivan v. Boerckel, ___ U.S. ___ (1999). There is no requirement, however, that certiorari be sought in the United States Supreme Court after a decision by the highest court of the state. Fay v. Noia, 372 U.S. 391 (1963).

**Page 780, substitute the following for the fourth paragraph of Note 2:**

There are adverse consequences, moreover, if the habeas petitioner failed to raise an available claim in previous state litigation. In O'Sullivan v. Boerckel, 526 U.S. 838 (1999), for example, the Court enforced a procedural foreclosure on three of the petitioner's six habeas claims. The reason was that he could have raised these claims in his application for discretionary review in the state Supreme Court but did not do so. His failure properly to exhaust his available state remedies, in other words, led to procedural foreclosure of his unexhausted claims. See also Edwards v. Carpenter, ___ U.S. ___ (2000).

**Page 786, add a footnote at the end of paragraph (b):**

**h.** The Court held in Slack v. McDaniel, ___ U.S. ___ (2000), that "a habeas petition which is filed after an initial petition was dismissed without adjudication on the merits for failure to exhaust state remedies is not a 'second or successive' petition as that term is understood in the habeas corpus context. Federal courts do, however, retain broad powers to prevent duplicative or unnecessary litigation." Justice Scalia, joined by Justice Thomas, dissented from this part of the Court's holding. The initial habeas case was filed before the effective date of the 1996 legislation.

**Page 786, add a new Note:**

**9. *Stewart v. Martinez–Villareal.*** In Stewart v. Martinez–Villareal, 523 U.S. 637 (1998), the Court answered one of the questions about *Rose v. Lundy* posed above. If Lundy allowed his federal petition to be dismissed, returned to state court to litigate his unexhausted claims, lost in state court, and then presented all his claims in a new federal petition, he would not, it appears, be subject to the limitations of § 2244(b).

Martinez–Villareal was convicted of murder and sentenced to death. The state courts affirmed on direct appeal, and a series of state-court habeas petitions were denied. Martinez–Villareal then filed three successive petitions for federal habeas, all of which were denied because they contained claims on which state remedies had not been exhausted. He then filed a fourth federal habeas petition. This petition asserted, among other claims, that Martinez–Villareal was not competent to be executed. He relied on Ford v. Wainwright, 477 U.S. 399 (1986), which held that the death penalty could not be inflicted on a prisoner who was insane.

The District Court dismissed the *Ford* claim on the ground that it was premature (no date of execution had yet been set). It then granted habeas relief on one of the other claims, but the Court of Appeals reversed and reinstated the conviction. Both courts indicated that they did not mean to foreclose a later assertion of the *Ford* claim.

Soon thereafter the state set a date of execution. After a hearing in state court on Martinez–Villareal's mental condition, it was determined that he was fit to be executed. He then renewed his *Ford* claim in federal court. This presented two questions: whether court of appeals permission to file the claim was required because it was a "second or successive application" under 28 U.S.C. § 2244(b)(3)[h]; and whether the limits of 28 U.S.C. § 2244(b)(1) and (2)[i] were applicable. The Court of Appeals held that § 2244(b) did not apply to a petition that raised only a competency to be executed claim, and accordingly remanded the case to the District Court for resolution of the merits. The state at this point successfully sought certiorari to review the Court of Appeals' decision.

The Supreme Court first held that it had jurisdiction (in spite of § 2244(b)(3)(E)) because the Court of Appeals had held § 2244(b) inapplicable. Chief Justice Rehnquist then wrote for the Court:

> "The state contends that because respondent has already had one 'fully-litigated habeas petition, the plain meaning of § 2244(b) . . . requires his new petition to be treated as successive.' Under that reading of the statute, respondent is entitled to only one merits judgment of his federal habeas claims. Because respondent has already presented a petition to the District Court, and the District Court and Court of Appeals have acted on that petition, § 2244(b) must apply to any subsequent request for federal habeas relief. . . .

**h.** "(A) Before a second or successive application permitted by this section is filed in the district court, the applicant shall move in the appropriate court of appeals for an order authorizing the district court to consider the application. . . .

"(E) The grant or denial of an authorization by a court of appeals to file a second or successive application shall not be appealable and shall not be the subject of a petition for rehearing or for a writ of certiorari."

**i.** "(1) A claim presented in a second or successive habeas corpus application under section 2254 that was presented in a prior application shall be dismissed.

"(2) A claim presented in a second or successive habeas corpus application under section 2254 that was not presented in a prior application shall be dismissed unless—

"(A) the applicant shows that the claim relies on a new rule of constitutional law, made retroactive to cases on collateral review by the supreme court, that was previously unavailable; or

"(B)(i) the factual predicate for the claim could not have been discovered previously through the exercise of due diligence; and

(ii) the facts underlying the claim, if proven and viewed in light of the evidence as a whole, would be sufficient to establish by clear and convincing evidence that, but for constitutional error, no reasonable factfinder would have found the applicant guilty of the underlying offense."

"This may have been the second time that respondent has asked the federal courts to provide relief on his *Ford* claim, but this does not mean that there were two separate applications, the second of which was necessarily subject to § 2244(b). There was only one application for habeas relief, and the District Court ruled (or should have ruled) on each claim at the time it became ripe. Respondent was entitled to an adjudication of all of the claims presented in his earlier . . . application for federal habeas relief. The Court of Appeals was therefore correct in holding that respondent was not required to get authorization to file a 'second or successive' application before his *Ford* claim could be heard.

"If the state's interpretation of 'second or successive' were correct, the implications for habeas practice would be far-reaching and seemingly perverse. [N]one of our cases expounding [the exhaustion] doctrine have ever suggested that a prisoner whose habeas petition was dismissed for failure to exhaust state remedies, and who then did exhaust those remedies and return to federal court, was by such action filing a successive petition. A court where such a petition was filed could adjudicate these claims under the same standard as would govern those made in any other first petition.

"We believe that respondent's *Ford* claim here—previously dismissed as premature—should be treated in the same manner as the claim of a petitioner who returns to a federal habeas court after exhausting state remedies. True, the cases are not identical; respondent's *Ford* claim was dismissed as premature, not because he had not exhausted state remedies, but because his execution was not imminent and therefore his competency to be executed could not be determined at that time. But in both situations, the habeas petitioner does not receive an adjudication of his claim. To hold otherwise would mean that a dismissal of a first habeas petition for technical procedural reasons would bar the prisoner from ever obtaining federal habeas review."

Justices Thomas and Scalia dissented. They thought the plain language of § 2244(b) required dismissal of the petition.

**10. Questions and Comments on *Martinez-Villareal*.** In a footnote in his opinion in *Martinez-Villareal*, Chief Justice Rehnquist said that "[t]his case does not present the situation where a prisoner raises a *Ford* claim for the first time in a petition filed after the federal courts have already rejected the prisoner's initial habeas application. Therefore, we have no occasion to decide whether such a filing would be a 'second or successive application' within the meaning of [§ 2244(b)]."

What possible difference could this make? Does the Court's reading of the language of § 2244(b) turn on the fact that Martinez–Villareal had sought *Ford* relief at a time when it was not available to him? Does the footnote mean that careful lawyers will now raise *Ford* claims routinely in all first habeas petitions just in case their clients lose their sanity as the time of execution approaches?

From another perspective, how, indeed, does the Court read the language of § 2244(b) to justify its decision? Does the "plain meaning" of the statute support any other view but the dissent's?

**Page 808, add to the citations in Note 2:**

Arleen Anderson, Responding to the Challenge of Actual Innocence Claims After *Herrera v. Collins*, 71 Temple L. Rev. 489 (1998) (proposing that it is "in the states' best interests to provide their own post-conviction procedures for reviewing claims of actual innocence").

**Page 808, add after the Notes on *Herrera v. Collins*:**

## Bousley v. United States

Supreme Court of the United States, 1998.
523 U.S. 614 .

■ CHIEF JUSTICE REHNQUIST delivered the opinion of the Court.

Petitioner pleaded guilty to "using" a firearm in violation of 18 U.S.C. § 924(c)(1) in 1990. Five years later we held in Bailey v. United States, 516 U.S. 137 (1995), that § 924(c)(1)'s "use" prong requires the government to show "active employment of the firearm." Petitioner meanwhile had sought collateral relief under 28 U.S.C. § 2255, claiming that his guilty plea was not knowing and intelligent because he was misinformed by the District Court as to the nature of the charged crime. We hold that, although this claim was procedurally defaulted, petitioner may be entitled to a hearing on the merits of it if he makes the necessary showing to relieve the default.

Following his arrest in March 1990, petitioner was charged with possession of methamphetamine with intent to distribute, in violation of 21 U.S.C. § 841(a)(1). A superseding indictment added the charge that he "knowingly and intentionally used ... firearms during and in relation to a drug trafficking crime," in violation of 18 U.S.C. § 924(c). Petitioner agreed to plead guilty to both charges while reserving the right to challenge the quantity of drugs used in calculating his sentence.

The District Court accepted petitioner's pleas, finding that he was "competent to enter [the] pleas, that [they were] voluntarily entered, and that there [was] a factual basis for them." Following a sentencing hearing, the District Court sentenced petitioner to 78 months' imprisonment on the drug count, a consecutive term of 60 months' imprisonment on the § 924(c) count, and four years of supervised release. Petitioner appealed his sentence, but did not challenge the validity of his plea. The Court of Appeals affirmed.

In June 1994, petitioner sought a writ of habeas corpus under 28 U.S.C. § 2241, challenging the factual basis for his guilty plea on the ground that neither the "evidence" nor the "plea allocution" showed a "connection between the firearms in the bedroom of the house, and the garage, where the drug trafficking occurred." A magistrate judge recommended that the petition be treated as a motion under 28 U.S.C. § 2255 and recommended dismissal, concluding that there was a factual basis for petitioner's guilty plea because the guns in petitioner's bedroom were in close proximity to drugs and were readily accessible. The District Court adopted the magistrate judge's Report and Recommendation and ordered that the petition be dismissed.

Petitioner appealed. While his appeal was pending, we held in *Bailey* that a conviction for use of a firearm under § 924(c)(1) requires the government to show "active employment of the firearm." As we explained, active employment includes uses such as "brandishing, displaying, bartering, striking with, and, most obviously, firing or attempting to fire" the weapon, but does not include mere possession of a firearm. Thus, a "defendant cannot be charged under § 924(c)(1) merely for storing a weapon near drugs or drug proceeds," or for "placement of a firearm to provide a sense of security or to embolden."

Following our decision in *Bailey*, the Court of Appeals appointed counsel to represent petitioner. Counsel argued that *Bailey* should be applied "retroactively," that petitioner's guilty plea was involuntary because he was misinformed about the elements of a § 924(c)(1) offense, that this claim was not waived by his guilty plea, and that his conviction should therefore be vacated. Nevertheless, the Court of Appeals affirmed the District Court's order of dismissal.

We then granted certiorari to resolve a split among the Circuits over the permissibility of post-*Bailey* collateral attacks on § 924(c)(1) convictions obtained pursuant to guilty pleas. Because the government disagreed with the Court of Appeals' analysis, we appointed amicus curiae to brief and argue the case in support of the judgment below.

A plea of guilty is constitutionally valid only to the extent it is "voluntary" and "intelligent." Brady v. United States, 397 U.S. 742, 748 (1970). We have long held that a plea does not qualify as intelligent unless a criminal defendant first receives "real notice of the true nature of the charge against him, the first and most universally recognized requirement of due process." Smith v. O'Grady, 312 U.S. 329, 334 (1941). Amicus contends that petitioner's plea was intelligently made because, prior to pleading guilty, he was provided with a copy of his indictment, which charged him with "using" a firearm. Such circumstances, standing alone, give rise to a presumption that the defendant was informed of the nature of the charge against him. Henderson v. Morgan, 426 U.S. 637, 647 (1976). Petitioner nonetheless maintains that his guilty plea was unintelligent because the District Court subsequently misinformed him as to the elements of a § 924(c)(1) offense. In other words, petitioner contends that the record reveals that neither he, nor his counsel, nor the court correctly understood the essential elements of the crime with which he was charged. Were this contention proven, petitioner's plea would be, contrary to the view expressed by the Court of Appeals, constitutionally invalid. . . .

Amicus urges us to apply the rule of Teague v. Lane, 489 U.S. 288 (1989), to petitioner's claim that his plea was not knowing and intelligent. In *Teague*, we held that "new constitutional rules of criminal procedure will not be applicable to those cases which have become final before the new rules are announced," unless the new rule "places 'certain kinds of primary, private individual conduct beyond the power of the criminal law-making authority to proscribe,'" or could be considered a "watershed rul[e] of criminal procedure." But we do not believe that *Teague* governs this case. The only constitutional claim made here is that petitioner's guilty plea was not knowing and intelligent. There is surely nothing new about this principle, enumerated as long ago as *Smith v. O'Grady*, supra. And because *Teague* by its terms applies only to procedural rules, we think it is inapplicable to the situation in which this Court decides the meaning of a criminal statute enacted by Congress.

This distinction between substance and procedure is an important one in the habeas context. The *Teague* doctrine is founded on the notion that one of the "principal functions of habeas corpus [is] 'to assure that no man has been incarcerated under a procedure which creates an impermissibly large risk that the innocent will be convicted.'" *Teague*, 489 U.S., at 312. Consequently, unless a new rule of criminal procedure is of such a nature that "without [it] the likelihood of an accurate conviction is seriously diminished," 489 U.S., at 313, there is no reason to apply the rule retroactively on habeas review. By contrast, decisions of this Court holding that a substantive federal criminal statute does not reach certain conduct, like decisions placing conduct "'beyond the power of the criminal law-making authority to proscribe,'" id., at 311, necessarily carry a significant risk that a defendant stands convicted of "an act that the law does not make criminal." Davis v. United States, 417 U.S. 333, 346 (1974). For under our federal system it is only Congress, and not the courts, which can make conduct criminal. United States v. Hudson & Goodwin, 11 U.S. (7 Cranch) 32 (1812). Accordingly, it would be inconsistent with the doctrinal underpinnings of habeas review to preclude petitioner from relying on our decision in *Bailey* in support of his claim that his guilty plea was constitutionally invalid.

Though petitioner's claim is not *Teague*-barred, there are nonetheless significant procedural hurdles to its consideration on the merits. We have strictly limited the circumstances under which a guilty plea may be attacked on collateral review. "It is well settled that a voluntary and intelligent plea of guilty made by an accused person, who has been advised by competent counsel, may not be collaterally attacked." Mabry v. Johnson,

467 U.S. 504, 508 (1984). And even the voluntariness and intelligence of a guilty plea can be attacked on collateral review only if first challenged on direct review. Habeas review is an extraordinary remedy and " 'will not be allowed to do service for an appeal.' " Reed v. Farley, 512 U.S. 339, 354 (1994). Indeed, "the concern with finality served by the limitation on collateral attack has special force with respect to convictions based on guilty pleas." United States v. Timmreck, 441 U.S. 780, 784 (1979). In this case, petitioner contested his sentence on appeal, but did not challenge the validity of his plea. In failing to do so, petitioner procedurally defaulted the claim he now presses on us.

In an effort to avoid this conclusion, petitioner contends that his claim falls within an exception to the procedural default rule for claims that could not be presented without further factual development. In Waley v. Johnston, 316 U.S. 101 (1942) (per curiam ), we held that there was such an exception for a claim that a plea of guilty had been coerced by threats made by a government agent, when the facts were "dehors the record and their effect on the judgment was not open to consideration and review on appeal." Petitioner's claim, however, differs significantly from that advanced in *Waley*. He is not arguing that his guilty plea was involuntary because it was coerced, but rather that it was not intelligent because the information provided him by the District Court at his plea colloquy was erroneous. This type of claim can be fully and completely addressed on direct review based on the record created at the plea colloquy.

Where a defendant has procedurally defaulted a claim by failing to raise it on direct review, the claim may be raised in habeas only if the defendant can first demonstrate either "cause" and actual "prejudice," Murray v. Carrier, 477 U.S. 478, 485 (1986); Wainwright v. Sykes, 433 U.S. 72, 87 (1977), or that he is "actually innocent," *Murray*, 477 U.S., at 496; Smith v. Murray, 477 U.S. 527, 537 (1986).

Petitioner offers two explanations for his default in an attempt to demonstrate cause. First, he argues that "the legal basis for his claim was not reasonably available to counsel" at the time his plea was entered. This argument is without merit. While we have held that a claim that "is so novel that its legal basis is not reasonably available to counsel" may constitute cause for a procedural default, Reed v. Ross, 468 U.S. 1, 16 (1984), petitioner's claim does not qualify as such. The argument that it was error for the District Court to misinform petitioner as to the statutory elements of § 924(c)(1) was most surely not a novel one. Indeed, at the time of petitioner's plea, the Federal Reporters were replete with cases involving challenges to the notion that "use" is synonymous with mere "possession."[2] Petitioner also contends that his default should be excused

**2.** Even were we to conclude that petitioner's counsel was unaware at the time that petitioner's plea colloquy was constitutionally deficient, "[w]here the basis of a . . . claim is available, and other defense counsel have perceived and litigated that claim, the because, "before *Bailey*, any attempt to attack [his] guilty plea would have been futile." This argument too is unavailing. As we clearly stated in Engle v. Isaac, 456 U.S. 107, 130 (1982), "futility cannot constitute cause if it means simply that a claim was 'unacceptable to that particular court at that particular time.' " Therefore, petitioner is unable to establish cause for his default.

Petitioner's claim may still be reviewed in this collateral proceeding if he can establish that the constitutional error in his plea colloquy "has probably resulted in the conviction of one who is actually innocent." *Murray v. Carrier*, 477 U.S., at 496. To establish actual innocence, petitioner must demonstrate that, " 'in light of all the evidence,' " "it is more likely than not that no reasonable juror would have convicted him." Schlup v. Delo, 513 U.S. 298, 327–28 (1995). The District Court failed to address petitioner's actual innocence, perhaps because petitioner failed to raise it initially in his § 2255 motion. However, the government does not contend that petitioner waived this claim by failing to raise it below. Accordingly, we believe it appropriate to remand this case to permit petitioner to attempt to make a showing of actual innocence.

It is important to note in this regard that "actual innocence" means factual innocence, not mere legal insufficiency. See Sawyer v. Whitley, 505 U.S. 333, 339 (1992). In other words, the government is not limited to the existing record to rebut any showing that petitioner might make. Rather, on remand, the government should be permitted to present any admissible evidence of petitioner's guilt even if that evidence was not presented during petitioner's plea colloquy and would not normally have been offered before our decision in *Bailey*.[3] In cases where the government has forgone more serious charges in the course of plea bargaining, petitioner's showing of actual innocence must also extend to those charges.

In this case, the government maintains that petitioner must demonstrate that he is actually innocent of both "using" and "carrying" a firearm in violation of § 924(c)(1). But petitioner's indictment charged him only with "using" firearms in violation of § 924(c)(1). And there is no record evidence that the government elected not to charge petitioner with "carrying" a firearm in exchange for his plea of guilty. Accordingly, petitioner need demonstrate no more than that he did not "use" a firearm as that term is defined in *Bailey*.

If, on remand, petitioner can make that showing, he will then be entitled to have his defaulted claim of an unintelligent plea considered on

demands of comity and finality counsel against labeling alleged unawareness of the objection as cause for a procedural default." Engle v. Isaac, 456 U.S. 107, 134 (1982).

**3.** Justice Scalia contends that this factual innocence inquiry will be unduly complicated by the absence of a trial transcript in the guilty plea context. We think his concerns are overstated. In the federal system, where this case arose, guilty pleas must be accompanied by proffers, recorded verbatim on the record, demonstrating a factual basis for the plea. See Fed. Rules Crim. Proc. 11(f), (g).

its merits. The judgment of the Court of Appeals is therefore reversed, and the case is remanded for further proceedings consistent with this opinion.

It is so ordered.

■ JUSTICE STEVENS, concurring in part and dissenting in part.

While I agree with the Court's central holding and with its conclusion that none of its judge-made rules foreclose petitioner's collateral attack on his conviction under 18 U.S.C. § 924(c), I believe there is a flaw in its analysis that will affect the proceedings on remand. Given the fact that the record now establishes that the plea of guilty to the § 924(c) charge was constitutionally invalid, petitioner remains presumptively innocent of that offense. Accordingly, unless he again pleads guilty, the burden is on the government to prove his unlawful use of a firearm.

I

This case does not raise any question concerning the possible retroactive application of a new rule of law, cf. Teague v. Lane, 489 U.S. 288 (1989), because our decision in Bailey v. United States, 516 U.S. 137 (1995), did not change the law. It merely explained what § 924(c) had meant ever since the statute was enacted. The fact that a number of Courts of Appeals had construed the statute differently is of no greater legal significance than the fact that 42 U.S.C. § 1981 had been consistently misconstrued prior to our decision in Patterson v. McLean Credit Union, 491 U.S. 164 (1989). Our comment on the significance of the pre-*Patterson* jurisprudence applies equally to the pre-*Bailey* cases construing § 924(c):

> "*Patterson* did not overrule any prior decision of this Court; rather, it held and therefore established that the prior decisions of the Courts of Appeals which read § 1981 to cover discriminatory contract termination were incorrect. They were not wrong according to some abstract standard of interpretive validity, but by the rules that necessarily govern our hierarchical federal court system. It is this Court's responsibility to say what a statute means, and once the Court has spoken, it is the duty of other courts to respect that understanding of the governing rule of law. A judicial construction of a statute is an authoritative statement of what the statute meant before as well as after the decision of the case giving rise to that construction." Rivers v. Roadway Express, Inc., 511 U.S. 298, 312–13 (1994).

Thus in 1990 when petitioner was advised by the trial judge, by his own lawyer, and by the prosecutor that mere possession of a firearm would support a conviction under § 924(c), he received critically incorrect legal advice. The fact that all of his advisers acted in good-faith reliance on existing precedent does not mitigate the impact of that erroneous advice. Its consequences for petitioner were just as severe, and just as unfair, as if the court and counsel had knowingly conspired to deceive him in order to induce him to plead guilty to a crime that he did not commit. Our cases make it perfectly clear that a guilty plea based on such misinformation is constitutionally invalid. Smith v. O'Grady, 312 U.S. 329, 334 (1941); Henderson v. Morgan, 426 U.S. 637, 644–45 (1976). Petitioner's conviction and punishment on the § 924(c) charge "are for an act that the law does not make criminal. There can be no room for doubt that such a circumstance 'inherently results in a complete miscarriage of justice' and 'present[s] exceptional circumstances' that justify collateral relief under [28 U.S.C.] § 2255." Davis v. United States, 417 U.S. 333, 346–47 (1974).

II

The government charges petitioner with "procedural default" because he did not challenge his guilty plea on direct appeal. The Court accepts this argument and therefore places the burden on petitioner to demonstrate either "cause and prejudice" or "actual innocence." Yet the Court cites no authority for its conclusion that "even the voluntariness and intelligence of a guilty plea can be attacked on collateral review only if first challenged on direct review."[1] Moreover, the primary case upon which the government relies, United States v. Timmreck, 441 U.S. 780 (1979), actually supports the contrary proposition: that a constitutionally invalid guilty plea may be set aside on collateral attack whether or not it was challenged on appeal.

Several years before we decided *Timmreck*, the Court had held that it is reversible error for a trial judge to accept a guilty plea without following the procedures dictated by Rule 11 of the Federal Rules of Criminal Procedure. McCarthy v. United States, 394 U.S. 459 (1969). The question in *Timmreck* was whether such an error was sufficiently serious to support a collateral attack under 28 U.S.C. § 2255. Because the error was neither jurisdictional nor constitutional, we held that collateral relief was unavailable. If we had thought that the failure to challenge the constitutionality of a guilty plea on direct appeal amounted to procedural default, there would have been no need in *Timmreck* to rely on the critical difference between reversible error and the more fundamental kind of error that can be corrected on collateral review. The opinion makes it clear that an ordinary Rule 11 violation must be challenged on appeal; the only criterion for collateral review that it mentions is that the error must be jurisdictional or constitutional. . . .

The Court has never held that the constitutionality of a guilty plea cannot be attacked collaterally unless it is first challenged on direct review. Moreover, as the facts of this case demonstrate, such a holding would be

1. The Court does cite Reed v. Farley, 512 U.S. 339, 354 (1994), for the general proposition that habeas review " 'will not be allowed to do service for an appeal.' " *Reed* is inapposite, however, as it involved neither a constitutional violation nor a guilty plea. In *Reed*, the Court rejected a state prisoner's statutory claim brought under 28 U.S.C. § 2254 on the grounds that the prisoner had neither made a timely objection nor suffered prejudice. . . .

unwise and would defeat the very purpose of collateral review. A layman who justifiably relied on incorrect advice from the court and counsel in deciding to plead guilty to a crime that he did not commit will ordinarily continue to assume that such advice was accurate during the time for taking an appeal. The injustice of his conviction is not mitigated by the passage of time. His plea should be treated as a nullity and the conviction based on such a plea should be voided.

Because the record in this case already unambiguously demonstrates that petitioner's plea to the § 924(c) charge is invalid as a matter of constitutional law, I would remand with directions to vacate his § 924(c) conviction and allow him to plead anew.

■ JUSTICE SCALIA, with whom JUSTICE THOMAS joins, dissenting.

I agree with the Court that petitioner has not demonstrated "cause" for failing to challenge the validity of his guilty plea on direct review. I disagree, however, that a defendant who has pleaded guilty can be given the opportunity to avoid the consequences of his inexcusable procedural default by having the courts inquire into whether " 'it is more likely than not that no reasonable juror would have convicted him' " of the offense to which he pleaded guilty.

No criminal-law system can function without rules of procedure conjoined with a rule of finality. Evidence not introduced, or objections not made, at the appropriate time cannot be brought forward to reopen the conviction after judgment has been rendered. In the United States, we have developed generous exceptions to the rule of finality, one of which permits reopening, via habeas corpus, when the petitioner shows "cause" excusing the procedural default, and "actual prejudice" resulting from the alleged error. We have gone even beyond that generous exception in a certain class of cases: cases that have actually gone to trial. There we have held that, "even in the absence of a showing of cause for the procedural default," habeas corpus will be granted "where a constitutional violation has probably resulted in the conviction of one who is actually innocent." Schlup v. Delo, 513 U.S. 298, 321 (1995). In every one of our cases that has considered the possibility of applying this so-called actual-innocence exception, a defendant had asked a habeas court to adjudicate a successive or procedurally defaulted constitutional claim after his conviction by a jury. [Citations omitted.]

There are good reasons for this limitation: First and foremost, it is feasible to make an accurate assessment of "actual innocence" when a trial has been had. In *Schlup*, for example, we said that to sustain an "actual innocence" claim the petitioner must "show that it is more likely than not that no reasonable juror would have convicted him *in the light of the new evidence*." 513 U.S., at 327 (emphasis added). That "new evidence" was to be evaluated, of course, along with the "old evidence," consisting of the transcript of the trial. The habeas court was to "make its determination concerning the petitioner's innocence in light of all the evidence, including that alleged to have been illegally admitted (but with due regard to any unreliability of it) and evidence tenably claimed to have been wrongly excluded or to have become available only after the trial." *Schlup*, supra, at 328. As the Court's opinion today makes clear, the government is permitted to supplement the trial record with any additional evidence of guilt, but the court begins with (and ordinarily ends with) a complete trial transcript to rely upon. But how is the court to determine "actual innocence" upon our remand in the present case, where conviction was based upon an admission of guilt? Presumably the defendant will introduce evidence (perhaps nothing more than his own testimony) showing that he did not "use" a firearm in committing the crime to which he pleaded guilty, and the government, eight years after the fact, will have to find and produce witnesses saying that he did. This seems to me not to remedy a miscarriage of justice, but to produce one.*

Secondly, the Court has given as one of its justifications for the supergenerous miscarriage-of-justice exception to inexcusable default, "the fact that habeas corpus petitions that advance a substantial claim of actual innocence are extremely rare." *Schlup*, supra, at 321. That may be true enough of petitions challenging jury convictions; it assuredly will not be true of petitions challenging the "voluntariness" of guilty pleas. I put "voluntariness" in quotation marks, because we are not dealing here with only coerced confessions, which may indeed be rare enough. The present case is here because, in Henderson v. Morgan, 426 U.S. 637, 644–46 (1976), this Court held that where neither the indictment, defense counsel, nor the trial court explained to the defendant that intent to kill was an element of

* The Court believes these concerns are overstated because, in the federal system, the court must be satisfied that there is a factual basis for the plea. This displays a sad lack of solicitude for state courts, which handle the overwhelming majority of criminal cases. But even in the federal system, the "factual basis" requirement will typically be of no use. Consider the factual basis for the guilty plea in the present case, as set forth in the plea agreement:

> "The parties ... agree that, on or about March 19, 1990, ... the defendant knowingly used firearms during and in relation to a drug-trafficking offense.... The following firearms were found in the defendant's bedroom near the 6.9 grams of methamphetamine: a loaded Walther PBK .380 caliber handgun, serial number A016494; and a loaded .22 caliber Advantage Arms 4–shot revolver. The defendant admits ownership and possession of these two guns. This conduct constituted a violation of Title 18, United States Code, Section 924(c). Three other firearms were found in the two briefcases containing the bulk of the methamphetamine: a loaded .22 caliber North American Arms handgun, serial number C7854; a loaded .45 caliber Colt Model 1911 semiautomatic handgun, serial number 244682; an unloaded Ruger .357 caliber revolver, serial number 151–36099. The defendant denies knowledge of these guns."

Of course "knowingly used" in this statement presumably means "knowingly used" in the erroneous sense that prompts this litigation. And that will almost always be the situation where the "involuntariness" of the plea is a consequence of subsequently clarified uncertainty in the law: the factual basis will not include a fact which, by hypothesis, the court and the parties think irrelevant.

second-degree murder, his plea to that offense was "involuntary." A plea, the Court explained, can "not be voluntary in the sense that it constitute[s] an intelligent admission that he committed the offense unless the defendant receive[s] 'real notice of the true nature of the charge against him, the first and most universally recognized requirement of due process.' " Of course the word "voluntary" had never been used (by precise speakers, at least) in that sense—in the sense of "intelligent"—and what the *Henderson* line of cases did was, by sleight-of-tongue, to obliterate the distinction between involuntary confessions and misinformed or even uninformed confessions. Once all those categories have been lumped together, the cases within them are not at all rare, but indeed exceedingly numerous.

It is well established that "when this Court construes a statute, it is explaining its understanding of what the statute has meant continuously since the date when it became law." Rivers v. Roadway Express, Inc., 511 U.S. 298, 313, n. 12 (1994). Thus, every time this Court resolves a Circuit split regarding the elements of a crime defined in a federal statute, most if not all defendants who pleaded guilty in those Circuits on the losing end of the split will have confessed "involuntarily," having been advised by the Court, or by their counsel, that the law was what (as it turns out) it was not—or even (since this would suffice for application of *Henderson*) merely not having been advised that the law was what (as it turns out) it was. Indeed the latter basis for "involuntariness" (mere lack of "real notice of the charge against him," *Henderson*, supra, at 665) might be available even to those defendants pleading guilty in the Circuits on the winning side of the split. Thus, our decision in Bailey v. United States, 516 U.S. 137 (1995), has generated a flood of 28 U.S.C. § 2255 habeas petitions, each asserting actual innocence of "using" a firearm in violation of 18 U.S.C. § 924(c). This term, we will resolve a Circuit split over the meaning of another element ("carry" a firearm) in the same statute. And we will also resolve Circuit splits over the requisite elements of five other federal criminal statutes.

To the undeniable fact that the claim of "actual innocence" is much more likely to be available in guilty-plea cases than in jury-trial cases, there must be added the further undeniable fact that guilty-plea cases are very much more numerous than jury-trial cases. Last year, 51,647 of the 55,648 defendants convicted and sentenced in federal court (or nearly 93 per cent) pleaded guilty. Administrative Office of the United States Courts, L. Mecham, Judicial Business of the United States Courts: 1997 Report of the Director 214.

When all these factors are taken into account, it could not be clearer that the premise for our adoption in *Schlup* of the super-generous "miscarriage of justice" exception to normal finality rules—viz., that the cases in which defendants seek to invoke the exception would be "extremely rare"—is simply not true when the exception is extended to guilty pleas. To the contrary, the cases will be extremely frequent, placing upon the criminal-justice system a burden it will be unable to bear—especially in light of the fact, discussed earlier, that on remand the habeas trial court will not have any trial record on the basis of which to make the "actual innocence" determination.

Not only does the disposition agreed upon today overload the criminal-justice system; it makes relief available where equity demands that relief be denied. When a defendant pleads guilty, he waives his right to have a jury make the requisite findings of guilt—typically in exchange for a lighter sentence or reduced charges. Thus, defendants plead guilty to charges that have not been proven—that perhaps could not be proven—in order to avoid conviction on charges of which they are "actually guilty," which carry a harsher penalty. Under today's holding, a defendant who is the "wheelman" in a bank robbery in which a person is shot and killed, and who pleads guilty in state court to the offense of voluntary manslaughter in order to avoid trial on felony-murder charges, is entitled to federal habeas review of his contention that his guilty plea was "involuntary" because he was not advised that intent-to-kill was an element of the manslaughter offense, and that he was "actually innocent" of manslaughter because he had no intent to kill. In such a case, it is excusing the petitioner from his procedural default, not holding him to it, that would be the miscarriage of justice.

The Court evidently seeks to avoid this absurd consequence by prescribing that the defendant's "showing of actual innocence must also extend" to any charge the government has "forgone." This is not even a fully satisfactory solution in theory, since it assumes that the "forgone" charge is identifiable. If, as is often the case, the bargaining occurred before the charge was filed ("charge-bargaining" instead of "plea-bargaining"), it will almost surely not be identifiable. And of course in practical terms, the solution is no solution at all. To avoid the patent inequity, the government will be called upon to refute, without any factual record to rely upon, not only the defendant's testimony of his innocence on the charge of conviction, but his testimony of innocence on the "forgone" charge as well—and as to the second, even the finding of "factual basis" required in federal courts will not exist. But even if rebuttal evidence existed, it is a bizarre waste of judicial resources to require mini-trials on charges made in dusty indictments (or indeed, if they could be identified, on charges never made), just to determine whether the defendant can litigate a procedurally defaulted challenge to a guilty plea on a different offense. Rube Goldberg would envy the scheme the Court has created.

* * *

It would be marvelously inspiring to be able to boast that we have a criminal-justice system in which a claim of "actual innocence" will always be heard, no matter how late it is brought forward, and no matter how much the failure to bring it forward at the proper time is the defendant's own fault. But of course we do not have such a system, and no society unwilling to devote unlimited resources to repetitive criminal litigation ever could. The "actual innocence" exception this Court has invoked to overcome inexcusable procedural default in cases decided by a jury "seeks to balance the societal interests in finality, comity, and conservation of scarce judicial resources with the individual interest in justice that arises in the extraordinary case." *Schlup*, 513 U.S., at 324. Since the balance struck there simply does not obtain in the guilty-plea context, today's decision is not a logical extension of *Schlup*, and it is a grave mistake. For these reasons, I respectfully dissent.

CHAPTER VIII

# STATE SOVEREIGN IMMUNITY AND THE 11TH AMENDMENT

**Page 825, add at the end of Note 5:**

See also David J. Bederman, Admiralty and the Eleventh Amendment, 72 Notre Dame L. Rev. 935 (1997) (arguing that both text and history of the 11th amendment confirm its inapplicability in admiralty).

An important recent article offers a new synthesis of 11th amendment history. See James E. Pfander, History and State Suability: An "Explanatory" Account of the Eleventh Amendment, 83 Corn. L. Rev. 1269 (1998). Pfander focuses on the substantial debts that states had incurred in fighting the Revolutionary War and finds that the framers of the Constitution adopted a "temporal compromise": "they imposed federal limits on future state fiscal policy, but left the states free to manage existing obligations as they saw fit...." What was so deeply shocking about *Chisholm*, says Pfander, was not so much that it allowed suits against states as that it allowed federal courts "to entertain suits to enforce obligations that the states had incurred under the Articles of Confederation." Pfander concludes that this historical understanding "strong[ly] supports" revisionist attacks on *Hans*.

Also of importance on these issues is Ann Woolhandler, The Common Law Origins of Constitutionally Compelled Remedies, 107 Yale L.J. 77 (1997). Following a comprehensive examination of the history, she concludes that *Ex parte Young* "did not fundamentally alter the role of the federal courts so much as [it] gradually changed the [label] under which litigants continued to do what they had done in the past." She finds a "historically settled consensus that the federal courts should administer a federalized set of rights and remedies for federal constitutional rights."

Finally, for an article that examines the role of officer suits under 42 U.S.C. § 1983 as an alternative to suits against states, see John C. Jeffries, Jr., In Praise of the Eleventh Amendment and Section 1983, 84 Va. L. Rev. 49 (1998).

**Page 879, delete the existing NOTES ON *SEMINOLE TRIBE* and replace with the following:**

## NOTE ON *SEMINOLE TRIBE*

Scholarly reaction to *Seminole Tribe* has been swift and varied. Many scholars linked *Seminole Tribe* to United States v. Lopez, 514 U.S. 549 (1995), and the revival of limits on congressional power under the commerce clause. See, e.g., Herbert Hovenkamp, Judicial Restraint and Constitutional Federalism: The Supreme Court's *Lopez* and *Seminole Tribe* Decisions, 96 Colum. L. Rev. 2213 (1996); Henry Paul Monaghan, The Sovereign Immunity "Exception," 110 Harv. L. Rev. 102 (1995); John C. Yoo, The Judicial Safeguards of Federalism, 70 Southern Cal. L. Rev. 1311 (1997). Monaghan viewed *Seminole Tribe* as perhaps reflecting "a visceral feeling among the majority on the Court that the role of the states in our federal structure has been so diminished as to become unintelligible."

Additional commentary appears in William A. Fletcher, The Eleventh Amendment: Unfinished Business, 75 Notre Dame L. Rev. 843 (2000) (arguing for *Union Gas* and against *Seminole Tribe* on the ground that state sovereign immunity from private suit is less justified when a state engages in commercial activity than when it exercises sovereign functions); Daniel J. Meltzer, The *Seminole* Decision and State Sovereign Immunity, 1996 Sup. Ct. Rev. 1 (exploring *Seminole Tribe*'s impact on 11th amendment doctrine); Carlos Manuel Vázquez, What Is Eleventh Amendment Immunity?, 106 Yale L.J. 1683 (1997) (analyzing *Seminole Tribe* as it bears on competing conceptions of the 11th amendment); Kit Kinports, Implied Waiver After *Seminole Tribe*, 82 Minn. L. Rev. 793 (1998) (pointing out that while Congress exercising article I power may not unilaterally abrogate 11th amendment immunity, it can use the conditional grant of federal funds to solicit state waivers); Wayne L. Baker, *Seminole* Speaks to Sovereign Immunity and *Ex Parte Young*, 71 St. John's L. Rev. 739 (1997) (concluding that Congress could easily evade *Seminole Tribe* by creating a private right of action against state officials); Katherine F. Nelson, Resolving Native American Land Claims and the Eleventh Amendment: Changing the Balance of Power, 39 Villanova L. Rev. 525 (1994) (a pre-*Seminole Tribe* consideration of 11th amendment problems in the particular context of Native American claims against states).

**Page 880, add after *Seminole Tribe*:**

## SECTION 2A: THE 1999 DECISIONS

### Alden v. Maine

Supreme Court of the United States, 1999.
527 U.S. 706.

■ JUSTICE KENNEDY delivered the opinion of the Court.

In 1992, petitioners, a group of probation officers, filed suit against their employer, the state of Maine, in the United States District Court for the District of Maine. The officers alleged the state had violated the overtime provisions of the Fair Labor Standards Act of 1938 (FLSA), 29 U.S.C. § 201 et seq., and sought compensation and liquidated damages. While the suit was pending, this Court decided Seminole Tribe v. Florida, 517 U.S. 44 (1996), which made it clear that Congress lacks power under article I to abrogate the states' sovereign immunity from suits commenced or prosecuted in the federal courts. Upon consideration of *Seminole Tribe*, the District Court dismissed petitioners' action, and the Court of Appeals affirmed. Petitioners then filed the same action in state court. The state trial court dismissed the suit on the basis of sovereign immunity, and the Maine Supreme Judicial Court affirmed. . . .

We hold that the powers delegated to Congress under article I of the United States Constitution do not include the power to subject nonconsenting states to private suits for damages in state courts. . . .

I

The 11th amendment makes explicit reference to the states' immunity from suits "commenced or prosecuted against one of the United States by Citizens of another State, or by Citizens or Subjects of any Foreign State." We have, as a result, sometimes referred to the states' immunity from suit as "11th amendment immunity." The phrase is convenient shorthand but something of a misnomer, for the sovereign immunity of the states neither derives from nor is limited by the terms of the 11th amendment. Rather, as the Constitution's structure, and its history, and the authoritative interpretations by this Court make clear, the states' immunity from suit is a fundamental aspect of the sovereignty which the states enjoyed before the ratification of the Constitution, and which they retain today (either literally or by virtue of their admission into the Union upon an equal footing with the other states) except as altered by the plan of the Convention or certain constitutional amendments.

A

. . . The federal system established by our Constitution preserves the sovereign status of the states in two ways. First, it reserves to them a substantial portion of the nation's primary sovereignty, together with the dignity and essential attributes inhering in that status. . . . Second, even as to matters within the competence of the national government, the constitutional design secures the founding generation's rejection of "the concept of a central government that would act upon and through the states" in favor of "a system in which the state and federal governments would exercise concurrent authority over the people—who were, in Hamilton's words, 'the only proper objects of government.' " Printz v. United States, 521 U.S. 898, 919 (1997) (quoting The Federalist No. 15, at 109). . . .

The states thus retain "a residuary and inviolable sovereignty." The Federalist No. 39, at 245. They are not relegated to the role of mere provinces or political corporations, but retain the dignity, though not the full authority, of sovereignty.

B

The generation that designed and adopted our federal system considered immunity from private suits central to sovereign dignity. When the Constitution was ratified, it was well established in English law that the Crown could not be sued without consent in its own courts. . . . Although the American people had rejected other aspects of English political theory, the doctrine that a sovereign could not be sued without its consent was universal in the states when the Constitution was drafted and ratified. See Chisholm v. Georgia, 2 U.S. (2 Dall.) 419, 434–35 (1793) (Iredell, J., dissenting). . . .

The leading advocates of the Constitution assured the people in no uncertain terms that the Constitution would not strip the states of sovereign immunity. One assurance was contained in The Federalist No. 81, written by Alexander Hamilton:

> "It is inherent in the nature of sovereignty not to be amenable to the suit of an individual *without its consent.* This is the general sense, and the general practice of mankind; and the exemption, as one of the attributes of sovereignty, is now enjoyed by the government of every state in the Union. Unless therefore, there is a surrender of this immunity in the plan of the convention, it will remain with the states, and the danger intimated must be merely ideal. . . . There is no color to pretend that the state governments would, by the adoption of that plan, be divested of the privilege of paying their own debts in their own way, free from every constraint but that which flows from the obligations of good faith. The contracts between a nation and individuals are only binding on the conscience of the sovereign, and have no pretensions to a compulsive force. They confer no right of action independent of the

sovereign will. To what purpose would it be to authorize suits against states for the debts they owe? How could recoveries be enforced? It is evident that it could not be done without waging war against the contracting state; and to ascribe to the federal courts, by mere implication, and in destruction of the preexisting right of the state governments, a power which would involve such a consequence, would be altogether forced and unwarrantable." Id. at 487–88 (emphasis in original).

At the Virginia ratifying convention, James Madison echoed this theme:

"Its jurisdiction in controversies between a state and citizens of another state is much objected to, and perhaps without reason. It is not in the power of individuals to call any state into court. . . .

". . . It appears to me that this [clause] can have no operation but this—to give a citizen a right to be heard in the federal courts, and if a state should condescend to be a party, this court may take cognizance of it." 3 J. Elliot, Debates on the Federal Constitution 533 (2d ed. 1854) (hereinafter Elliot's Debates).

When Madison's explanation was questioned, John Marshall provided immediate support:

"With respect to disputes between a state and the citizens of another state, its jurisdiction has been decried with unusual vehemence. I hope no gentleman will think that a state will be called at the bar of the federal court. Is there no such case at present? Are there not many cases in which the legislature of Virginia is a party, and yet the state is not sued? It is not rational to suppose, that the sovereign power shall be dragged before a court. The intent is, to enable states to recover claims of individuals residing in other states. I contend this construction is warranted by the words. But, say they, there will be partiality in it if a state cannot be defendant. . . . It is necessary to be so, and cannot be avoided. I see a difficulty in making a state defendant, which does not prevent its being plaintiff." Id., at 555.

. . . Despite the persuasive assurances of the Constitution's leading advocates . . ., this Court held, just five years after the Constitution was adopted, that article III authorized a private citizen of another state to sue the state of Georgia without its consent. Chisholm v. Georgia, 2 U.S. (2 Dall.) 419 (1793). . . .

It might be argued that the *Chisholm* decision was a correct interpretation of the constitutional design and that the 11th amendment represented a deviation from the original understanding. This, however, seems unsupportable. First, despite the opinion of Justice Iredell, the majority failed to address either the practice or the understanding that prevailed in the states at the time the Constitution was adopted. Second, even a casual reading of the opinions suggests the majority suspected the decision would be unpopular and surprising. Finally, two members of the majority acknowledged that the United States might well remain immune from suit despite article III's grant of jurisdiction over "Controversies to which the United States shall be a Party," see id. at 469 (Cushing, J.); id. at 478 (Jay, C.J.), and, invoking the example of actions to collect debts incurred before the Constitution was adopted, one raised the possibility of "exceptions," suggesting the rule of the case might not "extend to all the demands, and to every kind of action," see id. at 479 (Jay, C.J.). These concessions undercut the crucial premise that either the Constitution's literal text or the principal of popular sovereignty necessarily overrode widespread practice and opinion.

The text and history of the 11th amendment also suggest that Congress acted not to change but to restore the original constitutional design. Although earlier drafts of the amendment had been phrased as express limits on the judicial power granted in article III, see, e.g., 3 Annals of Congress 651–52 (1793) ("The Judicial Power of the United States shall not extend to any suits in law or equity, commenced or prosecuted against one of the United States . . ."), the adopted text addressed the proper interpretation of that provision of the original Constitution, see U.S. Const., amdt. 11 ("The Judicial Power of the United States shall not be construed to extend to any suit in law or equity, commenced or prosecuted against one of the United States . . ."). By its terms, then, the 11th amendment did not redefine the federal judicial power but instead overruled the Court. . . .

The text reflects the historical context and the congressional objective in endorsing the amendment for ratification. Congress chose not to enact language codifying the traditional understanding of sovereign immunity but rather to address the specific provisions of the Constitution that had raised concerns during the ratification debates and formed the basis of the *Chisholm* decision. Given the outraged reaction to *Chisholm* . . . , it is doubtful that if Congress meant to write a new immunity into the Constitution it would have limited that immunity to the narrow text of the 11th amendment:

> "Can we suppose that, when the 11th amendment was adopted, it was understood to be left open for citizens of a state to sue their own state in federal courts, whilst the idea of suits by citizens of other states, or of foreign states, was indignantly repelled? Suppose that Congress, when proposing the 11th amendment, had appended to it a proviso that nothing therein contained should prevent a state from being sued by its own citizens in cases arising under the Constitution or laws of the United States, can we imagine that it would have been adopted by the states? The supposition that it would is almost an absurdity on its face." Hans v. Louisiana, 134 U.S. 1, 14–15 (1890).

The more natural inference is that the Constitution was understood, in light of its history and structure, to preserve the states' traditional immunity from private suits. As the amendment clarified the only provisions of the Constitution that anyone had suggested might support a contrary understanding, there was no reason to draft with a broader brush. ...

Although the dissent attempts to rewrite history to reflect a different original understanding, its evidence is unpersuasive.... The views voiced during the ratification debates by Edmund Randolph and James Wilson, when reiterated by the same individuals in their respective capacities as advocate and Justice in *Chisholm*, were decisively rejected by the 11th amendment.... In short, the scanty and equivocal evidence offered by the dissent establishes no more than what is evident from the decision in *Chisholm*—that some members of the founding generation disagreed with Hamilton, Madison, Marshall, [and] Iredell.... The events leading to the adoption of the 11th amendment, however, make clear that the individuals who believed the Constitution stripped the states of their immunity from suit were at most a small minority.

Not only do the ratification debates and the events leading to the adoption of the 11th amendment reveal the original understanding of the states' constitutional immunity from suit, they also underscore the importance of sovereign immunity to the founding generation. Simply put, "[t]he Constitution never would have been ratified if the states and their courts were to be stripped of their sovereign authority except as expressly provided by the Constitution itself." Atascadero State Hospital v. Scanlon, 473 U.S. 234, 239, n. 2 (1985).

C

The Court has been consistent in interpreting the adoption of the 11th amendment as conclusive evidence "that the decision in *Chisholm* was contrary to the well-understood meaning of the Constitution," *Seminole Tribe*, 517 U.S. at 69.... Following this approach, the Court has upheld states' assertions of sovereign immunity in various contexts falling outside the literal text of the 11th amendment. In *Hans v. Louisiana*, supra, the Court held that sovereign immunity barred a citizen from suing his own state under the federal-question head of jurisdiction. The Court was unmoved by the petitioner's argument that the 11th amendment, by its terms, applied only to suits brought by citizens of other states.... Later decisions rejected similar requests to conform the principle of sovereign immunity to the strict language of the 11th amendment in holding that nonconsenting states are immune from suits brought by federal corporations, Smith v. Reeves, 178 U.S. 436 (1900), foreign nations, Principality of Monaco v. Mississippi, 292 U.S. 313 (1934), or Indian tribes, Blatchford v. Native Village of Noatak, 501 U.S. 775 (1991), and in concluding that sovereign immunity is a defense to suits in admiralty, though the text of the 11th amendment addresses only suits "in law or equity," Ex parte New York, 256 U.S. 490 (1921).

These holdings reflect a settled doctrinal understanding, consistent with the views of the leading advocates of the Constitution's ratification, that sovereign immunity derives not from the 11th amendment but from the structure of the original Constitution itself. The 11th amendment confirmed rather than established sovereign immunity as a constitutional principle; it follows that the scope of the states' immunity from suit is demarcated not by the text of the amendment alone but by fundamental postulates implicit in the constitutional design. As we explained in *Principality of Monaco*:

> "Manifestly, we cannot rest with a mere literal application of the words of § 2 of article III, or assume that the letter of the 11th amendment exhausts the restrictions upon suits against nonconsenting states. Behind the words of the constitutional provisions are postulates which limit and control. There is the essential postulate that the controversies, as contemplated, shall be found to be of a justiciable character. There is also the postulate that states of the Union, still possessing attributes of sovereignty, shall be immune from suits, without their consent, save where there has been 'a surrender of this immunity in the plan of the convention.' " 292 U.S. at 322–23 (quoting The Federalist No. 81, at 487) (footnote omitted). . . .

II

In this case we must determine whether Congress has the power, under article I, to subject nonconsenting states to private suits in their own courts. . . .

A

Petitioners contend the text of the Constitution and our recent sovereign immunity decisions establish that the states were required to relinquish this portion of their sovereignty. We turn first to these sources.

1

Article I, § 8 grants Congress broad power to enact legislation in several enumerated areas of national concern. The supremacy clause, furthermore, provides:

> "This Constitution, and the Laws of the United States which shall be made in Pursuance thereof . . ., shall be the supreme Law of the Land; and the Judges in every State shall be bound thereby, any Thing in the Constitution or Laws of any state to the Contrary notwithstanding." U.S. Const., art. VI.

It is contended that, by virtue of these provisions, where Congress enacts legislation subjecting the states to suit, the legislation by necessity overrides the sovereign immunity of the states.

As is evident from its text, however, the supremacy clause enshrines as "the supreme Law of the Land" only those federal acts that accord with the constitutional design. Appeal to the supremacy clause alone merely raises the question whether a law is a valid exercise of the national power. . . .

The Constitution, by delegating to Congress the power to establish the supreme law of the land when acting within its enumerated powers, does not foreclose a state from asserting immunity to claims arising under federal law merely because that law derives not from the state itself but from the national power. A contrary view could not be reconciled with *Hans v. Louisiana*, supra, which sustained Louisiana's immunity in a private suit arising under the Constitution itself . . . or with numerous other decisions to the same effect. We reject any contention that substantive federal law by its own force necessarily overrides the sovereign immunity of the states. When a state asserts its immunity to suit, the question is not the primacy of federal law but the implementation of the law in a manner consistent with the constitutional sovereignty of the states.

Nor can we conclude that the specific article I powers delegated to Congress necessarily include, by virtue of the necessary and proper clause or otherwise, the incidental authority to subject the states to private suits as a means of achieving objectives otherwise within the scope of the enumerated powers. Although some of our decisions had endorsed this contention, they have since been overruled, see *Seminole Tribe*, supra, at 63–67, 72; College Savings Bank v. Florida Prepaid Postsecondary Ed. Expense Bd., ___ U.S. ___, ___, 119 S.Ct. 2219 (1999).

The cases we have cited, of course, came at last to the conclusion that neither the supremacy clause nor the enumerated powers of Congress confer authority to abrogate the states' immunity from suit in federal court. The logic of the decisions, however, does not turn on the forum in which the suits were prosecuted but extends to state-court suits as well.

The dissenting opinion seeks to reopen these precedents, contending that state sovereign immunity must derive either from the common law (in which case the dissent contends it is defeasible by statute) or from natural law (in which case the dissent believes it cannot bar a federal claim). As should be obvious to all, this is a false dichotomy. The text and the structure of the Constitution protect various rights and principles. Many of these, such as the right to trial by jury and the prohibition on unreasonable searches and seizures, derive from the common law. The common-law lineage of these rights does not mean they are defeasible by statute or remain mere common-law rights, however. They are, rather, constitutional rights, and form the fundamental law of the land. . . .

Despite the dissent's assertion to the contrary, the fact that a right is not defeasible by statute means only that it is protected by the Constitution, not that it derives from natural law. Whether the dissent's attribution of our reasoning and conclusions to natural law results from analytical confusion or rhetorical device, it is simply inaccurate. We do not contend the founders could not have stripped the states of sovereign immunity and granted Congress power to subject them to private suit but only that they did not do so. By the same token, the contours of sovereign immunity are determined by the founders' understanding, not by the principles or limitations derived from natural law.

The dissent has offered no evidence that the founders believed sovereign immunity extended only to cases where the sovereign was the source of the right asserted. No such limitation existed on sovereign immunity in England, where sovereign immunity was predicated on a different theory altogether. It is doubtful whether the King was regarded, in any meaningful sense, as the font of the traditions and customs which formed the substance of the common law, yet he could not be sued on a common-law claim in his own courts. And it strains credibility to imagine that the King could have been sued in his own court on, say, a French cause of action. . . .

2

There are isolated statements in some of our cases suggesting that the 11th amendment is inapplicable in state courts. See Hilton v. South Carolina Public Railways Comm'n, 502 U.S. 197, 204–05 (1991); Will v. Michigan Dept. of State Police, 491 U.S. 58, 63 (1989); *Atascadero State Hospital v. Scanlon*, supra, 473 U.S. at 239–40, n. 2; Maine v. Thiboutot, 448 U.S. 1, 9 n. 7 (1980); Nevada v. Hall, 440 U.S. 410, 418–21 (1979). . . . Two of the cases discussing state-court immunity may be dismissed out of hand. The footnote digressions in *Atascadero State Hospital* and *Thiboutot* were irrelevant to either opinion's holding or rationale. The discussion in *Will* was also unnecessary to the decision; our holding that 42 U.S.C. § 1983 did not create a cause of action against the states rendered it unnecessary to determine the scope of the states' constitutional immunity from suit in their own courts. Our opinions in *Hilton* and *Hall*, however, require closer attention, for in those cases we sustained suits against states in state courts.

In *Hilton* we held that an injured employee of a state-owned railroad could sue his employer (an arm of the state) in state court under the Federal Employers' Liability Act (FELA), 45 U.S.C. §§ 51–60. Our decision was "controlled and informed" by stare decisis. A generation earlier we had held that because the FELA made clear that all who operated railroads would be subject to suit by injured workers, states that chose to enter the railroad business after the statute's enactment impliedly waived their sovereign immunity from such suits. See Parden v. Terminal R. Co., 377 U.S. 184 (1964). Some states had excluded railroad workers from the coverage of their workers' compensation statutes on the assumption that FELA provided adequate protection for those workers. Closing the courts to FELA suits against state employers would have dislodged settled expectations and required an extensive legislative response.

There is language in *Hilton* which gives some support to the position of petitioners here but our decision did not squarely address, much less resolve, the question of Congress' power to abrogate states' immunity from suit in their own courts. The respondent in *Hilton*, the South Carolina Public Railways Commission, neither contested Congress' constitutional authority to subject it to suits for money damages nor raised sovereign immunity as an affirmative defense. Nor was the state's litigation strategy surprising. *Hilton* was litigated and decided in the wake of Pennsylvania v. Union Gas, 491 U.S. 1 (1989), and before this Court's decisions in New York v. United States, 505 U.S. 144 (1992), *Printz*, and *Seminole Tribe*. At that time it may have appeared to the state that Congress' power to abrogate its immunity from suit in any court was not limited by the Constitution at all, so long as Congress made its intent sufficiently clear.

Furthermore, our decision in *Parden* was based on concepts of waiver and consent. Although later decisions have undermined the basis of *Parden*'s reasoning, see, e.g., *College Savings Bank*, supra, at ___ (overruling *Parden*'s theory of constructive waiver), we have not questioned the general proposition that a state may waive its sovereign immunity and consent to suit.

*Hilton*, then, must be read in light of the doctrinal basis of *Parden*, the issues presented and argued by the parties, and the substantial reliance interests drawn into question by the litigation. When so read, we believe the decision is best understood not as recognizing a congressional power to subject nonconsenting states to private suits in their own courts, nor even as endorsing the constructive waiver theory of *Parden*, but as simply adhering, as a matter of stare decisis and presumed historical fact, to the narrow proposition that certain states had consented to be sued by injured workers covered by the FELA, at least in their own courts.

In *Hall* we considered whether California could subject Nevada to suit in California's courts and determined the Constitution did not bar it from doing so. We noted that "the doctrine of sovereign immunity is an amalgam of two quite different concepts, one applicable to suits in the sovereign's own courts and the other to suits in the courts of another sovereign." 440 U.S., at 414.... Since we determined the Constitution did not reflect an agreement between the states to respect the sovereign immunity of one another, California was free to determine whether it would respect Nevada's sovereignty as a matter of comity.

Our opinion in *Hall* did distinguish a state's immunity from suit in federal court from its immunity in the courts of other states; it did not, however, address or consider any differences between a state's sovereign immunity in federal court and in its own courts. Our reluctance to find an implied constitutional limit on the power of the states cannot be construed, furthermore, to support an analogous reluctance to find implied constitutional limits on the power of the federal government. The Constitution, after all, treats the powers of the states differently from the powers of the federal government. As we explained in *Hall*:

> "In view of the 10th amendment's reminder that powers not delegated to the federal government nor prohibited to the states are reserved to the states or to the people, the existence of express limitations on state sovereignty may equally imply that caution should be exercised before concluding that unstated limitations on state power were intended by the framers." Id. at 425 (footnote omitted).

The federal government, by contrast, "can claim no powers which are not granted to it by the constitution, and the powers actually granted must be such as are expressly given, or given by necessary implication." Martin v. Hunter's Lessee, 14 U.S. (1 Wheat.) 304, 326 (1816).

Our decision in *Hall* thus does not support the argument urged by petitioners here. The decision addressed neither Congress' power to subject states to private suits nor the states' immunity from suit in their own courts. In fact, the distinction drawn between a sovereign's immunity in its own courts and its immunity in the courts of another sovereign, as well as the reasoning on which this distinction was based, are consistent with, and even support, the proposition urged by the respondent here—that the Constitution reserves to the states a constitutional immunity from private suits in their own courts which cannot be abrogated by Congress.

Petitioners seek support in two additional decisions. In Reich v. Collins, 513 U.S. 106. 108 (1994), we held that, despite its immunity from suit in federal court, a state which holds out what plainly appears to be "a clear and certain" postdeprivation remedy for taxes collected in violation of federal law may not declare, after disputed taxes have been paid in reliance on this remedy, that the remedy does not in fact exist. This case arose in the context of tax-refund litigation, where a state may deprive a taxpayer of all other means of challenging the validity of its tax laws by holding out what appears to be a "clear and certain" postdeprivation remedy. In this context, due process requires the state to provide the remedy it has promised. The obligation arises from the Constitution itself; *Reich* does not speak to the power of Congress to subject states to suits in their own courts.

In Howlett v. Rose, 496 U.S. 356 (1990), we held that a state court could not refuse to hear a § 1983 suit against a school board on the basis of sovereign immunity. The school board was not an arm of the state, however, so it could not assert any constitutional defense of sovereign immunity to which the state would have been entitled. See Mt. Healthy City Bd. of Ed. v. Doyle, 429 U.S. 274, 280 (1977). In *Howlett*, then, the only question was "whether a state-law defense of 'sovereign immunity' is available to a school board otherwise subject to suit in a Florida court even though such a defense would not be available if the action had been brought in a federal forum." 496 U.S. at 358–59. The decision did not address the question of Congress' power to compel a state court to entertain an action against a nonconsenting state.

B

Whether Congress has authority under article I to abrogate a state's immunity from suit in its own courts is, then, a question of first impression. In determining whether there is "compelling evidence" that this derogation of the states' sovereignty is "inherent in the constitutional compact," *Blatchford*, supra, 501 U.S. at 781, we continue our discussion of history, practice, precedent, and the structure of the Constitution.

1

We look first to evidence of the original understanding of the Constitution. Petitioners contend that because the ratification debates and the events surrounding the adoption of the 11th amendment focused on the states' immunity from suit in federal courts, the historical record gives no instruction as to the founding generation's intent to preserve the states' immunity from suit in their own courts.

We believe, however, that the founders' silence is best explained by the simple fact that no one, not even the Constitution's most ardent opponents, suggested the document might strip the states of the immunity. In light of the overriding concern regarding the states' war-time debts, together with the well known creativity, foresight, and vivid imagination of the Constitution's opponents, the silence is most instructive. It suggests the sovereign's right to assert immunity from suit in its own courts was a principle so well established that no one conceived it would be altered by the new Constitution. . . .

In light of the language of the Constitution and the historical context, it is quite apparent why neither the ratification debates nor the language of the 11th amendment addressed the states' immunity from suit in their own courts. The concerns voiced at the ratifying conventions, the furor raised by *Chisholm*, and the speed and unanimity with which the amendment was adopted, moreover, underscore the jealous care with which the founding generation sought to preserve the sovereign immunity of the states. To read this history as permitting the inference that the Constitution stripped the states of immunity in their own courts and allowed Congress to subject them to suit there would turn on its head the concern of the founding generation—that article III might be used to circumvent state-court immunity. In light of the historical record it is difficult to conceive that the Constitution would have been adopted if it had been understood to strip the states of immunity from suit in their own courts and cede to the federal government a power to subject nonconsenting states to private suits in these fora.

2

Our historical analysis is supported by early congressional practice, which provides "contemporaneous and weighty evidence of the Constitution's meaning." *Printz*, 521 U.S. at 905 (internal quotation marks omitted). Although early Congresses enacted various statutes authorizing federal suits in state court, we have discovered no instance in which they purported to authorize suits against nonconsenting states in these fora. . . .

Not only were statutes purporting to authorize private suits against nonconsenting states in state courts not enacted by early Congresses, statutes purporting to authorize such suits in any forum are all but absent from our historical experience. The first statute we confronted that even arguably purported to subject the states to private actions was the FELA. See *Parden*, supra. The provisions of the FLSA at issue here, which were enacted in the aftermath of *Parden*, are among the first statutory enactments purporting in express terms to subject nonconsenting states to private suits. Although similar statutes have multiplied in the last generation, "they are of such recent vintage that they are no more probative than the [FLSA] of a constitutional tradition that lends meaning to the text. Their persuasive force is far outweighed by almost two centuries of apparent congressional avoidance of the practice." *Printz*, 521 U.S. at 918.

Even the recent statutes, moreover, do not provide evidence of an understanding that Congress has a greater power to subject states to suit in their own courts than in federal courts. On the contrary, the statutes purport to create causes of actions against the states which are enforceable in federal, as well as state, court. To the extent recent practice thus departs from longstanding tradition, it reflects not so much an understanding that the states have surrendered their immunity from suit in their own courts as the erroneous view, perhaps inspired by *Parden* and *Union Gas*, that Congress may subject nonconsenting states to private suits in any forum.

3

The theory and reasoning of our earlier cases suggest the states do retain a constitutional immunity from suit in their own courts. We have often described the states immunity in sweeping terms, without reference to whether the suit was prosecuted in state or federal court [citing cases]. We have said on many occasions, furthermore, that the states retain their immunity from private suits prosecuted in their own courts [citing cases]. We have also relied on the states' immunity in their own courts as a premise in our 11th amendment rulings.

In particular, the exception to our sovereign immunity doctrine recognized in Ex parte Young, 209 U.S. 123 (1908), is based in part on the premise that sovereign immunity bars relief against states and their officers in both state and federal courts, and that certain suits for declaratory or injunctive relief against state officers must therefore be permitted if the Constitution is to remain the supreme law of the land. ... Had we not understood the states to retain a constitutional immunity from suit in their own courts, the need for the *Ex parte Young* rule would have been less pressing, and the rule would not have formed so essential a part of our sovereign immunity doctrine. See Idaho v. Coeur d'Alene Tribe of Idaho, 521 U.S. 261, 270–71 (1997) (principal opinion).

As it is settled doctrine that neither substantive federal law nor attempted congressional abrogation under article I bars a state from raising a constitutional defense of sovereign immunity in federal court, our decisions suggesting that the states retain an analogous constitutional immunity from private suits in their own courts support the conclusion that Congress lacks the article I power to subject the states to private suits in those fora.

4

Our final consideration is whether a congressional power to subject nonconsenting states to private suits in their own courts is consistent with the structure of the Constitution. We look both to the essential principles of federalism and to the special role of the state courts in the constitutional design.

Although the Constitution grants broad powers to Congress, our federalism requires that Congress treat the states in a manner consistent with their status as residuary sovereigns and joint participants in the governance of the nation. ... Petitioners contend that immunity from suit in federal court suffices to preserve the dignity of the states. Private suits against nonconsenting states, however, present "the indignity of subjecting a state to the coercive process of judicial tribunals at the instance of private parties," In re Ayers, 123 U.S. 443, 505 (1887), regardless of the forum. Not only must a state defend or default but also it must face the prospect of being thrust, by federal fiat and against its will, into the disfavored status of a debtor, subject to the power of private citizens to levy on its treasury or perhaps even government buildings or property which the state administers on the public's behalf.

In some ways, of course, a congressional power to authorize private suits against nonconsenting states in their own courts would be even more offensive to state sovereignty than a power to authorize the suits in a federal forum. Although the immunity of one sovereign in the courts of another has often depended in part on comity or agreement, the immunity of a sovereign in its own courts has always been understood to be within the sole control of the sovereign itself. See generally *Hall*, 440 U.S. at 414–18. A power to press a state's own courts into federal service to coerce the other branches of the state, furthermore, is the power first to turn the state against itself and ultimately to commandeer the entire political machinery of the state against its will and at the behest of individuals. Such plenary federal control of state governmental processes denigrates the separate sovereignty of the states.

It is unquestioned that the federal government retains its own immunity from suit not only in state tribunals but also in its own courts. In light of our constitutional system recognizing the essential sovereignty of the states, we are reluctant to conclude that the states are not entitled to a reciprocal privilege.

Underlying constitutional form are considerations of great substance. Private suits against nonconsenting states—especially suits for money damages—may threaten the financial integrity of the states. It is indisputable that, at the time of the founding, many of the states could have been forced into insolvency but for their immunity from private suits for money damages. Even today, an unlimited congressional power to authorize suits in state court to levy upon the treasuries of the states for compensatory damages, attorney's fees, and even punitive damages could create staggering burdens, giving Congress a power and a leverage over the states that is not contemplated by our constitutional design. The potential national power would pose a severe and notorious danger to the states and their resources. . . .

A general federal power to authorize private suits for money damages would place unwarranted strain on the states' ability to govern in accordance with the will of their citizens. Today, as at the time of the founding, the allocation of scarce resources among competing needs and interests lies at the heart of the political process. While the judgment creditor of the state may have a legitimate claim for compensation, other important needs and worthwhile ends compete for access to the public fisc. Since all cannot be satisfied in full, it is inevitable that difficult decisions involving the most sensitive and political of judgments must be made. If the principle of representative government is to be preserved to the states, the balance between competing interests must be reached after deliberation by the political process established by the citizens of the state, not by judicial decree mandated by the federal government and invoked by the private citizen. . . . When the federal government asserts authority over a state's most fundamental political processes, it strikes at the heart of the political accountability so essential to our liberty and republican form of government.

The asserted authority would blur not only the distinct responsibilities of the state and national governments but also the separate duties of the judicial and political branches of the state governments. . . . A state is entitled to order the processes of its own governance, assigning to the political branches, rather than the courts, the responsibility for directing the payment of debts. If Congress could displace a state's allocation of governmental power and responsibility, the judicial branch of the state, whose legitimacy derives from fidelity to the law, would be compelled to assume a role not only foreign to its experience but beyond its competence as defined by the very constitution from which its existence derives.

Congress cannot abrogate the states' sovereign immunity in federal court; were the rule to be different here, the national government would wield greater power in the state courts than in its own judicial instrumentalities.

The resulting anomaly cannot be explained by reference to the special role of the state courts in the constitutional design. Although Congress may not require the legislative or executive branches of the states to enact or administer federal regulatory programs, see *Printz*, supra, at 935; *New York*, 505 U.S. at 188, it may require state courts of "adequate and appropriate" jurisdiction, Testa v. Katt, 330 U.S. 386, 394 (1947), "to enforce federal prescriptions, insofar as those prescriptions relate to matters appropriate for the judicial power," *Printz*, supra, at 907. It would be an unprecedented step, however, to infer from the fact that Congress may declare federal law binding and enforceable in state courts the further principle that Congress' authority to pursue federal objectives through the state judiciaries exceeds not only its power to press other branches of the state into its service but even its control over the federal courts themselves. The conclusion would imply that Congress may in some cases act only through instrumentalities of the states. Yet, as Chief Justice Marshall explained, "[n]o trace is to be found in the constitution of an intention to create a dependence of the government of the union on those of the states, for the execution of the great powers assigned to it. Its means are adequate to its ends; and on those means alone was it expected to rely for the accomplishment of its ends." McCulloch v. Maryland, 17 U.S. (4 Wheat.) 316, 424 (1819). . . .

We have recognized that Congress may require state courts to hear only "matters appropriate for the judicial power," *Printz*, 521 U.S. at 907. Our sovereign immunity precedents establish that suits against nonconsenting states are not "properly susceptible of litigation in courts," *Hans*, 134 U.S. at 12, and, as a result, that "the 'entire judicial power granted by the Constitution' does not embrace authority to entertain such suits in the absence of the state's consent." *Principality of Monaco*, 292 U.S. at 329 (quoting *Ex parte New York*, 256 U.S. at 497). We are aware of no constitutional precept that would admit of a congressional power to require state courts to entertain federal suits which are not within the judicial power of the United States and could not be heard in federal courts. . . .

In light of history, practice, precedent, and the structure of the Constitution, we hold that the states retain immunity from private suit in their own courts, an immunity beyond the congressional power to abrogate by article I legislation.

III

The constitutional privilege of a state to assert its sovereign immunity in its own courts does not confer upon the state a concomitant right to disregard the Constitution or valid federal law. The states and their officers are bound by obligations imposed by the Constitution and by federal statutes that comport with the constitutional design. We are unwilling to assume the states will refuse to honor the Constitution or obey the binding laws of the United States. The good faith of the states thus provides an important assurance that "this Constitution, and the Laws of the United States which shall be made in Pursuance thereof . . . shall be the supreme Law of the Land." U.S. Const., art. VI.

Sovereign immunity, moreover, does not bar all judicial review of state compliance with the Constitution and valid federal law. Rather, certain limits are implicit in the constitutional principle of state sovereign immunity.

The first of these limits is that sovereign immunity bars suits only in the absence of consent. Many states, on their own initiative, have enacted statutes consenting to a wide variety of suits. . . . Nor, subject to constitutional limitations, does the federal government lack the authority or means to seek the states' voluntary consent to private suits. Cf. South Dakota v. Dole, 483 U.S. 203 (1987).

The states have consented, moreover, to some suits pursuant to the plan of the convention or to subsequent constitutional amendments. In ratifying the Constitution, the states consented to suits brought by other states or by the federal government. *Principality of Monaco*, supra, at 328–29 (collecting cases). . . . We have held also that in adopting the 14th amendment, the people required the states to surrender a portion of the sovereignty that had been preserved to them by the original Constitution, so that Congress may authorize private suits against nonconsenting states pursuant to its § 5 enforcement power. Fitzpatrick v. Bitzer, 427 U.S. 445 (1976). . . .

The second important limit to the principle of sovereign immunity is that it bars suits against states but not lesser entities. The immunity does not extend to suits prosecuted against a municipal corporation or other governmental entity which is not an arm of the state. See, e.g., Lincoln County v. Luning, 133 U.S. 529 (1890). Nor does sovereign immunity bar all suits against state officers. Some suits against state officers are barred by the rule that sovereign immunity is not limited to suits which name the state as a party if the suits are, in fact, against the state. The rule, however, does not bar certain actions against state officers for injunctive or declaratory relief. Compare *Ex parte Young*, supra, and *In re Ayers*, supra, with *Coeur d'Alene Tribe of Idaho*, supra, *Seminole Tribe*, supra, and Edelman v. Jordan, 415 U.S. 651 (1974). Even a suit for money damages may be prosecuted against a state officer in his individual capacity for unconstitutional or wrongful conduct fairly attributable to the officer himself, so long as the relief is sought not from the state treasury but from the officer personally. Scheuer v. Rhodes, 416 U.S. 232, 237–38 (1974).

The principle of sovereign immunity as reflected in our jurisprudence strikes the proper balance between the supremacy of federal law and the separate sovereignty of the states. Established rules provide ample means to correct ongoing violations of law and to vindicate the interests which animate the supremacy clause. That we have, during the first 210 years of our constitutional history, found it unnecessary to decide the question presented here suggests a federal power to subject nonconsenting states to private suits in their own courts is unnecessary to uphold the Constitution and valid federal statutes as the supreme law.

IV

The sole remaining question is whether Maine has waived its immunity. ... The state of Maine ... adheres to the general rule that "a specific authority conferred by an enactment of the legislature is requisite if the sovereign is to be taken as having shed the protective mantle of immunity," Cushing v. Cohen, 420 A.2d 919, 923 (Me.1980). Petitioners have not attempted to establish a waiver of immunity under this standard. Although petitioners contend the state has discriminated against federal rights by claiming sovereign immunity from this FLSA suit, there is no evidence that the state has manipulated its immunity in a systematic fashion to discriminate against federal causes of action. To the extent Maine has chosen to consent to certain classes of suits while maintaining its immunity from others, it has done no more than exercise a privilege of sovereignty concomitant to its constitutional immunity from suit. The state, we conclude, has not consented to suit.

V

This case at one level concerns the formal structure of federalism, but in a Constitution as resilient as ours form mirrors substance. Congress has vast power but not all power. When Congress legislates in matters affecting the states, it may not treat these sovereign entities as mere prefectures or corporations. Congress must accord states the esteem due to them as joint participants in a federal system, one beginning with the premise of sovereignty in both the central government and the separate states. Congress has ample means to ensure compliance with valid federal laws, but it must respect the sovereignty of the states.

In apparent attempt to disparage a conclusion with which it disagrees, the dissent attributes our reasoning to natural law. We seek to discover, however, only what the framers and those who ratified the Constitution sought to accomplish when they created a federal system. We appeal to no higher authority than the charter which they wrote and adopted. Theirs was the unique insight that freedom is enhanced by the creation of two governments, not one. We need not attach a label to our dissenting colleagues' insistence that the constitutional structure adopted by the founders must yield to the politics of the moment. Although the Constitution begins with the principle that sovereignty rests with the people, it does not follow that the national government becomes the ultimate, preferred mechanism for expressing the people's will. The states exist as a refutation of that concept. In choosing to ordain and establish the Constitution, the people insisted upon a federal structure for the very purpose of rejecting the idea that the will of the people in all instances is expressed by the central power, the one most remote from their control. The framers of the Constitution did not share our dissenting colleagues' belief that the Congress may circumvent the federal design by regulating the states directly when it pleases to do so, including by a proxy in which individual citizens are authorized to levy upon the state treasuries absent the states' consent to jurisdiction.

The case before us depends upon these principles. The state of Maine has not questioned Congress' power to prescribe substantive rules of federal law to which it must comply. Despite an initial good-faith disagreement about the requirements of the FLSA, it is conceded by all that the state has altered its conduct so that its compliance with federal law cannot now be questioned. The Solicitor General of the United States has appeared before this Court, however, and asserted that the federal interest in compensating the states' employees for alleged past violations of federal law is so compelling that the sovereign state of Maine must be stripped of its immunity and subjected to suit in its own courts by its own employees. Yet, despite specific statutory authorization, see 29 U.S.C. § 216(c), the United States apparently found the same interests insufficient to justify sending even a single attorney to Maine to prosecute this litigation. The difference between a suit by the United States on behalf of the employees and a suit by the employees implicates a rule that the national government must itself deem the case of sufficient importance to take action against the state; and history, precedent, and the structure of the Constitution make clear that, under the plan of the convention, the states have consented to suits of the first kind but not of the second. The judgment of the Supreme Judicial Court of Maine is

Affirmed.

■ JUSTICE SOUTER, with whom JUSTICE STEVENS, JUSTICE GINSBURG, and JUSTICE BREYER join, dissenting. . . .

Today's issue arises naturally in the aftermath of the decision in Seminole Tribe of Fla. v. Florida, 517 U.S. 44 (1996). The Court holds that the Constitution bars an individual suit against a state to enforce a federal statutory right under the Fair Labor Standards Act of 1938 (FLSA), 29 U.S.C. § 201 et seq., when brought in the state's courts over its objection. In thus complementing its earlier decision, the Court of course confronts the fact that the state forum renders the 11th amendment beside the point, and it has responded by discerning a simpler and more straightforward theory of state sovereign immunity than it found in *Seminole Tribe*: a state's sovereign immunity from all individual suits is a "fundamental aspect" of state sovereignty "confirmed" by the 10th amendment. As a consequence, *Seminole Tribe*'s contorted reliance on the 11th amendment and its background was presumably unnecessary; the 10th would have done the work with an economy that the majority in *Seminole Tribe* would have welcomed. . . .

The sequence of the Court's positions prompts a suspicion of error, and skepticism is confirmed by scrutiny of the Court's efforts to justify its holding. There is no evidence that the 10th amendment constitutionalized a concept of sovereign immunity as inherent in the notion of statehood, and no evidence that any concept of inherent sovereign immunity was understood historically to apply when the sovereign sued was not the font of the law. Nor does the Court fare any better with its subsidiary lines of reasoning, that the state-court action is barred by the scheme of American federalism, a result supposedly confirmed by a history largely devoid of precursors to the action considered here. The Court's federalism ignores the accepted authority of Congress to bind states under the FLSA and to provide for enforcement of federal rights in state court. The Court's history simply disparages the capacity of the Constitution to order relationships in a republic that has changed since the founding.

On each point the Court has raised it is mistaken, and I respectfully dissent from its judgment.

I

The Court rests its decision principally on the claim that immunity from suit was "a fundamental aspect of the sovereignty which the states enjoyed before the ratification of the Constitution," an aspect which the Court understands to have survived the ratification of the Constitution in 1788 and to have been "confirmed" and given constitutional status by the adoption of the 10th amendment in 1791. If the Court truly means by "sovereign immunity" what that term meant at common law, its argument would be insupportable. While sovereign immunity entered many new state legal systems as a part of the common law selectively received from England, it was not understood to be indefeasible or to have been given any such status by the new national Constitution, which did not mention it. Had the question been posed, state sovereign immunity could not have been thought to shield a state from suit under federal law on a subject committed to national jurisdiction by article I of the Constitution. Congress exercising its conceded article I power may unquestionably abrogate such immunity. I set out this position at length in my dissent in *Seminole Tribe* and will not repeat it here.

The Court does not, however, offer today's holding as a mere corollary to its reasoning in *Seminole Tribe*, substituting the 10th amendment for the 11th as the occasion demands, and it is fair to read its references to a "fundamental aspect" of state sovereignty as referring not to a prerogative inherited from the Crown, but to a conception necessarily implied by statehood itself. The conception is thus not one of common law so much as of natural law, a universally applicable proposition discoverable by reason. This, I take it, is the sense in which the Court so emphatically relies on Alexander Hamilton's reference in The Federalist No. 81 to the states' sovereign immunity from suit as an "inherent" right, a characterization that does not require, but is at least open to, a natural law reading.

I understand the Court to rely on the Hamiltonian formulation with the object of suggesting that its conception of sovereign immunity as a "fundamental aspect" of sovereignty was a substantially popular, if not the dominant, view in the periods of Revolution and Confederation. There is, after all, nothing else in the Court's opinion that would suggest a basis for saying that the ratification of the 10th amendment gave this "fundamental aspect" its constitutional status and protection against any legislative tampering by Congress. The Court's principal rationale for today's result, then, turns on history: was the natural law conception of sovereign immunity as inherent in any notion of an independent state widely held in the United States in the period preceding the ratification of 1788 (or the adoption of the 10th amendment in 1791)?

The answer is certainly no. There is almost no evidence that the generation of the framers thought sovereign immunity was fundamental in the sense of being unalterable. ... Some framers thought sovereign immunity was an obsolete royal prerogative inapplicable in a republic; some thought sovereign immunity was a common-law power defeasible, like other common-law rights, by statute; and perhaps a few thought, in keeping with a natural law view distinct from the common-law conception, that immunity was inherent in a sovereign because the body that made a law could not logically be bound by it. Natural law thinking on the part of a doubtful few will not, however, support the Court's position.

A

The American Colonies did not enjoy sovereign immunity, that being a privilege understood in English law to be reserved for the Crown alone. . . .

B

Starting in the mid-1760's, ideas about sovereignty in colonial America began to shift as Americans argued that, lacking a voice in Parliament, they had not in any express way consented to being taxed. The story of the subsequent development of conceptions of sovereignty is complex and uneven; here, it is enough to say that by the time independence was declared in 1776, the locus of sovereignty was still an open question, except that almost by definition, advocates of independence denied that sovereignty with respect to the American Colonies remained with the King in Parliament.

As the concept of sovereignty was unsettled, so was that of sovereign immunity. Some states appear to have understood themselves to be without immunity from suit in their own courts upon independence. Other new states understood themselves to be inheritors of the Crown's common-law sovereign immunity and so enacted statutes authorizing legal remedies against the state parallel to those available in England. . . .

Around the time of the Constitutional convention, then, there existed among the states some diversity of practice with respect to sovereign immunity; but despite a tendency among the state constitutions to announce and declare certain inalienable and natural rights of men and even of the collective people of a state, no state declared that sovereign immunity was one of those rights. To the extent that states were thought to possess immunity, it was perceived as a prerogative of the sovereign under common law. And where sovereign immunity was recognized as barring suit, provisions for recovery from the state were in order, just as they had been at common law in England.

C

At the Constitutional Convention, the notion of sovereign immunity, whether as natural law or as common law, was not an immediate subject of debate, and the sovereignty of a state in its own courts seems not to have been mentioned. This comes as no surprise, for although the Constitution required state courts to apply federal law, the framers did not consider the possibility that federal law might bind states, say, in their relations with their employees. In the subsequent ratification debates, however, the issue of jurisdiction over a state did emerge in the question whether states might be sued on their debts in federal court, and on this point, too, a variety of views emerged and the diversity of sovereign immunity conceptions displayed itself.

The only arguable support for the Court's absolutist view that I have found among the leading participants in the debate surrounding ratification was the one already mentioned, that of Alexander Hamilton in The Federalist No. 81, where he described the sovereign immunity of the states in language suggesting principles associated with natural law. . . .

In the Virginia ratifying convention, Madison . . . maintained that "it is not in the power of individuals to call any state into court," 3 J. Elliot, The Debates in the Several State Conventions on the Adoption of the Federal Constitution 533 (2d ed. 1836) (hereinafter Elliot's Debates), and thought that the phrase "in which a State shall be a Party" in article III, § 2, must be interpreted in light of that general principle, so that "the only operation it can have, is that, if a state should wish to bring a suit against a citizen, it must be brought before the federal court." Ibid. n15. John Marshall argued along the same lines against the possibility of federal jurisdiction over private suits against states, and he invoked the immunity of a state in its own courts in support of his argument. . . .

There was no unanimity among the Virginians either on state-or federal-court immunity, however, for Edmund Randolph anticipated the position he would later espouse as plaintiff's counsel in Chisholm v. Georgia, 2 U.S. (2 Dall.) 419 (1793). . . .

At the farthest extreme from Hamilton, James Wilson made several comments in the Pennsylvania convention that suggested his hostility to any idea of state sovereign immunity. . . . Wilson laid out his view that sovereignty was in fact not located in the states at all: "Upon what principle is it contended that the sovereign power resides in the state governments? The honorable gentleman has said truly, that there can be no subordinate sovereignty. Now, if there cannot, my position is, that the sovereignty resides in the people; they have not parted with it; they have only dispensed such portions of the power as were conceived necessary for the public welfare." 2 Elliot's Debates at 443. While this statement did not specifically address sovereign immunity, it expressed the major premise of what would later become Justice Wilson's position in *Chisholm*: that because the people, and not the states, are sovereign, sovereign immunity has no applicability to the states.

From a canvass of this spectrum of opinion expressed at the ratifying conventions, one thing is certain. No one was espousing an indefeasible, natural law view of sovereign immunity. The controversy over the enforceability of state debts subject to state law produced emphatic support for sovereign immunity from eminences as great as Madison and Marshall, but neither of them indicated adherence to any immunity conception outside the common law.

D

At the close of the ratification debates, the issue of the sovereign immunity of the states under article III had not been definitively resolved, and in some instances the indeterminacy led the ratification conventions to respond in ways that point to the range of thinking about the doctrine. Several state ratifying conventions proposed amendments and issued declarations that would have exempted states from subjection to suit in federal court. [T]he state ratifying conventions' felt need for clarification on the question of state suability demonstrates that uncertainty surrounded the matter even at the moment of ratification. This uncertainty set the stage for the divergent views expressed in *Chisholm*.

E

If the natural law conception of sovereign immunity as an inherent characteristic of sovereignty enjoyed by the states had been broadly accepted at the time of the founding, one would expect to find it reflected somewhere in the five opinions delivered by the Court in *Chisholm v. Georgia*, supra. Yet that view did not appear in any of them. And since a bare two years before *Chisholm*, the Bill of Rights had been added to the original Constitution, if the 10th amendment had been understood to give federal constitutional status to state sovereign immunity so as to endue it with the equivalent of the natural law conception, one would be certain to find such a development mentioned somewhere in the *Chisholm* writings. In fact, however, not one of the opinions espoused the natural law view, and not one of them so much as mentioned the 10th amendment. Not even Justice Iredell, who alone among the Justices thought that a state could not be sued in federal court, echoed Hamilton or hinted at a constitutionally immutable immunity doctrine....

[I]n *Chisholm* two Justices (Jay and Wilson), both of whom had been present at the Constitutional Convention, took a position suggesting that states should not enjoy sovereign immunity (however conceived) even in their own courts; one (Cushing) was essentially silent on the issue of sovereign immunity in state court; one (Blair) took a cautious position affirming the pragmatic view that sovereign immunity was a continuing common law doctrine and that states would permit suit against themselves as of right; and one (Iredell) expressly thought that state sovereign immunity at common-law rightly belonged to the sovereign states. Not a single Justice suggested that sovereign immunity was an inherent and indefeasible right of statehood....

The Court, citing Hans v. Louisiana, 134 U.S. 1 (1890), says that the 11th amendment "overruled" *Chisholm*, but the animadversion is beside the point. The significance of *Chisholm* is its indication that in 1788 and 1791 it was not generally assumed (indeed, hardly assumed at all) that a state's sovereign immunity from suit in its own courts was an inherent, and not merely a common-law, advantage. On the contrary, the testimony of five eminent legal minds of the day confirmed that virtually everyone who understood immunity to be legitimate saw it as a common-law prerogative (from which it follows that it was subject to abrogation by Congress as to a matter within Congress's article I authority).

The Court does no better with its trio of arguments to undercut *Chisholm*'s legitimacy: that the *Chisholm* majority "failed to address either the practice or the understanding that prevailed in the states at the time the Constitution was adopted"; that "the majority suspected the decision would be unpopular and surprising"; and that "two members of the majority acknowledged that the United States might well remain immune from suit despite" article III. These three claims do not, of course, go to the question whether state sovereign immunity was understood to be "fundamental" or "inherent," but in any case, none of them is convincing. ...

Nor can the Court make good on its claim that the enactment of the 11th amendment retrospectively reestablished the view that had already been established at the time of the framing (though eluding the perception of all but one member of the Supreme Court)... .There was nothing "established" about the position espoused by Georgia in the effort to repudiate its debts, and the Court's implausible suggestion to the contrary merely echoes the brio of its remark in *Seminole Tribe* that *Chisholm* was "contrary to the well-understood meaning of the Constitution." 517 U.S. at

69. The fact that *Chisholm* was no conceptual aberration is apparent from the ratification debates and the several state requests to rewrite article III. There was no received view either of the role this sovereign immunity would play in the circumstances of the case or of a conceptual foundation for immunity doctrine at odds with *Chisholm*'s reading of article III. As an author on whom the Court relies, has it, "there was no unanimity among the framers that immunity would exist," D. Currie, The Constitution in the Supreme Court: The First Century 19 (1985). . . .

II

The Court's rationale for today's holding based on a conception of sovereign immunity as somehow fundamental to sovereignty or inherent in statehood fails for the lack of any substantial support for such a conception in the thinking of the founding era. The Court cannot be counted out yet, however, for it has a second line of argument looking not to a clause-based reception of the natural law conception or even to its recognition as a "background principle," see *Seminole Tribe*, 517 U.S. at 72, but to a structural basis in the Constitution's creation of a federal system. Immunity, the Court says, "inheres in the system of federalism established by the Constitution," its "contours [being] determined by the founders' understanding, not by the principles or limitations derived from natural law." Again, "we look both to the essential principles of federalism and to the special role of the state courts in the constitutional design." That is, the Court believes that the federal constitutional structure itself necessitates recognition of some degree of state autonomy broad enough to include sovereign immunity from suit in a state's own courts, regardless of the federal source of the claim asserted against the state. If one were to read the Court's federal structure rationale in isolation from the preceding portions of the opinion, it would appear that the Court's position on state sovereign immunity might have been rested entirely on federalism alone. If it had been, however, I would still be in dissent, for the Court's argument that state court sovereign immunity on federal questions is inherent in the very concept of federal structure is demonstrably mistaken.

A

[T]he general scheme of delegated sovereignty as between the two component governments of the federal system was clear, and was succinctly stated by Chief Justice Marshall: "In America, the powers of sovereignty are divided between the government of the union, and those of the states. They are each sovereign, with respect to the objects committed to it, and neither sovereign with respect to the objects committed to the other." McCulloch v. Maryland, 17 U.S. (4 Wheat.) 316, 410 (1819).

Hence the flaw in the Court's appeal to federalism. The state of Maine is not sovereign with respect to the national objective of the FLSA.[1] It is

1. It is therefore sheer circularity for the Court to talk of the "anomaly" that would arise if a state could be sued on federal law in its own courts, when it may not be

not the authority that promulgated the FLSA, on which the right of action in this case depends. That authority is the United States acting through the Congress, whose legislative power under article I of the Constitution to extend FLSA coverage to state employees has already been decided, see Garcia v. San Antonio Metropolitan Transit Authority, 469 U.S. 528 (1985), and is not contested here.

Nor can it be argued that because the state of Maine creates its own court system, it has authority to decide what sorts of claims may be entertained there, and thus in effect to control the right of action in this case. Maine has created state courts of general jurisdiction; once it has done so, the supremacy clause of the Constitution, which requires state courts to enforce federal law and state-court judges to be bound by it, requires the Maine courts to entertain this federal cause of action. Maine has advanced no " 'valid excuse,' " Howlett v. Rose, 496 U.S. 356, 369 (1990) (quoting Douglas v. New York, N. H. & H. R. Co., 279 U.S. 377, 387–88 (1929)), for its courts' refusal to hear federal-law claims in which Maine is a defendant, and sovereign immunity cannot be that excuse, simply because the state is not sovereign with respect to the subject of the claim against it. The Court's insistence that the federal structure bars Congress from making states susceptible to suit in their own courts is, then, plain mistake.[2]

B

It is symptomatic of the weakness of the structural notion proffered by the Court that it seeks to buttress the argument by relying on "the dignity and respect afforded a state, which the immunity is designed to protect" (quoting Idaho v. Coeur d'Alene Tribe of Idaho, 521 U.S. 261, 268 (1997)). . . .It would be hard to imagine anything more inimical to the republican conception, which rests on the understanding of its citizens precisely that the government is not above them, but of them, its actions

sued under federal law in federal court, *Seminole Tribe*, supra. The short and sufficient answer is that the anomaly is the Court's own creation: the 11th amendment was never intended to bar federal-question suits against the states in federal court. The anomaly is that *Seminole Tribe*, an opinion purportedly grounded in the 11th amendment, should now be used as a lever to argue for state sovereign immunity in state courts, to which the 11th amendment by its terms does not apply.

**2.** Perhaps as a corollary to its view of sovereign immunity as to some degree indefeasible because "fundamental," the Court frets that the "power to press a state's own courts into federal service to coerce the other branches of the state . . . is the power first to turn the state against itself and ultimately to commandeer the entire political machinery of the state against its will and at the behest of individuals." But this is to forget that the doctrine of separation of powers prevails in our Republic. When the state judiciary enforces federal law against state officials, as the supremacy clause requires it to do, it is not turning against the state's executive any more than we turn against the federal executive when we apply federal law to the United States: it is simply upholding the rule of law. There is no "commandeering" of the state's resources where the state is asked to do no more than enforce federal law.

being governed by law just like their own. Whatever justification there may be for an American government's immunity from private suit, it is not dignity.

It is equally puzzling to hear the Court say that "federal power to authorize private suits for money damages would place unwarranted strain on the states' ability to govern in accordance with the will of their citizens." So long as the citizens' will, expressed through state legislation, does not violate valid federal law, the strain will not be felt; and to the extent that state action does violate federal law, the will of the citizens of the United States already trumps that of the citizens of the state: the strain then is not only expected, but necessarily intended.

Least of all does the Court persuade by observing that "other important needs" than that of the "judgment creditor" compete for public money. The "judgment creditor" in question is not a dunning bill-collector, but a citizen whose federal rights have been violated, and a constitutional structure that stints on enforcing federal rights out of an abundance of delicacy toward the states has substituted politesse in place of respect for the rule of law.

III

If neither theory nor structure can supply the basis for the Court's conceptions of sovereign immunity and federalism, then perhaps history might. The Court apparently believes that because state courts have not historically entertained commerce clause-based federal-law claims against the states, such an innovation carries a presumption of unconstitutionality. At the outset, it has to be noted that this approach assumes a more cohesive record than history affords. In Hilton v. South Carolina Public Railways Comm'n, 502 U.S. 197 (1991) (Kennedy, J.), a case the Court labors mightily to distinguish, we held that a state-owned railroad could be sued in state court under the Federal Employers' Liability Act, 45 U.S.C. §§ 51–60, notwithstanding the lack of an express congressional statement, because " 'the 11th amendment does not apply in state courts.' " *Hilton*, supra, at 205 (quoting Will v. Michigan Dept. of State Police, 491 U.S. 58, 63–64 (1989)). But even if the record were less unkempt, the problem with arguing from historical practice in this case is that past practice, even if unbroken, provides no basis for demanding preservation when the conditions on which the practice depended have changed in a constitutionally relevant way.

It was at one time, though perhaps not from the framing, believed that "Congress' authority to regulate the states under the commerce clause" was limited by "certain underlying elements of political sovereignty ... deemed essential to the states' 'separate and independent existence.' " See *Garcia*, 469 U.S. at 547–58 (quoting Lane County v. Oregon, 74 U.S. (7 Wall.) 71, 76 (1869)). On this belief, the preordained balance between state and federal sovereignty was understood to trump the terms of article I and preclude Congress from subjecting states to federal law on certain subjects. . . .

Today, however, in light of *Garcia*, supra (overruling National League of Cities v. Usery, 426 U.S. 833 (1976)), the law is settled that federal legislation enacted under the commerce clause may bind the states without having to satisfy a test of undue incursion into state sovereignty. . . . Because the commerce power is no longer thought to be circumscribed, the dearth of prior private federal claims entertained against the states in state courts does not tell us anything, and reflects nothing but an earlier and less expansive application of the commerce power.

Least of all is it to the point for the Court to suggest that because the framers would be surprised to find states subjected to a federal-law suit in their own courts under the commerce power, the suit must be prohibited by the Constitution. . . . If the framers would be surprised to see states subjected to suit in their own courts under the commerce power, they would be astonished by the reach of Congress under the commerce clause generally. The proliferation of government, state and federal, would amaze the framers, and the administrative state with its reams of regulations would leave them rubbing their eyes. But the framers' surprise at, say, the FLSA, or the Federal Communications Commission, or the Federal Reserve Board is no threat to the constitutionality of any one of them, for a very fundamental reason:

> "When we are dealing with words that also are a constituent act, like the Constitution of the United States, we must realize that they have called into life a being the development of which could not have been foreseen completely by the most gifted of its begetters. It was enough for them to realize or to hope that they had created an organism; it has taken a century and has cost their successors much sweat and blood to prove that they created a nation. The case before us must be considered in the light of our whole experience and not merely in that of what was said a hundred years ago." Missouri v. Holland, 252 U.S. 416, 433 (1920) (Holmes, J.). . . .

IV

A

[T]here is much irony in the Court's profession that it grounds its opinion on a deeply rooted historical tradition of sovereign immunity, when the Court abandons a principle nearly as inveterate, and much closer to the hearts of the framers: that where there is a right, there must be a remedy. . . . Blackstone considered it "a general and indisputable rule, that where there is a legal right, there is also a legal remedy, by suit or action at law, whenever that right is invaded." 3 Blackstone * 23. The generation of the framers thought the principle so crucial that several states put it into their constitutions. And when Chief Justice Marshall asked about Marbury, "[i]f he has a right, and that right has been violated, do the laws of his country afford him a remedy?," Marbury v. Madison, 5 U.S. (1 Cranch) 137, 162 (1803), the question was rhetorical, and the answer clear:

> "The very essence of civil liberty certainly consists in the right of every individual to claim the protection of the laws, whenever he receives an injury. One of the first duties of government is to afford that protection. In Great Britain the king himself is sued in the respectful form of a petition, and he never fails to comply with the judgment of his court." Id. at 163.

Yet today the Court has no qualms about saying frankly that the federal right to damages afforded by Congress under the FLSA cannot create a concomitant private remedy. ... It will not do for the Court to respond that a remedy was never available where the right in question was against the sovereign. A state is not the sovereign when a federal claim is pressed against it, and even the English sovereign opened itself to recovery and, unlike Maine, provided the remedy to complement the right. ... Far from defaulting on debt to eyes-open creditors, Maine is simply withholding damages from private citizens to whom they appear to be due. ... Why the state of Maine has not rendered this case unnecessary by paying damages to petitioners under the FLSA of its own free will remains unclear to me. The Court says that "it is conceded by all that the state has altered its conduct so that its compliance with federal law cannot now be questioned." But the ambiguous qualifier "now" allows the Court to avoid the fact that whatever its forward-looking compliance, the state still has not paid damages to petitioners; had it done so, the case before us would be moot.

V

[I]f the present majority had a defensible position one could at least accept its decision with an expectation of stability ahead. As it is, any such expectation would be naive. The resemblance of today's state sovereign immunity to the *Lochner* era's industrial due process is striking. The Court began this century by imputing immutable constitutional status to a conception of economic self-reliance that was never true to industrial life and grew insistently fictional with the years, and the Court has chosen to close the century by conferring like status on a conception of state sovereign immunity that is true neither to history nor to the structure of the Constitution. I expect the Court's late essay into immunity doctrine will prove the equal of its earlier experiment in laissez-faire, the one being as unrealistic as the other, as indefensible, and probably as fleeting.[a]

---

**a.** For a predictive analysis of *Alden* that anticipated the Court's result and much of its reasoning, see Richard H. Seamon, The Sovereign Immunity of States in Their Own Courts, 37 Brandeis L.J. 319 (1998–99). [Footnote by eds.]

## College Savings Bank v. Florida Prepaid Postsecondary Education Expense Board

Supreme Court of the United States, 1999.
527 U.S. 666.

JUSTICE SCALIA delivered the opinion of the Court.

The Trademark Remedy Clarification Act (TRCA), 106 Stat. 3567, subjects the states to suits brought under § 43(a) of the Trademark Act of 1946 (Lanham Act) for false and misleading advertising, 15 U.S.C. § 1125(a). The question presented in this case is whether that provision is effective to permit suit against a state for its alleged misrepresentation of its own product—either because the TRCA effects a constitutionally permissible abrogation of state sovereign immunity, or because the TRCA operates as an invitation to waiver of such immunity which is automatically accepted by a state's engaging in the activities regulated by the Lanham Act.

I

[W]e have recognized only two circumstances in which an individual may sue a state. First, Congress may authorize such a suit in the exercise of its power to enforce the 14th amendment—an amendment enacted after the 11th amendment and specifically designed to alter the federal-state balance. Fitzpatrick v. Bitzer, 427 U.S. 445 (1976). Second, a state may waive its sovereign immunity by consenting to suit. Clark v. Barnard, 108 U.S. 436, 447–48 (1883). This case turns on whether either of these two circumstances is present.

II

Section 43(a) of the Lanham Act, 15 U.S.C. § 1125(a), enacted in 1946, created a private right of action against "any person" who uses false descriptions or makes false representations in commerce. The TRCA amends § 43(a) by defining "any person" to include "any State, instrumentality of a State or employee of a State or instrumentality of a State acting in his or her official capacity." § 3(c), 106 Stat. 3568. The TRCA further amends the Lanham Act to provide that such state entities "shall not be immune, under the 11th amendment of the Constitution of the United States or under any other doctrine of sovereign immunity, from suit in federal court by any person, including any governmental or nongovernmental entity for any violation under this act," and that remedies shall be available against such state entities "to the same extent as such remedies are available ... in a suit against" a nonstate entity. § 3(b) (codified in 15 U.S.C. § 1122).

Petitioner College Savings Bank is a New Jersey chartered bank located in Princeton, New Jersey. Since 1987, it has marketed and sold CollegeSure certificates of deposit designed to finance the costs of college education. College Savings holds a patent upon the methodology of administering its CollegeSure certificates. Respondent Florida Prepaid Postsecondary Education Expense Board (Florida Prepaid) is an arm of the state of Florida. Since 1988, it has administered a tuition prepayment program designed to provide individuals with sufficient funds to cover future college expenses. College Savings brought a patent infringement action against Florida Prepaid in United States District Court in New Jersey. That action is the subject of today's decision in Florida Prepaid Postsecondary Ed. Expense Bd. v. College Savings Bank, ___ U.S. ___ (1999). In addition, and in the same court, College Savings filed the instant action alleging that Florida Prepaid violated § 43(a) of the Lanham Act by making misstatements about its own tuition savings plans in its brochures and annual reports.

Florida Prepaid moved to dismiss this action on the ground that it was barred by sovereign immunity. ... The United States intervened to defend the constitutionality of the TRCA. ... The District Court ... granted Florida Prepaid's motion to dismiss. The Court of Appeals affirmed. We granted certiorari.

III

We turn first to the contention that Florida's sovereign immunity was validly abrogated. Our decision three terms ago in Seminole Tribe of Fla. v. Florida, 517 U.S. 44 (1996), held that the power "to regulate Commerce" conferred by article I of the Constitution gives Congress no authority to abrogate state sovereign immunity. As authority for the abrogation in the present case, petitioner relies upon § 5 of the 14th amendment, which we held in *Fitzpatrick v. Bitzer*, supra, and reaffirmed in *Seminole Tribe*, 517 U.S. at 72–73, could be used for that purpose.

Section 1 of the 14th amendment provides that no state shall "deprive any person of ... property ... without due process of law." Section 5 provides that "the Congress shall have power to enforce, by appropriate legislation, the provisions of this article." We made clear in City of Boerne v. Flores, 521 U.S. 507, ___, ___ (1997), that the term "enforce" is to be taken seriously—that the object of valid § 5 legislation must be the carefully delimited remediation or prevention of constitutional violations. Petitioner claims that, with respect to § 43(a) of the Lanham Act, Congress enacted the TRCA to remedy and prevent state deprivations without due process of two species of "property" rights: (1) a right to be free from a business competitor's false advertising about its own product, and (2) a more generalized right to be secure in one's business interests. Neither of these qualifies as a property right protected by the due process clause.

As to the first: The hallmark of a protected property interest is the right to exclude others. That is "one of the most essential sticks in the bundle of rights that are commonly characterized as property." Kaiser Aetna v. United States, 444 U.S. 164, 176 (1979). That is why the right that we all possess to use the public lands is not the "property" right of anyone—hence the sardonic maxim, explaining what economists call the "tragedy of the commons," res publica, res nullius. The Lanham Act may well contain provisions that protect constitutionally cognizable property interests—notably, its provisions dealing with infringement of trademarks, which are the "property" of the owner because he can exclude others from using them. The Lanham Act's false-advertising provisions, however, bear no relationship to any right to exclude; and Florida Prepaid's alleged misrepresentations concerning its own products intruded upon no interest over which petitioner had exclusive dominion. . . .

Petitioner argues that the common-law tort of unfair competition "by definition" protects property interests and thus the TRCA "by definition" is designed to remedy and prevent deprivations of such interests in the false-advertising context. Even as a logical matter, that does not follow, since not everything which *protects* property interests is designed to remedy or prevent *deprivations* of those property interests. A municipal ordinance prohibiting billboards in residential areas protects the property interests of homeowners, although erecting billboards would ordinarily not deprive them of property. To sweep within the 14th amendment the elusive property interests that are "by definition" protected by unfair-competition law would violate our frequent admonition that the due process clause is not merely a "font of tort law." Paul v. Davis, 424 U.S. 693, 701 (1976).

Petitioners second assertion of a property interest rests upon an argument similar to the one just discussed, and suffers from the same flaw. Petitioner argues that businesses are "property" within the meaning of the due process clause, and that Congress legislates under § 5 when it passes a law that prevents state interference with business (which false advertising does). The assets of a business (including its good will) unquestionably are property, and any state taking of those assets is unquestionably a "deprivation" under the 14th amendment. But business in the sense of *the activity of doing business*, or *the activity of making a profit* is not property in the ordinary sense—and it is only *that*, and not any business asset, which is impinged upon by a competitors' false advertising.

Finding that there is no deprivation of property at issue here, we need not pursue the follow-on question that *City of Boerne* would otherwise require us to resolve: whether the prophylactic measure taken under purported authority of § 5 (viz., prohibition of states' sovereign-immunity claims, which are not in themselves a violation of the 14th amendment) was genuinely necessary to prevent violation of the 14th amendment. We turn next to the question whether Florida's sovereign immunity, though not abrogated, was voluntarily waived.

IV

We have long recognized that a state's sovereign immunity is "a personal privilege which it may waive at pleasure." *Clark v. Barnard*, 108

U.S. at 447. The decision to waive that immunity, however, "is altogether voluntary on the part of the sovereignty." Beers v. Arkansas, 61 U.S. (20 How.) 527 (1858). Accordingly, our "test for determining whether a state has waived its immunity from federal-court jurisdiction is a stringent one." Atascadero State Hospital v. Scanlon, 473 U.S. 234, 241 (1985). Generally, we will find a waiver either if the state voluntarily invokes our jurisdiction or else if the state makes a "clear declaration" that it intends to submit itself to our jurisdiction. Thus, a state does not consent to suit in federal court merely by consenting to suit in the courts of its own creation. Smith v. Reeves, 178 U.S. 436, 441–45 (1900). Nor does it consent to suit in federal court merely by stating its intention to "sue and be sued," Florida Dept. of Health and Rehabilitative Servs. v. Florida Nursing Home Assn., 450 U.S. 147, 149–50 (1981) (per curiam), or even by authorizing suits against it "in any court of competent jurisdiction," Kennecott Copper Corp. v. State Tax Comm'n, 327 U.S. 573, 577–79 (1946). We have even held that a state may, absent any contractual commitment to the contrary, alter the conditions of its waiver and apply those changes to a pending suit. *Beers v. Arkansas*, supra.

There is no suggestion here that respondent Florida Prepaid expressly consented to being sued in federal court. ... Rather, petitioner College Savings and the United States both maintain that Florida Prepaid has "impliedly" or "constructively" waived its immunity from Lanham Act suit. They do so on the authority of Parden v. Terminal R. Co. of Ala. Docks Dept., 377 U.S. 184 (1964)—an elliptical opinion that stands at the nadir of our waiver (and, for that matter, sovereign immunity) jurisprudence. In *Parden*, we permitted employees of a railroad owned and operated by Alabama to bring an action under the Federal Employers' Liability Act (FELA) against their employer. Despite the absence of any provision in the statute specifically referring to the states, we held that the act authorized suits against the states by virtue of its general provision subjecting to suit "every common carrier by railroad ... engaging in commerce between ... the several States," 45 U.S.C. § 51. We further held that Alabama had waived its immunity from FELA suit even though Alabama law expressly disavowed any such waiver:

> "By enacting the [FELA] Congress conditioned the right to operate a railroad in interstate commerce upon amenability to suit in federal court as provided by the act; by thereafter operating a railroad in interstate commerce, Alabama must be taken to have accepted that condition and thus to have consented to suit." 377 U.S. at 192. ...

Only nine years later, in Employees of Dept. of Public Health and Welfare of Mo. v. Department of Public Health and Welfare of Mo., 411 U.S. 279 (1973), we began to retreat from *Parden*. That case held—in an opinion written by one of the *Parden* dissenters over the solitary dissent of *Parden*'s author—that the state of Missouri was immune from a suit brought under the Fair Labor Standards Act by employees of its state health facilities. Although the statute specifically covered the state hospitals in question and such coverage was unquestionably enforceable in federal court by the United States, we did not think that the statute expressed with clarity Congress's intention to supersede the states' immunity from suits brought by individuals. We "put to one side" the *Parden* case, which we characterized as involving "dramatic circumstances" and "a rather isolated state activity," unlike the provision of the Fair Labor Standards Act in question that applied to a broad class of state employees. ... We also distinguished the railroad in *Parden* on the ground that it was "operated for profit" "in the area where private persons and corporations normally ran the enterprise." 411 U.S. at 284. ...

Several terms later, in Welch v. Texas Dept. of Highways and Public Transp., 483 U.S. 468 (1987), although we expressly avoided addressing the constitutionality of Congress's conditioning a state's engaging in commerce-clause activity upon the state's waiver of sovereign immunity, we said there was "no doubt that *Parden*'s discussion of congressional intent to negate 11th amendment immunity is no longer good law," and overruled *Parden* "to the extent [it] is inconsistent with the requirement that an abrogation of 11th amendment immunity by Congress must be expressed in unmistakably clear language," 483 U.S. at 478, and n.8.

College Savings and the United States [contend that a] *Parden*-style waiver of immunity, they say, is still possible after *Employees* and *Welch* so long as the following two conditions are satisfied: First, Congress must provide unambiguously that the state will be subject to suit if it engages in certain specified conduct governed by federal regulation. Second, the state must voluntarily elect to engage in the federally regulated conduct that subjects it to suit. In this latter regard, their argument goes, a state is never deemed to have constructively waived its sovereign immunity by engaging in activities that it cannot realistically choose to abandon, such as the operation of a police force; but constructive waiver is appropriate where a state runs an enterprise for profit, operates in a field traditionally occupied by private persons or corporations, engages in activities sufficiently removed from "core [state] functions" or otherwise acts as a "market participant" in interstate commerce. On this theory, Florida Prepaid constructively waived its immunity from suit by engaging in the voluntary and nonessential activity of selling and advertising a for-profit educational investment vehicle in interstate commerce after being put on notice by the clear language of the TRCA that it would be subject to Lanham Act liability for doing so.

We think that the constructive-waiver experiment of *Parden* was ill conceived, and see no merit in attempting to salvage any remnant of it. ... *Parden* broke sharply with prior cases, and is fundamentally incompatible with later ones. We have never applied the holding of *Parden* to another statute, and in fact have narrowed the case in every subsequent opinion in which it has been under consideration. In short, *Parden* stands as an anomaly in the jurisprudence of sovereign immunity, and indeed in the jurisprudence of constitutional law. Today, we drop the other shoe: Whatever may remain of our decision in *Parden* is expressly overruled.

To begin with, we cannot square *Parden* with our cases requiring that a state's express waiver of sovereign immunity be unequivocal. ... There is a fundamental difference between a state's expressing unequivocally that it waives its immunity, and Congress's expressing unequivocally its intention that if the state takes certain action it shall be deemed to have waived that immunity. ...

Indeed, *Parden*-style waivers are simply unheard of in the context of *other* constitutionally protected privileges. As we said in Edelman v. Jordan, 415 U.S. 651, 673 (1974), "constructive consent is not a doctrine commonly associated with the surrender of constitutional rights." ...

Given how anomalous it is to speak of the "constructive waiver" of a constitutionally protected privilege, it is not surprising that the very cornerstone of the *Parden* opinion was the notion that state sovereign immunity is not constitutionally grounded. ... Our more recent decision in *Seminole Tribe* expressly repudiates that proposition, and in formally overruling *Parden* we do no more than make explicit what that case implied.

Recognizing a congressional power to exact constructive waivers of sovereign immunity through the exercise of article I powers would also, as a practical matter, permit Congress to circumvent the antiabrogation holding of *Seminole Tribe*. Forced waiver and abrogation are not even different sides of the same coin—they are the same side of the same coin. ... There is little more than a verbal distinction between saying that Congress can make Florida liable to private parties for false or misleading advertising in interstate commerce of its prepaid tuition program, and saying the same thing but adding at the end "if Florida chooses to engage in such advertising." ...

Nor do we think that the constitutionally grounded principle of state sovereign immunity is any less robust where, as here, the asserted basis for constructive waiver is conduct that the state realistically could choose to abandon, that is undertaken for profit, that is traditionally performed by private citizens and corporations, and that otherwise resembles the behavior of "market participants." Permitting abrogation or constructive waiver of the constitutional right only when these conditions exist would of course limit the evil—but it is hard to say that that limitation has any more support in text or tradition than, say, limiting abrogation or constructive waiver to the last Friday of the month. Since sovereign immunity itself was not traditionally limited by these factors, and since they have no bearing upon the voluntariness of the waiver, there is no principled reason why they should enter into our waiver analysis. ...

The "market participant" cases from our dormant-commerce-clause jurisprudence, relied upon by the United States, are inapposite. Those cases hold that, where a state acts as a participant in the private market, it may prefer the goods or services of its own citizens, even though it could not do so while acting as a market regulator. ... The "market participant" exception to judicially created dormant-commerce-clause restrictions makes sense because the evil addressed by those restrictions—the prospect that states will use custom duties, exclusionary trade regulations, and other exercises of governmental power (as opposed to the expenditure of state resources) to favor their own citizens—is entirely absent where the states are buying and selling in the market. In contrast, a suit by an individual against an unconsenting state is the very evil at which the 11th amendment is directed—and it exists whether or not the state is acting for profit, in a traditionally "private" enterprise, and as a "market participant." In the sovereign-immunity context, moreover, "evenhandness" between individuals and states is not to be expected: "The constitutional role of the states sets them apart from other employers and defendants." *Welch*, 483 U.S. at 477. ...

V

The principal thrust of Justice Breyer's dissent is an attack upon the very legitimacy of state sovereign immunity itself. In this regard, Justice Breyer and the other dissenters proclaim that they are "not *yet* ready" (emphasis added), to adhere to the still-warm precedent of *Seminole Tribe* and to the 110–year-old decision in *Hans* that supports it. Accordingly, Justice Breyer reiterates (but only in outline form, thankfully) the now-fashionable revisionist accounts of the 11th amendment set forth in other opinions in a degree of repetitive detail that has despoiled our northern woods. Compare post with *Atascadero*, 473 U.S. at 258–302 (Brennan, J., dissenting); *Welch*, 483 U.S. at 504–16 (Brennan, J., dissenting); *Seminole Tribe*, 517 U.S. at 76–99 (Stevens, J., dissenting); id. at 100–85 (Souter, J., dissenting). But see *Alden v. Maine*, 527 U.S. 706, ___ (1999) (Souter, J., dissenting). The arguments recited in these sources have been soundly refuted, and the position for which they have been marshaled has been rejected by constitutional tradition and precedent as clear and conclusive, and almost as venerable, as that which consigns debate over whether *Marbury v. Madison* was wrongly decided to forums more other-worldly than ours. On this score, we think nothing further need be said except two minor observations peculiar to this case.

First, Justice Breyer and the other dissenters have adopted a decidedly perverse theory of stare decisis. While finding themselves entirely unconstrained by a venerable precedent such as *Hans*, imbedded within our legal system for over a century, at the same time they cling desperately to an anomalous and severely undermined decision (*Parden*) from the 1960's. Surely this approach to stare decisis is exactly backwards—unless, of course, one wishes to use it as a weapon rather than a guide, in which case any old approach will do. Second, while we stress that the following observation has no bearing upon our resolution of this case, we find it puzzling that Justice Breyer would choose this occasion to criticize our sovereign-immunity jurisprudence as being ungrounded in constitutional text, since the present lawsuit that he would allow to go forward—having apparently been commenced against a state (Florida) by a citizen of another state—seems to fall four square within the literal text of the 11th amendment. . . .

As for the more diffuse treatment of the subject of federalism contained in the last portion of Justice Breyer's opinion: It is alarming to learn that so many members of this Court subscribe to a theory of federalism that rejects "the details of any particular federalist doctrine"—which it says can and should "change to reflect the nation's changing needs"—and that puts forward as the only "unchanging goal" of federalism worth mentioning "the protection of liberty," which it believes is most directly achieved by "promoting the sharing among citizens of governmental decision-making authority," which in turn demands (we finally come to the point) "necessary legislative flexibility" for the people's representatives in Congress. . . . Legislative flexibility on the part of Congress will be the touchstone of federalism when the capacity to support combustion becomes the acid test of a fire extinguisher. Congressional flexibility is desirable, of course—but only within the *bounds of federal power* established by the Constitution. Beyond those bounds (the theory of our Constitution goes), it is a menace. Our opinion today has sought to discern what the bounds are; the dissent denies them any permanent place. . . .

Concluding, for the foregoing reasons, that the sovereign immunity of the state of Florida was neither validly abrogated by the Trademark Remedy Clarification Act, nor voluntarily waived by the state's activities in interstate commerce, we hold that the federal courts are without jurisdiction to entertain this suit against an arm of the state of Florida. The judgment of the Third Circuit dismissing the action is affirmed.

■ JUSTICE STEVENS, dissenting. . . .

The procedural posture of this case requires the Court to assume that Florida Prepaid is an "arm of the state" of Florida because its activities relate to the state's educational programs. But the validity of that assumption is doubtful if the Court's jurisprudence in this area is to be based primarily on present-day assumptions about the status of the doctrine of sovereign immunity in the 18th century. Sovereigns did not then play the kind of role in the commercial marketplace that they do today. In future cases, it may therefore be appropriate to limit the coverage of state sovereign immunity by treating the commercial enterprises of the states like the commercial activities of foreign sovereigns under the Foreign Sovereign Immunities Act of 1976. . . .

■ JUSTICE BREYER, with whom JUSTICE STEVENS, JUSTICE SOUTER, and JUSTICE GINSBURG join, dissenting.

The Court holds that Congress, in the exercise of its commerce power, cannot require a state to waive its immunity from suit in federal court even where the state engages in activity from which it might readily withdraw, such as federally regulated commercial activity. This Court has previously held to the contrary. Parden v. Terminal R. Co. of Ala. State Docks Dept., 377 U.S. 184 (1964). I would not abandon that precedent.

I

Thirty-five years ago this Court unanimously subscribed to the holding that the Court today overrules. Justice White, writing for four members of the Court who dissented on a different issue, succinctly described that holding as follows:

> "It is within the power of Congress to condition a state's permit to engage in the interstate transportation business on a waiver of the state's sovereign immunity from suits arising out of such business. Congress might well determine that allowing regulable conduct such as the operation of a railroad to be undertaken by a body legally immune from liability directly resulting from these operations is so inimical to the purposes of its regulation that the state must be put to the option of either foregoing participation in the conduct or consenting to legal responsibility for injury caused thereby." 377 U.S. at 198 (opinion of White, J., joined by Douglas, Harlan, and Stewart, JJ.). . . .

Far from being anomalous, *Parden*'s holding finds support in reason and precedent. When a state engages in ordinary commercial ventures, it acts like a private person, outside the area of its "core" responsibilities, and in a way unlikely to prove essential to the fulfillment of a basic governmental obligation. A Congress that decides to regulate those state commercial activities rather than to exempt the state likely believes that an exemption, by treating the state differently from identically situated private persons, would threaten the objectives of a federal regulatory program aimed primarily at private conduct. And a Congress that includes the state not only within its substantive regulatory rules but also (expressly) within a related system of private remedies likely believes that a remedial exemption would similarly threaten that program. It thereby avoids an enforcement gap which, when allied with the pressures of a competitive marketplace, could place the state's regulated private competitors at a significant disadvantage.

These considerations make Congress' need to possess the power to condition entry into the market upon a waiver of sovereign immunity (as "necessary and proper" to the exercise of its commerce power) unusually strong, for to deny Congress that power would deny Congress the power effectively to regulate *private* conduct. At the same time they make a state's need to exercise sovereign immunity unusually weak, for the state is unlikely to *have to* supply what private firms already supply, nor may it fairly demand special treatment, even to protect the public purse, when it does so. Neither can one easily imagine what the Constitution's founders would have thought about the assertion of sovereign immunity in this special context. These considerations, differing in kind or degree from those that would support a general congressional "abrogation" power, indicate that *Parden*'s holding is sound, irrespective of this Court's decisions in Seminole Tribe of Fla. v. Florida, 517 U.S. 44 (1996), and Alden v. Maine, ___ U.S. ___ (1999). . . .

The majority is . . . wrong to say that this Court has "narrowed" *Parden* in its "subsequent opinions," at least in any way relevant to today's decision. *Parden* considered two separate issues: (1) Does Congress have the *power* to require a state to waive its immunity? (2) How *clearly* must Congress speak when it does so? The Court has narrowed *Parden* only in respect to the second issue, not the first; but today we are concerned only with the first. The Court in Employees of Dept. of Public Health and Welfare of Mo. v. Department of Public Health and Welfare of Mo., 411 U.S. 279 (1973), for example, discussed whether Congress *had, or had not,* "lifted" sovereign immunity, not whether it *could, or could not,* have done so. . . . In short, except for those in today's majority, no member of this Court had ever questioned the holding of *Parden* that the Court today discards because it cannot find "merit in attempting to salvage any remnant of it."

*Parden* had never been questioned because, *Seminole Tribe* or not, it still makes sense. The line the Court today rejects has been drawn by this Court to place states outside the ordinary dormant commerce clause rules when they act as "market participants." And Congress has drawn this same line in the related context of foreign state sovereign immunity. 28 U.S.C. § 1605(a)(2). . . . Indeed, given the widely accepted view among modern nations that when a state engages in ordinary commercial activity sovereign immunity has no significant role to play, it is today's holding, not *Parden*, that creates the legal "anomaly."

II

I resist all the more strongly the Court's extension of *Seminole Tribe* in this case because, although I accept this Court's pre-*Seminole Tribe* sovereign immunity decisions, I am not yet ready to adhere to the proposition of law set forth in *Seminole Tribe*. In my view, Congress does possess the authority to abrogate a state's sovereign immunity where "necessary and proper" to the exercise of an article I power. My reasons include those that Justices Stevens and Souter already have described in detail [in their *Seminole Tribe* dissents]. . . .

By interpreting the Constitution as rendering immutable this one common-law doctrine (sovereign immunity), *Seminole Tribe* threatens the nation's ability to enact economic legislation needed for the future in much the way that Lochner v. New York, 198 U.S. 45 (1905), threatened the nation's ability to enact social legislation over 90 years ago. ... The similarity to *Lochner* lies in the risk that *Seminole Tribe* and the Court's subsequent cases will deprive Congress of necessary legislative flexibility. Their rules will make it more difficult for Congress to create, for example, a decentralized system of individual private remedies, say a private remedial system needed to protect intellectual property, including computer-related educational materials, irrespective of the need for, or importance of, such a system in a 21st century advanced economy. Yet ... Congress needs this kind of flexibility if it is to achieve one of federalism's basic objectives.

That basic objective should not be confused with the details of any particular federalist doctrine, for the contours of federalist doctrine have changed over the course of our nation's history. Thomas Jefferson's purchase of Louisiana, for example, reshaped the great debate about the need for a broad, rather than a literal, interpretation of federal powers; the Civil War effectively ended the claim of a state's right to "nullify" a federal law; the Second New Deal, and its ultimate judicial ratification, showed that federal and state legislative authority were not mutually exclusive; this Court's "civil rights" decisions clarified the protection against state infringement that the 14th amendment offers to basic human liberty. In each instance the content of specific federalist doctrines had to change to reflect the nation's changing needs (territorial expansion, the end of slavery, the Great Depression, and desegregation).

But those changing doctrines reflect at least one unchanging goal: the protection of liberty. Federalism helps to protect liberty not simply in our modern sense of helping the individual remain free of restraints imposed by a distant government, but more directly by promoting the sharing among citizens of governmental decisionmaking authority. ...

In today's world, legislative flexibility is necessary if we are to protect this kind of liberty. Modern commerce and the technology upon which it rests needs large markets and seeks government large enough to secure trading rules that permit industry to compete in the global market place, to prevent pollution that crosses borders, and to assure adequate protection of health and safety by discouraging a regulatory "race to the bottom." Yet local control over local decisions remains necessary. Uniform regulatory decisions about, for example, chemical waste disposal, pesticides, or food labeling, will directly affect daily life in every locality. But they may reflect differing views among localities about the relative importance of the wage levels or environmental preferences that underlie them. Local control can take account of such concerns and help to maintain a sense of community despite global forces that threaten it. Federalism matters to ordinary citizens seeking to maintain a degree of control, a sense of community, in an increasingly interrelated and complex world.

Courts can remain sensitive to these needs when they interpret statutes and apply constitutional provisions, for example, the dormant commerce clause. But courts cannot easily draw the proper basic lines of authority. The proper local/national/international balance is often highly context specific. And judicial rules that would allocate power are often far too broad. Legislatures, however, can write laws that more specifically embody that balance. Specific regulatory schemes, for example, can draw lines that leave certain local authority untouched, or that involve states, local communities, or citizens directly through the grant of funds, powers, rights, or privileges. Depending upon context, Congress may encourage or require interaction among citizens working at various levels of government. That is why the modern substantive federalist problem demands a flexible, context-specific legislative response (and it does not help to constitutionalize an ahistoric view of sovereign immunity that, by freezing its remedial limitations, tends to place the state beyond the reach of law).

I recognize the possibility that Congress may achieve its objectives in other ways. Ex parte Young, 209 U.S. 123 (1908), is still available, though effective only where damages remedies are not important. Congress, too, might create a federal damages-collecting "enforcement" bureaucracy charged with responsibilities that Congress would prefer to place in the hands of states or private citizens. Or perhaps Congress will be able to achieve the results it seeks (including decentralization) by embodying the necessary state "waivers" in federal funding programs—in which case, the Court's decisions simply impose upon Congress the burden of rewriting legislation, for no apparent reason.

But none of these alternatives is satisfactory. Unfortunately, *Seminole Tribe*, and today's related decisions, separate one formal strand from the federalist skein—a strand that has been understood as anti-Republican since the time of Cicero—and they elevate that strand to the level of an immutable constitutional principle more akin to the thought of James I than of James Madison. They do so when the role sovereign immunity once played in helping to assure the states that their political independence would remain even after joining the union no longer holds center stage. They do so when a federal court's ability to enforce its judgment against a state is no longer a major concern. And they do so without adequate legal support grounded in either history or practical need. To the contrary, by making that doctrine immune from congressional article I modification, the Court makes it more difficult for Congress to decentralize governmental decisionmaking and to provide individual citizens, or local communities, with a variety of enforcement powers. By diminishing congressional flexibility to do so, the Court makes it somewhat more difficult to satisfy modern federalism's more important liberty-protecting needs. In this sense, it is counterproductive.

### III

I do not know whether the state has engaged in false advertising or unfair competition as College Savings Bank alleges. But this case was dismissed at the threshold. Congress has clearly said that College Savings

Bank may bring a Lanham Act suit in these circumstances. For the reasons set forth in this opinion, I believe Congress has the constitutional power so to provide. I would therefore reverse the judgment of the Court of Appeals.

---

## Florida Prepaid Postsecondary Education Expense Board v. College Savings Bank

Supreme Court of the United States, 1999.
527 U.S. 627.

■ CHIEF JUSTICE REHNQUIST delivered the opinion of the Court.

In 1992, Congress amended the patent laws and expressly abrogated the states' sovereign immunity from claims of patent infringement. Respondent College Savings then sued the state of Florida for patent infringement, and the Court of Appeals held that Congress had validly abrogated the state's sovereign immunity from infringement suits pursuant to its authority under § 5 of the 14th amendment. We hold that, under City of Boerne v. Flores, 521 U.S. 507 (1997), the statute cannot be sustained as legislation enacted to enforce the guarantees of the 14th amendment's due process clause, and accordingly reverse the decision of the Court of Appeals.

I

Since 1987, respondent College Savings Bank, a New Jersey chartered savings bank located in Princeton, New Jersey, has marketed and sold certificates of deposit known as the CollegeSure CD, which are essentially annuity contracts for financing future college expenses. College Savings obtained a patent for its financing methodology, designed to guarantee investors sufficient funds to cover the costs of tuition for colleges. Petitioner Florida Prepaid Postsecondary Education Expenses Board (Florida Prepaid) is an entity created by the state of Florida that administers similar tuition prepayment contracts available to Florida residents and their children. College Savings claims that, in the course of administering its tuition prepayment program, Florida Prepaid directly and indirectly infringed College Savings' patent.

College Savings brought an infringement action under 35 U.S.C. § 271(a) against Florida Prepaid in the United States District Court for the District of New Jersey in November 1994. By the time College Savings filed its suit, Congress had already passed the Patent and Plant Variety Protection Remedy Clarification Act (Patent Remedy Act), 35 U.S.C. §§ 271(h), 296(a), ... to "clarify that States, instrumentalities of States, and officers and employees of States acting in their official capacity, are subject to suit in Federal court by any person for infringement of patents and plant variety protections." Pub. L. 102–560, preamble. ... Section 296(a) addresses the sovereign immunity issue ... specifically:

> "Any state, any instrumentality of a state, and any officer or employee of a state or instrumentality of a state acting in his official capacity, shall not be immune, under the 11th amendment of the Constitution of the United States or under any other doctrine of sovereign immunity, from suit in federal court by any person ... for infringement of a patent under section 271, or for any other violation under this title." ...

After this Court decided Seminole Tribe of Fla. v. Florida, 517 U.S. 44 (1996), Florida Prepaid moved to dismiss the action on the grounds of sovereign immunity. Florida Prepaid argued that the Patent Remedy Act was an unconstitutional attempt by Congress to use its article I powers to abrogate state sovereign immunity. College Savings responded that Congress had properly exercised its power pursuant to § 5 of the 14th amendment to enforce the guarantees of the due process clause in § 1 of the amendment. The United States intervened to defend the constitutionality of the statute. Agreeing with College Savings, the District Court denied Florida Prepaid's motion to dismiss, and the Federal Circuit affirmed. ...

II

... College Savings and the United States ... contend that Congress' enactment of the Patent Remedy Act validly abrogated the states' sovereign immunity. To determine the merits of this proposition, we must answer two questions: "first, whether Congress has 'unequivocally expressed its intent to abrogate the immunity,' ... and second, whether Congress has acted 'pursuant to a valid exercise of power.' " *Seminole Tribe*, supra, at 55. We agree with the parties and the Federal Circuit that in enacting the Patent Remedy Act, Congress has made its intention to abrogate the states' immunity " 'unmistakably clear in the language of the statute.' " Dellmuth v. Muth, 491 U.S. 223, 228 (1989). ...

Whether Congress had the power to compel states to surrender their sovereign immunity for these purposes, however, is another matter. Congress justified the Patent Remedy Act under three sources of constitutional authority: the patent clause, art. I, § 8, cl. 8; the interstate commerce clause, art. I, § 8, cl. 3; and § 5 of the 14th amendment. ...*Seminole Tribe* makes clear that Congress may not abrogate state sovereign immunity pursuant to its article I powers; hence the Patent Remedy Act cannot be sustained under either the commerce clause or the patent clause. ...

Instead, College Savings and the United States argue that the Federal Circuit properly concluded that Congress enacted the Patent Remedy Act to secure the 14th amendment's protections against deprivations of property without due process of law. The 14th amendment provides in relevant part:

> "Section 1. ... No State shall ... deprive any person of life, liberty, or property, without due process of law. ...

Section 5. The Congress shall have power to enforce, by appropriate legislation, the provisions of this article."

... We have held that "the 'provisions of this article,' to which § 5 refers, include the due process clause of the 14th amendment." *City of Boerne v. Flores*, 521 U.S. at 519.

But the legislation must nonetheless be "appropriate" under § 5 as that term was construed in *City of Boerne*. ... There, this Court held that the Religious Freedom Restoration Act of 1993 (RFRA), 42 U.S.C. § 2000bb et seq., exceeded Congress' authority under § 5 of the 14th amendment, insofar as RFRA was made applicable to the states. ...

We thus held that for Congress to invoke § 5, it must identify conduct transgressing the 14th amendment's substantive provisions, and must tailor its legislative scheme to remedying or preventing such conduct. ...

Can the Patent Remedy Act be viewed as remedial or preventive legislation aimed at securing the protections of the 14th amendment for patent owners? Following *City of Boerne*, we must first identify the 14th amendment "evil" or "wrong" that Congress intended to remedy, guided by the principle that the propriety of any § 5 legislation "must be judged with reference to the historical experience ... it reflects." The underlying conduct at issue here is state infringement of patents and the use of sovereign immunity to deny patent owners compensation for the invasion of their patent rights. It is this conduct then—unremedied patent infringement by the states—that must give rise to the 14th amendment violation that Congress sought to redress in the Patent Remedy Act.

In enacting the Patent Remedy Act, however, Congress identified no pattern of patent infringement by the states, let alone a pattern of constitutional violations. ... Though patents may be considered "property" for purposes of our analysis, the legislative record still provides little support for the proposition that Congress sought to remedy a 14th amendment violation in enacting the Patent Remedy Act. ... This Court has ... held that "in procedural due process claims, the deprivation by state action of a constitutionally protected interest ... is not in itself unconstitutional; what is unconstitutional is the deprivation of such an interest without due process of law." Zinermon v. Burch, 494 U.S. 113, 125 (1990) (emphasis deleted).

Thus, under the plain terms of the clause and the clear import of our precedent, a state's infringement of a patent, though interfering with a patent owner's right to exclude others, does not by itself violate the Constitution. Instead, only where the state provides no remedy, or only inadequate remedies, to injured patent owners for its infringement of their patent could a deprivation of property without due process result. See Parratt v. Taylor, 451 U.S. 527, 539–31 (1981).

Congress, however, barely considered the availability of state remedies for patent infringement and hence whether the states' conduct might have amounted to a constitutional violation under the 14th amendment. It did hear a limited amount of testimony to the effect that the remedies available in some states were uncertain.

The primary point made by these witnesses, however, was not that state remedies were constitutionally inadequate, but rather that they were less convenient than federal remedies, and might undermine the uniformity of patent law.

Congress itself said nothing about the existence or adequacy of state remedies in the statute or in the Senate Report, and made only a few fleeting references to state remedies in the House Report, essentially repeating the testimony of the witnesses. . . .

The legislative record thus suggests that the Patent Remedy Act does not respond to a history of "widespread and persisting deprivation of constitutional rights" of the sort Congress has faced in enacting proper prophylactic § 5 legislation. *City of Boerne*, 521 U.S. at 526. Instead, Congress appears to have enacted this legislation in response to a handful of instances of state patent infringement that do not necessarily violate the Constitution. Though the lack of support in the legislative record is not determinative, identifying the targeted constitutional wrong or evil is still a critical part of our § 5 calculus because "strong measures appropriate to address one harm may be an unwarranted response to another, lesser one," id. at 530. Here, the record at best offers scant support for Congress' conclusion that states were depriving patent owners of property without due process of law by pleading sovereign immunity in federal-court patent actions.

Because of this lack, the provisions of the Patent Remedy Act are "so out of proportion to a supposed remedial or preventive object that [they] cannot be understood as responsive to, or designed to prevent, unconstitutional behavior." Id. at 532. . . .

The historical record and the scope of coverage therefore make it clear that the Patent Remedy Act cannot be sustained under § 5 of the 14th amendment. The examples of states avoiding liability for patent infringement by pleading sovereign immunity in a federal-court patent action are scarce enough, but any plausible argument that such action on the part of the state deprived patentees of property and left them without a remedy under state law is scarcer still. The statute's apparent and more basic aims were to provide a uniform remedy for patent infringement and to place states on the same footing as private parties under that regime. These are proper article I concerns, but that article does not give Congress the power to enact such legislation after *Seminole Tribe*.

The judgment of the Court of Appeals is reversed, and the case is remanded for proceedings consistent with this opinion.

It is so ordered.

■ JUSTICE STEVENS, with whom JUSTICE SOUTER, JUSTICE GINSBURG, and JUSTICE BREYER join, dissenting.

The Constitution vests Congress with plenary authority over patents and copyrights ... This Court's recent decision in City of Boerne v. Flores, 521 U.S. 507 (1997), amply supports congressional authority to enact the Patent Remedy Act... .Before discussing *City of Boerne*, however, I shall comment briefly on the principle that undergirds all aspects of our patent system: national uniformity.

I

... Sound reasons support both Congress' authority over patents and its subsequent decision in 1800 to vest exclusive jurisdiction over patent infringement litigation in the federal courts. The substantive rules of law that are applied in patent infringement cases are entirely federal. ... There is, accordingly, a strong federal interest in an interpretation of the patent statutes that is both uniform and faithful to the constitutional goals of stimulating invention and rewarding the disclosure of novel and useful advances in technology. Federal interests are threatened, not only by inadequate protection for patentees, but also when overprotection may have an adverse impact on a competitive economy. Therefore, consistency, uniformity, and familiarity with the extensive and relevant body of patent jurisprudence are matters of overriding significance in this area of the law. ...

II

Our recent decision in *City of Boerne* sets out the general test for determining whether Congress has enacted "appropriate" legislation pursuant to § 5 of the 14th amendment. "There must be a congruence and proportionality between the injury to be prevented or remedied and the means adopted to that end." The first step of the inquiry, then, is to determine what injury Congress sought to prevent or remedy with the relevant legislation.

As the Court recognizes, Congress' authority under § 5 of the 14th amendment extends to enforcing the due process clause of that amendment. Congress decided, and I agree, that the Patent Remedy Act was a proper exercise of this power.

The Court acknowledges, as it must, that patents are property. ... The question presented by this case ... is whether the Patent Remedy Act, which clarified Congress' intent to subject state infringers to suit in federal court, may be applied to willful infringement.

As I read the Court's opinion, its negative answer to that question ... relies entirely on perceived deficiencies in the evidence reviewed by Congress before it enacted the clarifying amendment. "In enacting the Patent Remedy Act ... Congress identified no pattern of patent infringement by the states, let alone a pattern of constitutional violations."

It is quite unfair for the Court to strike down Congress' act based on an absence of findings supporting a requirement this Court had not yet articulated. The legislative history of the Patent Remedy Act makes it abundantly clear that Congress was attempting to hurdle the then-most-recent barrier this Court had erected in the 11th amendment course—the "clear statement" rule of Atascadero State Hospital v. Scanlon, 473 U.S. 234 (1985).

Nevertheless, Congress did hear testimony about inadequate state remedies for patent infringement when considering the Patent Remedy Act. ... Congress heard other general testimony that state remedies would likely be insufficient to compensate inventors whose patents had been infringed. ... In addition, Congress found that state infringement of patents was likely to increase. ...

It is true that, when considering the Patent Remedy Act, Congress did not review the remedies available in each state for patent infringements and surmise what kind of recovery a plaintiff might obtain in a tort suit in all 50 jurisdictions. But, it is particularly ironic that the Court should view this fact as support for its holding. Given that Congress had long ago pre-empted state jurisdiction over patent infringement cases, it was surely reasonable for Congress to assume that such remedies simply did not exist. Furthermore, it is well known that not all states have waived their sovereign immunity from suit, and among those states that have, the contours of this waiver vary widely.

Even if such remedies might be available in theory, it would have been "appropriate" for Congress to conclude that they would not guarantee patentees due process in infringement actions against state defendants. State judges have never had the exposure to patent litigation that federal judges have experienced for decades, and, unlike infringement actions brought in federal district courts, their decisions would not be reviewable in the Court of Appeals for the Federal Circuit. Surely this Court would not undertake the task of reviewing every state court decision that arguably misapplied patent law. And even if 28 U.S.C. § 1338 is amended or construed to permit state courts to entertain infringement actions when a state is named as a defendant, given the Court's opinion in Alden v. Maine, 527 U.S. 706 (1999), it is by no means clear that state courts could be required to hear these cases at all. ...

III

In my view, Congress had sufficient evidence of due process violations, whether actual or potential, to meet the requirement we expressed in *City of Boerne* that Congress can act under § 5 only to "remedy or prevent unconstitutional actions." See 521 U.S. at 519. The Court's opinion today threatens to read Congress' power to pass prophylactic legislation out of § 5 altogether; its holding is unsupported by *City of Boerne* and in fact conflicts with our reasoning in that case. ...

By enacting [the Religious Freedom Restoration Act], Congress sought to change the meaning of the free exercise clause of the first amendment as it had been interpreted by this Court, rather than to remedy or to prevent violations of the clause as we had interpreted it. ... The Patent Remedy Act, however, was passed to prevent future violations of due process, based on the substantiated fear that states would be unable or unwilling to provide adequate remedies for their own violations of patent-holders' rights. ...

*City of Boerne* also identified a "proportionality" component to "appropriate" legislation under § 5. Our opinion expressly recognized that "preventive rules are sometimes appropriate" if there is "a congruence between the means used and the ends to be achieved. ... Strong measures appropriate to address one harm may be an unwarranted response to another, lesser one." ...

Again, the contrast between RFRA and the act at issue in this case could not be more stark. The sole purpose of this amendment is to abrogate the states' sovereign immunity as a defense to a charge of patent infringement. It has no impact whatsoever on any substantive rule of state law, but merely effectuates settled federal policy to confine patent infringement litigation to federal judges. There is precise congruence between "the means used" (abrogation of sovereign immunity in this narrow category of cases) and "the ends to be achieved" (elimination of the risk that the defense of sovereign immunity will deprive some patentees of property without due process of law).

That congruence is equally precise whether infringement of patents by state actors is rare or frequent. If they are indeed unusual, the statute will operate only in those rare cases. But if such infringements are common, or should become common as state activities in the commercial arena increase, the impact of the statute will likewise expand in precise harmony with the growth of the problem that Congress anticipated and sought to prevent. In either event the statute will have no impact on the states' enforcement of their own laws. None of the concerns that underlay our decision in *City of Boerne* are even remotely implicated in this case. ...

IV

For these reasons, I am convinced that the 1992 act should be upheld even if full respect is given to the Court's recent cases cloaking the states with increasing protection from congressional legislation. I do, however, note my continuing dissent from the Court's aggressive sovereign immunity jurisprudence; today, this Court once again demonstrates itself to be the champion of states' rights. In this case, it seeks to guarantee rights the states themselves did not express any particular desire in possessing: during Congress' hearings on the Patent Remedy Act, although invited to do so, the states chose not to testify in opposition to the abrogation of their immunity.

The statute that the Court invalidates today was only one of several "clear statements" that Congress enacted in response to the decision in *Atascadero State Hospital*, supra. In each of those clarifications Congress was fully justified in assuming that it had ample authority to abrogate sovereign immunity defenses to federal claims, an authority that the Court squarely upheld in Pennsylvania v. Union Gas Co., 491 U.S. 1 (1989). It was that *holding*—not just the "plurality opinion"—that was overruled in Seminole Tribe of Fla. v. Florida, 517 U.S. 44 (1996). The full reach of that case's dramatic expansion of the judge-made doctrine of sovereign immunity is unpredictable; its dimensions are defined only by the present majority's perception of constitutional penumbras rather than constitutional text. Until this expansive and judicially crafted protection of states' rights runs its course, I shall continue to register my agreement with the views expressed in the *Seminole* dissents and in the scholarly commentary on that case.

I respectfully dissent.[a]

NOTES ON THE 1999 DECISIONS

1. ***Kimel v. Florida Board of Regents.*** The *College Savings Bank* cases were followed in Kimel v. Florida Board of Regents, ___ U.S. ___ (2000), which held that Congress could not constitutionally authorize damage actions against states for violation of the Age Discrimination in Employment Act. As originally passed in 1967, that statute covered only private employers. A 1974 enactment, however, extended the statute to public agencies, including states. A majority of the Supreme Court, excepting only Justices Thomas and Kennedy, found the requisite "clear statement" to authorize damage actions against states. In an opinion by Justice O'Connor, joined by Chief Justice Rehnquist and by Justices Scalia, Kennedy, and Thomas, the Court then held that the Age Discrimination in Employment Act, although undoubtedly within Congress's article I power, was not "appropriate legislation" under § 5 of the 14th amendment. The Court reasoned that since age discrimination generally did not violate equal protection (unless irrational), legislation to prohibit age discrimination in employment could not be justified as an attempt as "responsive to, or designed to prevent, unconstitutional behavior." City of Boerne v. Flores,

a. For early analysis of the effect of *Seminole Tribe* on federal remedies for misappropriation of intellectual property, see Christina Bohannon and Thomas F. Cotter, When the State Steals Ideas: Is the Abrogation of State Sovereign Immunity from Federal Infringement Claims Constitutional in Light of *Seminole Tribe*?, 67 Fordham L. Rev. 1435 (1999) (correctly anticipating that federal attempts to authorize private infringement actions against states exceeds federal § 5 power); Paul J. Heald and Michael L. Wells, Remedies for the Misappropriation of Intellectual Property by State and Municipal Governments Before and After *Seminole Tribe*: The Eleventh Amendment and Other Immunity Doctrines, 55 W. & L.L. Rev. 849 (1998) (concluding, notwithstanding the doctrinal complexity, that federal law will provide remedies for most violations of intellectual property rights). [Footnote by eds.]

521 U.S. 507, 532 (1997). Justices Stevens, Souter, Ginsburg, and Breyer dissented on grounds of continued disagreement with *Seminole Tribe* and reiterated their view that article I power sufficed to override state sovereign immunity against private suits.

2. **Bibliography.** For an interesting reaction to *Alden* and the *Florida Prepaid* cases, see Ann Woolhandler, Old Property, New Property, and Sovereign Immunity, 75 Notre Dame L. Rev. 919 (2000). Woolhandler provides a historical defense of these decisions, arguing that due process requires damages remedies (either against states or state officers) for deprivations of "old property" but not necessarily for deprivations of "new property." "Old property" is shorthand for traditional property interests, while "new property" refers to "statutorily created expectations of compliance with federal law." While all "property" might be entitled to some due process protection, only traditional property interests necessarily trigger a constitutional right to compensation. On this view, the Supreme Court's decisions upholding state sovereign immunity against claims for violations of "new property" rights can be defended. For criticism of Woolhandler's approach, see Vicki C. Jackson, Principle and Compromise in Constitutional Adjudication: The Eleventh Amendment and State Sovereign Immunity, 75 Notre Dame L. Rev. 953 (2000).

For additional analysis of *Alden* in the same issue of the Notre Dame Law Review, see James E. Pfander, Once More Unto the Breach: Eleventh Amendment Scholarship and the Court, 75 Notre Dame L. Rev. 817 (2000) (introducing a symposium on state sovereign immunity and exploring the implications of *Alden* for Eleventh Amendment scholarship); Carlos Manuel Vázquez, Eleventh Amendment Schizophrenia, 75 Notre Dame L. Rev. 859 (2000) (exploring the "schizophrenia" of saying on the one hand that state sovereign immunity from private suits is constitutionally fundamental and beyond Congressional control and allowing on the other hand unlimited federal enforcement actions against states, as well as private suits against state officers); Daniel J. Meltzer, State Sovereign Immunity: Five Authors in Search of a Theory, 75 Notre Dame L. Rev. 1011 (2000) (criticizing the Court's efforts to promote federalism by limiting the enforcement of valid federal laws against states rather than by restricting the reach of federal legislative authority as "fail[ing] to promote any coherent conception of states' rights or state autonomy while harming legitimate national objectives"); John E. Nowak, The Gang of Five & the Second Coming of an Anti–Reconstruction Supreme Court, 75 Notre Dame L. Rev. 1091 (2000) (comparing recent decisions to those that dismantled or curtailed Reconstruction-era legislation); Suzanna Sherry, States Are People Too, 75 Notre Dame L. Rev. 1121 (2000) (criticizing analogies between state sovereign immunity and individuals rights); Daniel A. Farber, Pledging a New Allegiance: An Essay on Sovereignty and the New Federalism, 75 Notre Dame L. Rev. 1133 (2000) (examining *Alden* as reflecting a "new federalism" credo of state sovereignty); John V. Orth, History and the Eleventh Amendment, 75 Notre Dame L. Rev. 1147 (2000) (examining the use of history to justify various positions on state sovereign immunity); Jay Tidmarsh, A Dialogic Defense of *Alden*, 75 Notre Dame L. Rev. 1161 (2000) (defending the result in *Alden* as "within the range of permissible constitutional choice").

For other interesting reactions to these cases, see Pamela S. Karlan, The Irony of Immunity: The Eleventh Amendment, Irreparable Injury, and Section 1983, 53 Stan. L. Rev. ___ (2001) (forthcoming) (pointing out that precluding money damages for the victims of violations of federal statutes creates "irreparable injury" that would justify injunctive relief and suggesting that injunctions against state agencies are potentially broader and more intrusive than damage actions); Carlos Manuel Vázquez, Sovereign Immunity, Due Process, and the *Alden* Trilogy, 109 Yale L.J. 1927 (2000) (suggesting that *Florida Prepaid v. College Savings Bank* may have undermined *Alden* by interpreting due process to require that states provide remedies when they intentionally deprive persons of (at least some forms of) liberty or property in violation of federal law); Jonathan R. Siegel, Congress's Power to Authorize Suits Against States, 68 Geo. Wash. L. Rev. 44 (1999) (arguing that Congress could avoid the restrictions of Seminole Tribe and Alden by authorizing the federal government to espouse claims by private parties in suits against states).

Also see Christina Bohannan & Thomas F. Cotter, When the State Steals Ideas: Is the Abrogation of State Sovereign Immunity from Federal Infringement Claims Constitutional in Light of *Seminole Tribe*?, 67 Fordham L. Rev. 1435 (1999) (a predictive analysis of the issues presented in the *Florida Prepaid* decisions); Paul J. Heald & Michael L. Wells, Remedies for the Misappropriation of Intellectual Property by State and Municipal Governments Before and After *Seminole Tribe*: The Eleventh Amendment and Other Immunity Doctrines, 55 W. & L. L. Rev. 849 (1998) (analyzing federal remedies for violations of intellectual property rights before the *Florida Prepaid* cases).

**Page 880, add at the beginning of Section 3, immediately before *Idaho v. Coeur d'Alene Tribe*:**

## INTRODUCTORY NOTE ON *COEUR D'ALENE TRIBE*

Of all the oddities in 11th amendment jurisprudence, none is stranger than *Seminole Tribe*'s treatment of *Ex parte Young*. For nearly a century, *Ex parte Young* has allowed prospective relief against states by resort to the fiction of suing a state officer. The *Seminole Tribe* Court purported not to question *Ex parte Young* but only to hold that Congress intended to preclude that option in the Indian Gaming Regulatory Act. Since prospective enforcement against state officers, as *Young* allows, would have implemented precisely the intention manifest in the statute, the Court's insistence that Congress actually intended to forbid this solution struck some as "singularly unpersuasive," Daniel J. Meltzer, The *Seminole* Decision and

State Sovereign Immunity, 1996 Sup. Ct. Rev. 1, 43, and other, less polite observers as "wilfully perverse." John C. Jeffries, Jr., In Praise of the Eleventh Amendment and Section 1983, 84 Va. L. Rev. 47, 52 n.19 (1998).

So long as *Ex parte Young* remains generally intact, the practical significance of *Seminole Tribe* for questions of injunctive relief will be limited. Indeed, from all that appears, Congress could overrule *Seminole Tribe* simply by clarifying its intention to allow—or more accurately not to disallow—officer suits. On the other hand, *Seminole Tribe* and its progeny would mean a great deal if they portended any general limitation on *Ex parte Young*. That possibility was raised in the next main case.[a]

**Page 903, add a footnote at the end of the first full paragraph:**

**d.** For an argument that the current remedies available to taxpayers who pay unconstitutional state taxes are inadequate and a proposal that Congress should enact legislation to correct the problem, see John F. Coverdale, Remedies for Unconstitutional State Taxes, 32 Conn. L. Rev. 73 (1999).

**a.** For commentary on the relation of *Seminole Tribe* and *Ex Parte Young*, see Vicki L. Jackson, *Seminole Tribe*, the Eleventh Amendment, and the Potential Evisceration of *Ex Parte Young*, 72 N.Y.U. L. Rev. 495 (1997) (emphasizing the dangers of curtailing officer suits); David P. Currie, Response: *Ex Parte Young* After *Seminole Tribe*, 72 N.Y.U. L. Rev. 547 (1997) (offering a more optimistic response); Laura S. Fitzgerald, Beyond *Marbury*: Jurisdictional Self–Dealing in *Seminole Tribe*, 52 Vand. L. Rev. 407 (1999) (arguing that the Court has assumed a unilateral power to control its own jurisdiction in suits against states).

CHAPTER IX

# 42 U.S.C. § 1983

**Page 919, add at the end of footnote g:**

For recent investigation and reinterpretation of the history of § 1983, see David Achtenberg, A "Milder Measure of Villainy": The Unknown History of 42 U.S.C. § 1983 and the Meaning of "Under Color of" Law, 1999 Utah L. Rev. 1 (concluding that history "should dispel the remarkably persistent myth that the Forty–Second Congress never intended the provision to cover constitutional wrongs unless those wrongs were actually authorized by state law").

**Page 937, add a new Note:**

**6a. *Crawford–El v. Britton.*** At issue in Crawford–El v. Britton, 523 U.S. 574 (1998), was whether *Harlow*-inspired protections against discovery and trial should apply where improper motivation is alleged, not to overcome the defense of qualified immunity, but to establish the underlying constitutional violation. Examples are claims of racial discrimination, which require proof of discriminatory animus, and first amendment retaliation, which require proof of a retaliatory purpose.

Casually, almost as an aside, and apparently without dissent, the Court resolved the ambiguity in *Harlow* against any opportunity to overcome qualified immunity by proof of malice. After quoting *Harlow*'s statement that "bare allegations of malice should not suffice to subject government officials either to the costs of trial or to the burdens of broad-reaching discovery," the *Crawford–El* Court announced:

> "Under that standard, a defense of qualified immunity may not be rebutted by evidence that the defendant's conduct was malicious or otherwise improperly motivated. Evidence concerning the defendant's subjective intent is simply irrelevant to that defense."

On the question whether *Harlow* required analogous restrictions on proof of improper motivation where required by the underlying constitutional claim, the *Crawford–El* Court was a bit murky. At issue was the D.C. Circuit's ruling that a plaintiff alleging a constitutional violation requiring proof of improper motive had to prove that motive by clear and convincing evidence. By a vote of five to four, the Supreme Court disapproved that requirement. Speaking through Justice Stevens, the Court said that any *Harlow*-like adjustment in pleading, discovery, or summary judgment practice should come from the legislature, not the courts. Later in its opinion, however, the Court suggested several ways in which trial judges could constrain discovery and trial based on "bare allegations" of improper motivation. One such mechanism was to "insist that the plaintiff 'put forward specific, nonconclusory factual allegations' that establish improper motive causing cognizable injury in order to survive a prediscovery motion for dismissal or summary judgment," citing Siegert v. Gilley, 500 U.S. 226, 236 (1991) (Kennedy, J., concurring in the judgment). This remark raises the possibility that heightened *proof* may not be required in unconstitutional-motive cases but that heightened *pleading* may be. Apparently, another Supreme Court decision will required to resolve that question.

**Page 940, add at the end of Note 7:**

For additional criticism of the Supreme Court's immunity decisions, see Sheldon Nahmod, The Restructuring of Narrative and Empathy in Section 1983 Cases, 72 Chi.–Kent L. Rev. 819 (1997). Nahmod examines immunity decisions "from the perspective of narrative empathy" and concludes that the Court has "instruct[ed] the decision-maker, the judge (and *not* the jury), to empathize with the defendant . . ., thus forcing § 1983 plaintiffs to bear their own losses even when their constitutional rights are violated."

For analysis of qualified immunity through the lens of the familiar distinction between rules and standards, see Alan K. Chen, The Ultimate Standard: Qualified Immunity in the Age of Constitutional Balancing Tests, 81 Iowa L. Rev. 261 (1995), which concludes that the "ultimate standard" of qualified immunity doctrine should be replaced by a more rule-oriented approach.

For analysis of qualified immunity from the perspective of a comparison with the criminal law, see Barbara E. Armacost, Qualified Immunity: Ignorance Excused, 51 Vand. L. Rev. 583 (1998). She examines qualified immunity in a variety of contexts and concludes that, "[t]he recognition that qualified immunity is about notice and that notice functions as a surrogate for fault—in much the same way that fair notice in criminal law acts as a proxy for fault—helps to explain the courts' analyses in constitutional damages cases."

Finally, for criticism of the Court's one-size-fits-all approach to qualified immunity and an argument that constitutional tort liability should take account of the presence or absence of alternative remedies, see John C. Jeffries, Jr., Disaggregating Constitutional Torts, 110 Yale L.J. ___ (2000) (forthcoming). And for criticism of qualified immunity and of the whole scheme of officer liability, see Cornelia T.L. Pillard, Taking Fiction Seriously: The Strange Results of Public Officials' Individual Liability Under *Bivens*, 88 Geo. L.J. 65 (1999).

**Page 941, add a new Note:**

**7a. Unnecessary Merits Adjudication?** As *Anderson v. Creighton* suggests, and subsequent decisions make plain, there is an unusual sequence of decision in qualified immunity cases. First, a court determines whether a constitutional right was violated. If so, the court then decides whether the defendant's conduct was nevertheless protected by qualified immunity. Under this procedure, courts adjudicate constitutional claims on the merits even when the merits do not affect the outcome of damages actions.

A good example is Wilson v. Layne, 526 U.S. 603 (1999). Plaintiffs claimed that their fourth amendment rights had been violated when police invited *Washington Post* reporters to accompany them on a lawful search. The Court ruled first that such media "ride-alongs" violated the fourth amendment. The Court then found that, since the unconstitutionality of such actions was not clearly established at the time they were taken the defendants were protected by qualified immunity. Note that the second conclusion rendered the first unnecessary. Given that the law was not clearly established, the defendants would prevail against a claim for money damages whether or not their conduct violated the Constitution. Yet, the Court requires that the merits of constitutional tort claims be decided before consideration of qualified immunity. Why?

An answer to this question is attempted in John C. Jeffries, Jr., The Right–Remedy Gap in Constitutional Law, 109 Yale L.J. 87 (1999), which argues that the limitation of money damages by the law of qualified immunity is a two-edged sword. On the one hand, qualified immunity reduces the incentives for government officers to comply with existing constitutional requirements, whatever they may be. On the other hand, qualified immunity facilitates the growth and development of constitutional law by reducing the cost of innovation. New rules apply to future cases but do not trigger damages liability for past failure to comply with the new standards. The result, Jeffries argues, is not only to reduce the cost of constitutional innovation, but also to tilt constitutional adjudication from reparation toward reform, as societal resources are continually shifted away from cash compensation for past injury and toward the prevention of future harm. Obviously, this concern for the growth and direction of constitutional law would be entirely defeated if the existence of qualified immunity precluded adjudication of the merits.

For argument in a similar vein, see John M.M. Greabe, *Mirabile Dictum!*: The Case for "Unnecessary" Constitutional Ruling in Civil Rights Damages Actions, 74 Notre Dame L. Rev. 403 (1999) (arguing against "merits by-pass" and in favor of "not-strictly-necessary" constitutional adjudication).

**Page 954, add the following at the end of Section 2:**

Congress recently amended §§ 1983 and 1988 to overrule *Pulliam*. Section 1983 now provides that the person acting under color of state law "shall be liable to the party injured in an action at law, suit in equity, or other proper proceeding for redress, *except that in any action brought against a judicial officer for an act or omission taken in such officer's judicial capacity, injunctive relief shall not be granted unless a declaratory decree was violated or declaratory relief was unavailable.*" (Emphasis added.) Section 1988(b) now provides that the court may allow "a reasonable attorney's fee as part of the costs, *except that in any action brought against a judicial officer for an act or omission taken in such officer's judicial capacity, such officer shall not be held liable for any costs, including attorney's fees, unless such action was clearly in excess of such officer's jurisdiction.*" (Emphasis added.) Is anything left of *Pulliam* after this?

**Page 1015, add at the end of footnote a:**

For an elaborate criticism this aspect of *Swint* and an argument in favor of a properly circumscribed doctrine of pendent appellate jurisdiction applicable to all categories of interlocutory review, see Joan Steinman, The Scope of Appellate Jurisdiction: Pendent Appellate Jurisdiction Before and After *Swint*, 49 Hastings L.J. 1337 (1998).

**Page 1017, add at the end of Note 2:**

In addition, two recent symposia address issues of municipal liability from a variety of perspectives. Volume 48 of the DePaul Law Review published a symposium on Municipal Liability in Civil Rights Litigation, with contents as follows: Susan Bandes, Introduction: The Emperor's New Clothes, 48 DePaul L. Rev. 619 (1999); Jack M. Beermann, Municipal Responsibility for Constitutional Torts, id. at 627; Michael J. Gerhardt, Institutional Analysis of Municipal Liability Under Section 1983, id. at 669; Karen M. Blum, Municipal Liability: Derivative or Direct? Statutory or Constitutional? Distinguishing the *Canton* Case from the *Collins* Case, id. at 687; David F. Hamilton, The Importance and Overuse of Policy and Custom Claims: A View from One Trench, id. at 723; G. Flint Taylor, A Litigator's View of Discovery and Proof in Police Misconduct Policy and Practice Cases, id. at 747. Volume 31 of the Urban Lawyer published a symposium on Reconsidering *Monell*'s Limitation on Municipal Liability for Civil Rights Violations, with an introduction by David M. Gelfand, 31 Urb. Law. 395 (1999) and the following articles: Robert J. Kaczorowski, Reflections on *Monell*'s Analysis of the Legislative History of Section 1983, id. at 407; Barbara Kritchevsky, Reexamining *Monell*: Basing Section 1983 Municipal Liability Doctrine on the Statutory Language, id. at 437; Robert E. Manley, Effective But Messy, *Monell* Should Endure, id. at 481; Oscar G. Chase and Arlo Monell Chase, *Monell*: The Story Behind the Landmark, id. at 491; Ronald Turner, Employer Liability for Supervisory Hostile Environment Sexual Harassment: Comparing Title VII's and Section 1983's Regulatory Regimes, id. at 503; Laura Oren, If *Monell* Were Reconsidered: Sexual Abuse and the Scope-of-Employment Doctrine in the Common Law, id. at 527.

Finally, for an interesting recent article that calls for renewed attention to "custom" as a basis of municipal liability, see Myriam E. Gilles, Breaking the Code of Silence: Rediscovering "Custom" in Section 1983 Municipal Liability, 80 B.U. L. Rev. 17 (2000). Gilles focuses particularly on the "police code of silence" as a "custom" that "causes" constitutional violations.

**Page 1035, add at the beginning of footnote a:**

For a recent reinterpretation of *Paul*, see Barbara E. Armacost, Race and Reputation: The Real Legacy of *Paul v. Davis*, 85 Va. L. Rev. 569 (1999) (arguing that much of the "scholarly hand-wringing" is misdirected, because most of the claims excluded from due process by *Paul* are redirected to other constitutional "homes").

**Page 1040, add a new Note:**

6. ***County of Sacramento v. Lewis.*** In other contexts as well, the availability of damages under § 1983 prompts special attention to the definition of the underlying right. At issue in County of Sacramento v. Lewis, 523 U.S. 833 (1998), was police liability for causing death in a high-speed automobile chase. The Supreme Court adopted a restrictive standard that effectively bars federal liability in such cases.

Sheriff's deputies encountered two boys on a motorcycle approaching at high speed. The deputies ordered the motorcycle to stop, but the boys evaded the patrol cars and drove away. Although the boys were suspected of nothing more serious than failure to stop, a deputy gave chase, following the motorcycle as close as 100 feet and reaching speeds as fast as 100 miles per hour. When the motorcycle tipped over, Philip Lewis, a 16–year-old boy who had been riding the motorcycle as a passenger, fell into the path of the patrol car and was killed. Lewis's parents sued the deputy and the county, alleging a violation of the boy's substantive due process right to life. Faced with these facts, the Ninth Circuit ruled that liability would be established on proof of "deliberate indifference to, or reckless disregard for, a person's right to life," but the Supreme Court disagreed.

Speaking through Justice Souter, the Court held that the proper standard for substantive due process analysis was not "deliberate indifference" but whether the deputy had been guilty of an abuse of power which "shocks the conscience." In the specific context of a high-speed automobile chase to apprehend suspected offenders, that standard required proof of an intent to harm the suspects. Justice Scalia, with whom Justice Thomas joined, objected to the Court's resuscitation of the "ne plus ultra, the Napoleon Brandy, the Mahatma Ghandi, the Celophane [citing Cole Porter] of subjectivity, th' ol' 'shocks the conscience' test," but agreed as to the result. Justice Stevens also concurred in the judgment on the ground that, because of uncertainty as to the legal standard, the defendant was entitled to qualified immunity. There was no dissent.

**Page 1126, add a footnote at the end of *City of Burlington v. Dague*:**

**a.** The impact of *Dague* is assessed in Julie Davies, Federal Civil Rights Practice in the 1990's: The Dichotomy Between Reality and Practice, 48 Hastings L.J. 197 (1997). Davies reports that the reactions of civil rights lawyers are surprisingly mixed. Plaintiffs' lawyers generally agreed that *Dague* had lowered their leverage in settlement negotiations, but many viewed the loss of multipliers as relatively insignificant. Several "stated that under the lodestar formulation, they are paid at a high hourly rate, and that courts have adjusted for the lack of a multiplier by awarding them a greater percentage of the hours billed." Davies finds, however, that the lack of fee enhancement does affect lawyers bringing class actions, especially in cases requiring expert witnesses.

For a sophisticated economic analysis of the question of multipliers, see Peter H. Huang, A New Options Theory for Risk Multipliers of Attorney's Fees in Federal Civil Rights Litigation, 73 N.Y.U. L. Rev. 1943 (1998) (arguing on the basis of options theory that fee enhancement should be allowed but that multipliers should be set at "less than the initial reciprocal of the probability of the plaintiff prevailing in the lawsuit").

CHAPTER X

# Remedial Interactions

**Page 1183, add at the end of the first full paragraph:**

For a more recent article building on the work of Ronan Degnan and Stephen Burbank, see Howard M. Erichson, Interjurisdictional Preclusion, 96 Mich. L. Rev. 945 (1998).

APPENDIX B

# Selected Federal Statutes

**Page B–33, replace the text of 42 U.S.C. § 1983 with the following:**

## § 1983. Civil action for deprivation of rights

Every person who, under color of any statute, ordinance, regulation, custom, or usage, of any State or Territory or the District of Columbia, subjects, or causes to be subjected, any citizen of the United States or other person within the jurisdiction thereof to the deprivation of any rights, privileges, or immunities secured by the Constitution and laws, shall be liable to the party injured in an action at law, suit in equity, or other proper proceeding for redress, except that in any action brought against a judicial officer for an act or omission taken in such officer's judicial capacity, injunctive relief shall not be granted unless a declaratory decree was violated or declaratory relief was unavailable. For the purposes of this section, any Act of Congress applicable exclusively to the District of Columbia shall be considered to be a statute of the District of Columbia.

**Page B–35, replace the text of § 1988(b) with the following:**

### (b) Attorney's fees

In any action or proceeding to enforce a provision of sections 1981, 1981a, 1982, 1983, 1985, and 1986 of this title, title IX of Public Law 92–318, the Religious Freedom Restoration Act of 1993, title VI of the Civil Rights Act of 1964, or section 40302 of the Violence Against Women Act of 1994, or section 13981 of this title, the court, in its discretion, may allow the prevailing party, other than the United States, a reasonable attorney's fee as part of the costs, except that in any action brought against a judicial officer for an act or omission taken in such officer's judicial capacity, such officer shall not be held liable for any costs, including attorney's fees, unless such action was clearly in excess of such officer's jurisdiction.

*

APPENDIX C

# JUDICIAL REVIEW

**Page C–10, add to footnote d:**

See also John Harrison, The Constitutional Origins and Implications of Judicial Review, 84 Va. L. Rev. 333 (1998) (providing a closely reasoned and persuasive derivation of *Marbury's* conclusion from the text of the Constitution).

†